DEC 1 7 2010

Christmas

Christmas

FESTIVAL OF INCARNATION

Donald Heinz

GLENVIEW PUBLIC LIBRARY
1930 Glenview Road
Glenview, IL 60025

Fortress Press
Minneapolis

CHRISTMAS
Festival of Incarnation

Copyright © 2010 Fortress Press, an imprint of Augsburg Fortress. All rights reserved. Except for brief quotations in critical articles or reviews, no part of this book may be reproduced in any manner without prior written permission from the publisher. Visit http://www.augsburgfortress.org/copyrights/contact.asp or write to Permissions, Augsburg Fortress, Box 1209, Minneapolis, MN 55440.

Scripture quotations are from the New Revised Standard Version Bible, copyright © 1989 by the Division of Christian Education of the National Council of the Churches of Christ in the USA. Used by permission. All rights reserved.

Cover image: Angel fresco, Bernardino Luini (c.1480–1532), Pinacoteca di Brera, Milan, Italy. Photo © Bridgeman Art Collection.
Cover design: Laurie Ingram
Book design: Douglas Schmitz

Pages 24–25: Reprinted with the permission of Scribner, a division of Simon and Schuster, Inc., from *The Collected Works of W. B. Yeats, Volume 1: The Poems,* Revised and edited by Richard Finneran. Copyright © 1933 by the Macmillan Company, copyright renewed © 1961 by Bertha Georgie Yeats. All rights reserved.

Page 19 and page 63: "For the Time Being," copyright 1944 and renewed 1972 by W. H. Auden, from *Collected Poems of W. H. Auden* by W. H. Auden. Used by permission of Random House, Inc.

Library of Congress Cataloging-in-Publication Data
Heinz, Donald.
Christmas : festival of Incarnation / Donald Heinz.
p. cm.
Includes bibliographical references and index.
ISBN 978-0-8006-9733-4 (alk. paper)
1. Christmas. 2. Incarnation. I. Title.
BV45.H44 2010
232.92—dc22
2010011707

The paper used in this publication meets the minimum requirements of American National Standard for Information Sciences—Permanence of Paper for Printed Library Materials, ANSI Z329.48-1984.

Manufactured in the U.S.A.

14 13 12 11 10 1 2 3 4 5 6 7 8 9 10

To my children, Stephen, Katherine, Rebekah, Anna
Who have known the enchantment of Christmas

Contents

Preface

Every year comes a happy array of books for Christmas. They line up home decorating and fancy parties, poems and stories and cookies, the latest ways to stimulate the children, proper lamentations on materialism, even a dose of piety—all the necessary rehearsals required for playing a great festival. This is a different play.

This book is a religious and historical accounting of Christmas as an ever-evolving festival of Incarnation. Generically, Incarnation refers to any divine being who takes on human form (literally, flesh) and comes to live on earth for a time. In Christian theology, Incarnation refers to the belief that Jesus Christ, identified as the second person of the Trinity of Father, Son, and Holy Spirit, came to earth as fully divine and fully human. As such, Christ represents and demonstrates the fully human presence of God on earth, enacting a divine plan for the redemption and salvation of humankind. The drama of Incarnation, a central theme of this book, is the *risk* God takes in becoming human and fully immersed in and committed to a material world. This book tells the amazing story of how an original religious festival celebrating the one-time Incarnation of God that is the heart of Christianity relentlessly expanded the divine investment in material culture and laid down vast deposits in the Western tradition. The incarnational plot opens with the original Christmas story and its protagonists embedded in the texts of the New Testament. In the second act, Christianity comes to understand itself as a theater of Incarnation with the church as its festival house. Finally, spilling far beyond sacred pages and liturgical auspices, there spreads across time and place, to cathedral square and market and home, an expanding range of human celebration until all the world becomes the stage for Christmas.

That the daring idea of Incarnation, thought by Christians to represent a surprising and profound divine departure and soon enough embodied in the church's teaching and practice, should become a pregnant theme from which unending and unauthorized development flows—this is the fullness of Christmas to which I bear witness. The Incarnation was not going to remain a pristine idea in the mind of God, or even in the flesh of Jesus Christ, or even in the church that calls itself the body of Christ. The Incarnation would become a divine-human venture, including not only marches of pilgrims drawn to festival but every imaginable prop piling up on stages everywhere.

My account must become greater than the sum of its parts, and the ambitions of this story run to a large stage. I hope to offer readers much more than they have been prepared to expect and to surprise them with how little of the panoply of Christmas the December crowds see. *More* is the underlying theme, in a jaded time that wonders if that's all there is.

To be sure, Christmas is resplendent even from afar and a ready delight. It is easy to see and hear and feel the festival well before getting around to believing it up close. Like the figure of Christ, Christmas is a treasure trove embedded in the history of the West. But where is the treasure today? How much of the gold is left? Some say that Christmas has dwindled into a festival of consumerism, and they call it the "civil religion of capitalism." Indeed, Christmas without religion is now more imaginable than Christmas without shopping. Others, in order to provide good holiday value for a pluralist society, change the subject to winter holiday. And many domesticate religious festival as "good family times."

Shopping, solstice, sociability—is that all there is? Even if one buys the view that the American Christmas is an "invented tradition" of questionable provenance, or that it has been turned into a seasonal commodity bought and sold in the global market, the hope may linger that there is more to it, more than meets the acquisitive holiday eye. This book displays the more. A contemporary visitor to St. Paul's in London pauses at the tomb of the cathedral's great architect, Christopher Wren, to make out the epitaph: "If you seek his monument, look around." A festival of Incarnation invites wide-angled amazement.

To offer a fully dimensional account of Christmas in the human landscape, some triangulations are necessary—what is today called an interdisciplinary approach. *Theology* has an ear for distinctly spiritual ideas and practices and does not reduce religion to its footprints in politics or popular culture or economics. The *sociological imagination* finds a way into the resilience, the homeliness, and the ambiguity of what is lately called "lived Christianity," meaning a humanly constructed church channeling God on the ground. With a keen eye for festival and for ritual, *anthropology* spots the formation of a distinctive Christian culture inside the church and the exuberant and uncontrollable impulse to carry material culture and deep play into every human precinct. Great religious festivals spin God into every matter, and religion becomes complicit in forces it cannot control. But simply to plot Christmas as capitalist religion misses too much of the story and wrongly implies that the values of the market are the final stage of human evolution.

One might have thought that beginning the study of a religious festival with its theology would be obvious. But much of contemporary scholarship fails to get Christmas because its angles of approach are too narrow. A distinctively religious approach to Christmas is an overdue assignment. Curators who mount exhibitions of religious art find that their audiences must unlearn modern assumptions and relearn what people in other times knew by heart. Just as musicians today try to recover the "performance practices" of earlier times, a retrieval of the "audience practices" of historic Christmases would be fruitful for those who seek a full hearing of Christmas today. Neither concert halls nor museums nor even the town square and market were the seminal festival sites.

But the social sciences also offer indispensable insights. Anthropologists claim that looking closely into "great cultural performances" (like religious festivals) offers large payoffs in human self-understanding. We come to see the dramas that run beneath life in society and the fuller proportions of the human project. The stories we tell ourselves and the rituals in which we annually act them out are ideal locations to mine an understanding of our attempts to create meaning in the world, to spin ourselves in webs of significance.

A thick description of Christmas offers something for everyone, if also the larger portrait that has gone missing. Christians may trace the contours of liturgical celebration and fret whether Christianity's major festival is slipping through their fingers. Aesthetes who love Christmas for its visual art or music find much on display here. Celebrators of popular culture and revisionists of kitsch can greet them in these pages. Fans of C. S. Lewis or Tolkien and those who believe "magical realism" can save a disenchanted world can renew their hopes. Boundary-tenders on the church-state patrol can sharpen their watch. Political and economic commentators can register hope or dismay in Christmas as the site where the rival civilizations of religion and the market clash. Those of dramatic bent may imagine that the guerrilla theater that is liturgy and ritual could stage authentic alternatives to commodified culture. Curmudgeons can hear their own echoes in all those who have said no to Christmas. Those who believe human renewal lies in the good old days will find less and more. Even bon vivants who only want to match guests with food and wine will find fulfillment.

Christmas inaugurates and plays out the risks and realizations of Incarnation. To watch the festival of Christmas over time is to glimpse the descent of God into human festival, the religious spinning of the divine into matter. One could imagine religious festival as fluorescent—absorbing light of invisible wave length and emitting light of visible, though sometimes flickering, wavelength. To join those audiences who take to the lighted stage of the great festival house is to enlist in the disturbing ambiguities of religion and accept parts in the play called the spiritual quest. To pour out into the streets where Christmas is also staged is to encounter the disturbing course of Incarnation in the world. Will it ruin things for the reader if I reveal now that it turns out that the celebration of Christmas becomes the uneasy record of how God and religion and humans are faring in the modern world?

Part One

Plotting Incarnation

Divine Scripts and Human Actors

Today Christmas is wrapped in modern culture, but it was born in sacred texts written two thousand years ago that proclaimed the Incarnation of God as Christianity's seminal idea. How did this come to be? How did Incarnation turn into Christmas? How does Christmas reveal the long march of Incarnation?

God's apparent change of heart brought Jesus into the world as a startling new divine self-revelation. In the Christian view, a fusing of God-as-God with God-becoming-human turned the world upside down and was proclaimed as good news for the human condition. The poignant story of Jesus as God undergoing change, for humanity's sake, required the uniquely Christian sacred texts that the church came to call the *New* Testament.

The New Testament is the original source for the Incarnation and the authorization for celebrations of Christmas that make God matter everywhere. The great festival emerged, as did the New Testament itself, in oral tradition, written word, liturgical celebration, and lived religion. Early Christianity celebrated Christmas listening to Matthew and Luke read in public worship, and the words achieved incantatory power for hearers already distanced from the time of Christ.

Would things turn out over time? This book closes worrying about *the risk of Incarnation*. That is, has the festival of Christmas turned out the way God intended? The great idea that Christianity calls the Incarnation requires that God suffer the consequences of coming out in earthly context, from the crucifixion of Jesus to the unsteadiness of his followers. The New Testament and early Christianity tell the stories of the divine Child taken into the hands of strangers. Extended over time, the festival of Christmas plays the unpredictable descent of the divine into every human matter.

Incarnational change and development were inevitable. Sacred narratives do not stay put, as subsequent readers and hearers carry them, with the Child, into new worlds. Their theological definitions and their leading characters come loose from ancient moorings, escape ecclesiastical control, and evolve in response to changing human contexts. Incarnations, or "inculturations," as missionaries call them, keep happening. This is witness to the carrying capacity of Incarnation, if also its susceptibility to reckless adventure. Playing out the point and peril of Incarnation, Christian history demonstrates a continuing return to the sources, for return of the people of God from their many detours and for the renewal of their iconic festivals.

Although some people can still recite Luke's account by heart from hearing it read in church, or annually by Charlie Brown, it is mostly not the custom in the modern, self-confident West to look back to earlier times and sources for present direction. It is said that Americans are innocent of historical perspective and that truism may apply to Bible-believers as well. Attempts to understand a festival rooted in ancient, not to mention sacred, history are likely to be overwhelmed by present manifestations. Christmas *now* overwhelms Christmas *then,* and may be mostly discontinuous. Although ancient Christians made pilgrimages to Bethlehem in order to keep their holy texts alive, it is a challenge for twenty-first-century celebrators to cross the threshold of everyday experience into the lost world of the first sightings (and sitings and citings).

To be sure, Christianity believes that the Incarnation of God proclaimed in the New Testament has authorized a trajectory that reaches far beyond Bethlehem and well beyond ancient texts as well. Christmas has turned into an entire Christian culture and taken up residences beyond lived Christianity as well. That is the larger story of this book.

The Christian tradition in the West was always a tension between original intention and contemporary realization. So too with Christmas. Chapter 1 offers close readings of the first constructions of Christmas in the sacred texts of the New Testament and then discusses how the Bible came to be a normative, if also ignored, source for the staging of religious festival, as well as a primary object of Christian material culture itself. Chapter 2 portrays the characters of Christmas as ever-shifting shapes in the life of Christianity and in the imagination of artists and theologians. Texts that anchor a great idea (the Incarnation) must watch its accompanying dramatis personae migrate far beyond their pages. The "ship with cargo precious" of which the carol sings visits many a foreign port.

1

The Original Texts of Christmas

If you want to read Scripture right, see to it that you find Christ in it.
I want to hear of no other God than this Mary's child.
—Martin Luther

They all were looking for a king
To slay their foes and lift them high:
Thou cam'st, a little baby thing
That made a woman cry.
—George MacDonald

Much of the Christian New Testament proclaims the life, death, and resurrection of Jesus Christ and the theological and ethical meaning of his coming, but only two of the four Gospels actually tell a Christmas story. The infancy narratives in Matthew and Luke are the only original manger we still possess today.

Matthew

Matthew is the first book of the New Testament, but this Gospel opens as if it were reprising the original creation story. Matthew 1:1 could be rendered as "This is the book of the new Genesis, wrought in Jesus Christ, son of David and Abraham." Portraying the coming of Jesus as a latter-day miracle from God, Matthew pulls together God's earlier actions, in what Christians came to call the Old Testament, and God's recent doings.

A complicated opening genealogy (1:2-17) establishes this newborn child's ancestry. It is a long parade, all these ancestors, and it runs from the first covenant God made with Abraham, to the throne of King David, to the time of Israel's exile, and now to the time of restoration. Jesus as the promised Messiah appears as the climax and fulfillment of patriarchal hope and prophetic vision.

The birth of Jesus is presented through the eyes of Joseph the just Israelite, though orchestrated by angels. The figure of Joseph establishes Jesus' legal Davidic ancestry, while the child's divine sonship comes through the Virgin Mary and the Holy Spirit. When Joseph discovers that his betrothed is pregnant and decides to break the engagement, an angel appears in a dream and calls Joseph to go along with God's design: "Do not be afraid to take Mary as your wife" (1:20). Matthew adopts a literary fashion of promise (Old Testament) and fulfillment (New Testament), in order to connect Mary's messianic pregnancy to a prophecy from Isaiah, "Behold a virgin shall conceive" (Isaiah 7:14, quoted in Matthew 1:23).

The birth of Jesus is a cosmic event, so the night sky reveals the arrival of a change in the universe. Magi see a new star and set out on the long-foretold "pilgrimage of the nations," bringing gifts to Zion from Arabia, Babylon, or Persia. Their presence and their worship are meant to reveal the universal dimensions of this birth. But Matthew's account dislocates Jerusalem as the focus of ancient hope to point instead to Bethlehem. The little town is to be the place of new creation, while God's incarnational plot challenges the vested interests of the holy city. In Jerusalem, the magi confuse the religious authorities with their inquiry, "Where is the child who has been born king of the Jews? For we observed his star at its rising, and have come to pay him homage" (2:2). Invoking a new king of the Jews plants a political charge in the story.

The magi quickly take their leave from court and are overjoyed when their star stops at Bethlehem. They enter the house, see baby Jesus and his mother, and kneel in homage—a scene that will stimulate countless Christian artists. The gifts of the magi are gold, frankincense, and myrrh, the first presents of a new age (2:8-11), which later times would endlessly mythologize.

King Herod is enraged when they do not report back. He orders all Bethlehem babies under a certain age to be slaughtered. So do the powerful exercise violence over those who threaten their dominion. As Rachel, Israel personified, once wept at the Jewish exile, she now weeps for the holy innocents slain for reasons of state (2:16-18). This opening scene is book-ended by the last chapters of Matthew's Gospel, when Jesus again comes up against the leader of the whole world, Caesar, through his subordinate Pontius Pilate (27:11-26). Only two dramatis personae are named in the ancient creeds alongside Jesus Christ: the Virgin Mary and Pilate. Matthew deliberately makes a shadow fall over the baby's crib: one day, this new king will have a crown, but of thorns, and his seat of power will be a cross.

Modern commentators assert that the New Testament writers are men of their times, not simply secretaries for God's dictations. In these infancy narratives Matthew's first-century readers will see not only the fate of Jesus but also that of early Christianity mirrored. It is not an idyllic Christmas scene Matthew paints but one filled with the turmoil and peril also experienced in the early church. Matthew wants to assure his readers that God is in charge even amidst great danger to the new Christian movement. Saved by the dreams that come to Joseph and to the magi, the baby becomes a refugee, and his parents safely escape to Egypt. The upright Joseph, prompted three times by dream-borne angels, holds the narrative together, protecting the baby from hostile forces and bringing him safely at last to Galilee (2:13-15, 19-23) and to his portentous future.

It is thought that the community for whom Matthew first wrote were Jewish-Christians trying to grasp their role in a larger story underway in the last quarter of the first century C.E. The Gospel of

Matthew would come to rest in a two-testament Bible. The story of Christ claims the center of this triptych, with the Old Testament on the left and these New Testament believers on the right. Because their roots are in Judaism and their future course in Christianity, Matthew's hearers want to find the connection, to see that Jesus is Israel in person, that in the events of his infancy he is reliving ancient history and also anchoring a new age. As foretold, salvation is coming to all the nations. They themselves are part of the plot.

Contemporary biblical exegesis strives, with difficulty, to carry the modern reader into the political drama of the first century and back again to the too-frequently unnoticed political conflict between the New Testament message and the ethos of the modern world. *Then and now*, not everything is going well in the Christian community. Then, Matthew offers—will modern readers now see it—a narrative of resistance, written from and for a minority community of disciples who see Jesus Christ as the agent of a new reign of God but are uncertain of their part. So this Gospel shapes its audience into a counterculture to Roman imperial power and the old religious establishment. To identify with Jesus is to side with an unexpected movement of God begun on the margins and plotted to break through to the center. Matthew closes his Gospel anticipating Jesus' return when God's reign over all, including Rome, is to be established. All these are surprising and perhaps unwelcome accoutrements of Christmas to modern sensibilities, which have adjusted to different tellings and make their peace with different circumstances.

The inclusion of the infancy narrative probably came at the end of Matthew's theological reflection on the meaning of Christ, just as Christmas followed Easter in the long process through which Christianity came to terms with its experiences of Jesus and his role in the Incarnation God was plotting. Mature reflections on the person of Christ were carried by Matthew and Luke back to earthbound Christmas stories, even as the Gospel of John's cosmic account made of Christ the eternal Word at the beginning of the universe (John 1:1-14).

When an ancient text, especially one considered sacred, is read today, the question is always what to do with it, how to understand or apply it. Is it spiritual inspiration, good news with a claim, pious legend, seasonal decoration? Millions who know little of Matthew's theological purposes do know this story. The obedient Joseph, stage-directing angels, exotic wise men, indifferent priests, an evil king, and the refugee baby are unforgettable. They have left permanent residues in the Western imagination and laid down deep deposits in Christian art and music. In the near wings of this stage set, Matthew's first readers would have recognized their own times and perhaps themselves, just as modern preachers invite Christmas Eve congregations to make the connections and position themselves near the stage. A connection rarely made in happy worship is between the baby in the manger and the Christ on the cross. But Matthew's portrayal of King Herod lends itself to what is called *biblical realism*—the unblinking realization that darkness always seeks to snuff out the light.

Modern directors expect that their audiences will "get" classical dramas and be shaken by them. Matthew, too, is meant to disturb readers and hearers with unexpected visions and consequences. A Gospel that wants to hammer its point theologically may be unfit for a party. Incarnation came to a world that dominates, oppresses, marginalizes, and destroys. The turning point in this not-harmless tale comes when the audience joins the narrator in unmasking the everyday and submitting to God's revolutionary dreams. To stage a Gospel is to extend religion's claims beyond the personal piety of a good seat in the house. To focus, for example, on Matthew's historicity (what about that star) or the charm of children at Christmas is to fall seriously short of the author's intention. Matthew wanted to shape his audience into disciples who could become Matthew's story. This Gospel is *formational rather than informational.*

Luke

Drawing from eyewitnesses, other orderly accounts, and his own literary abilities, Luke sets out to compose a theological account of the events surrounding Jesus Christ and how they brought the Christian church into being, all set on the stage of world history (Luke 1:1-4). His Christmas story is different from Matthew's. Luke makes John the Baptist the hinge of his opening story, recapitulating the role of the great prophet Elijah in the Old Testament and preparing Israel to make ready for the appearance of the Messiah. Such an important figure as John gets his own dramatic birth narrative. John's mother Elizabeth has been barren her whole marriage and now is an old woman. When the angel Gabriel appears to Zechariah—her husband and a temple priest—with the news that their prayers have been answered and a son will be born, Zechariah seems doubtful. For that, he is struck dumb until the birth of his son (1:5-24).

Then comes the announcement of the birth of Jesus—and of the Jesus Movement that became Christianity. In the midst of Elizabeth's pregnancy, the same angel Gabriel appears to a young virgin named Mary. The angel startles Mary with the words: "Greetings, favored one! The Lord is with you" (1:28). As she braces for what is coming (a bodily posture deftly drawn in much Christian art), the angel says, "Do not be afraid, Mary, for you have found favor with God. And now, you will conceive in your womb and bear a son, and you will name him Jesus" (1:30-31). This baby will be called the Son of God and be the royal successor to King David. When Mary asks, "How can this be?" (1:34) and gently reminds the angel she is still a virgin, Gabriel answers, "The Holy Spirit will come upon you, and the power of the Most High will overshadow you" (1:35). Since Mary accepts the angel's reminder that nothing is impossible with God, she bows in consent, "Here am I, the servant of the Lord; let it be with me according to your word" (1:38). Luke portrays "the Word become flesh," as the Gospel of John expresses it (1:14), in the dramatic dialogue between Mary as the chosen one and the angel Gabriel as the emissary of God. While reminiscent of older, well-beloved stories from classical antiquity, Luke's account bears no resemblance to gods who deal roughly with earthly women.

Luke interrupts the action several times with sung reflection, just as arias in Handel and Bach piously comment on the action narrated in historical recitative. Old Testament theophanies had also often inspired songs of praise. When Mary hurries to her cousin with the good news, John the Baptist leaps in Elizabeth's womb. Elizabeth ejaculates words that pious Catholics will be repeating two thousand years later, "Blessed are you among women, and blessed is the fruit of your womb" (1:42). Then Mary breaks into song. The opening words, "My soul magnifies the Lord" (1:46), give the song its enduring Latin name, *Magnificat*. Contemporary scholars set this song among the lowly who look to God for divine favor to raise them up. The radical lyrics sing of scattering the proud, bringing down the mighty and lifting up the lowly, of filling the hungry with good things while sending the rich away empty. To keep it in the church's mind, Mary's song has been chanted in nightly vespers, whispered in monasteries, and set to trumpets and kettledrums by Bach. How ironic that the song occasioned by a divine in-breaking and sung by a pregnant woman should so often be disembodied, elevated to pieties that float safely above the ground of social history and speak only to the believer's heart.

There are more Christmas songs. When John the Baptist is born, his father's tongue is unloosed in time to name him John. And to sing what will be called the *Benedictus*: "Blessed be the Lord God of Israel, for he has looked favorably on his people and redeemed them" (1:68). It is a song of salvation history in which the imminent birth of Jesus is seen as Old Testament prophecy coming true. The covenant with Abraham and the promise to David are now renewed and fulfilled.

Luke's account of the birth of Jesus at the opening of his second chapter is the best-known story in the New Testament. An imperial census brings Mary and Joseph to Bethlehem, their lineage town, just as it is time for Mary to deliver. "And she gave birth to her firstborn son and wrapped him in bands of cloth, and laid him in a manger, because there was no place for them in the inn" (2:7). Probably Mary and Joseph have ended up in the worst room of a peasant house, in which people and animals share the same space, or perhaps a cave out back. (Or was Joseph denied hospitality among relatives because the news was out about the illegitimate pregnancy?) So overcrowded are things that the baby gets the feeding trough. "No room in the inn" (2:7) is the pregnant phrase that delivers a million future sermons.

Angels and shepherds materialize like a Greek chorus to witness and interpret the action. In lonely hills, to people at the bottom of the ladder of power or privilege—not the temple in the holy city—angels from heaven announce a new rendezvous point for God and humans. This is good news to all the peoples, all now designated recipients of divine favor (2:8-10). The shepherds must first be calmed down: "Do not be afraid" (2:10). Then the birth announcement: "See, I am bringing you good news of great joy for all the people; to you is born this day in the city of David a Savior, who is the Messiah, the Lord" (2:10-11). The heavens cannot hold back. A whole host of angels break into the *Gloria in excelsis Deo,* still sung every Sunday in many Christian liturgies: "Glory to God in the highest heaven, and on earth peace among those whom he favors" (2:14). As soon as the heavenly singing ends, the shepherds go straight to the village of Bethlehem, looking for a baby in a feeding trough. Luke makes it their role to spread the news, and the world's to be amazed. Mary spends much time pondering what it all means and what lies in the future for herself and for this child (2:15-20).

A few days later, Mary and Joseph properly present their newborn in the temple. Simeon and Anna, saints of the old order, witness with their own eyes the coming of salvation but foretell conflict and suffering on the horizon. Again Luke provides a song. It is Simeon taking leave of the old age and indeed of his own life on earth: "Master, now you are dismissing your servant in peace, according to your word; for my eyes have seen your salvation, which you have prepared in the presence of all peoples, a light for revelation to the Gentiles and for glory to your people Israel" (2:29-32). Monastic communities still sing these words as their last song to God before going to sleep. Ominously, Simeon has another word for Mary: "This child is destined for the falling and the rising of many . . . and a sword will pierce your own soul too" (2:34-35). A prophetess there, Anna, is moved to praise and sings out to all who look for new redemption (2:36-38). The family returns to Nazareth, and Luke's Christmas story closes (2:39-40).

Biblical scholars mark Luke's setting in the vortex of early first-century forces. The mighty emperor in distant Rome is exercising his authority to count and control his subjects. State power brings Mary and Joseph to Bethlehem, where an astonishing scene unfolds. The announcement of Jesus' birth goes not to powerful elites but to mangy shepherds. Luke will show that one day

Jesus himself will shepherd the flock of Israel. In another reversal, the titles Savior and Lord, always reserved for the emperor, are reassigned to the newborn baby in a manger. Luke's late first-century hearers would not miss the implication. Although no one knows it at the time, Christians came to conclude that a transfer of sovereignty has occurred, from Rome to Bethlehem. In Luke's second volume, the New Testament book of Acts, Jesus becomes the name above all names under heaven that promises salvation to earth (Acts 4:12)—but that too had been the Emperor's claim. The reader is being prepared for a confrontation and a reversal, between an apparently weak kingdom of God and an apparently powerful kingdom of this world.

As with Matthew, contemporary biblical commentators want readers to see Luke's agenda of theological proclamation and church growth set into the life experienced by his hearers at the end of the first century. The messianic era has been introduced not by special effects, as apocalyptic enthusiasts might expect, but by preparing people for a role in God's new age and for cast-calls for people of faith, uprightness, and conviction. Just as Matthew wrote to shape a new community, Luke portrays a people being prepared to welcome the age of Christ, not Caesar.

The modern reader likely catches Luke's story on the run, while the earliest hearers of Luke's Christmas proclamation would be sitting in Sunday worship with fellow believers and inquirers. Listening to Luke was a prominent feature in the early lectionaries, the list of scriptures to be read aloud each week. Early Christian scholars would write whole commentaries on these readings so that preachers could get their expositions right. Great books and great texts, certainly in the Western tradition, are best understood in their original settings before too quickly rushing to what they might mean to the modern reader or hearer. But today the Christmas stories are most likely to be decontextualized, unencumbered by settings of worship, theological proclamation, and moral application.

As the church kept reading or hearing the Gospel stories, it aspired to turn into them, to become a community worthy of its founding narratives. After early centuries of hearing these Christmas accounts, there developed the religious festival of Christmas in the lived experience of Christianity. Rehearing Luke in a churchly context today recenters the original story. In the performance space of the church, the story resonates differently: Mary's womb is like the tabernacle housing the eucharistic bread; the Holy Spirit who came upon Mary is the one who still troubles the water of the baptismal font; the community wants to be the manger that now houses the baby; banners, vestments, and great art model the divine-human synergy authorized by the Incarnation.

Christ in Words: The Bible as Incarnation

The Bible—the cradle in which the Child lies, as Luther liked to say—became itself a divine incarnation as the church's book, further authorization and confirmation of the coming of God in human form. The history of Christianity could be written as a succession of new or recovered meanings of the biblical message. Like Christmas and like Christ himself, the Bible would become the site for endless contests over Christian meanings and divine intentions.

Students of great texts struggle to find the way back to their original intentions, as do scholars and judges who study the U.S. Constitution. How does one read the Bible today? Does an age of reason and science relegate these tales to the childhood of the human race? Does capitalism abduct the Christmas story for its own uses? Do the churches remove the powder before safely passing once-explosive shells around, as Albert Schweitzer wrote at the conclusion of his quest for the historical Jesus? Are the Christmas stories middle-class collectibles? Is it possible to read Homer or Virgil or Augustine or Dante without unknowingly reframing them in the social, economic, and political situation of modern times? Will eyeglasses that cannot be removed determine what is seen? "Reader response theory" refers to how living texts keep acquiring new meanings in their diverse and unauthorized interactions with new readers and hearers.

The Bible and Christmas, in the view of early Christianity, were meant for each other. While inviting a childlike faith, the Bible also provides the antidote to the cultural infantilization of the Christmas season. Once their self-understanding as astonishingly "good news for all the peoples" is conceded, the texts of Christmas cannot easily be stripped of their earthly import. Jesus was not born in a Holiday Inn. Christmas unwrapped is like a nested Russian doll that keeps opening to further images—Jesus as divine child and refugee from state power, Jesus announcing that the kingdom of God is dawning, Jesus provoking a crisis of decision, Jesus offering wholeness to all creation, Jesus telling stories that trap his hearers in assumptions from which only God can spring them, Jesus dying and rising for the cosmos. All these images Matthew and Luke embroider into the life of early Christianity. Some critics once viewed the infancy stories as embarrassing accretions or harmless folktales, but these days they are seen again as essential elements of literary and theological masterpieces by Matthew and Luke. The Bible does not consent to remain beside the point of religious festival. In the first great stagings of Christmas, Matthew and Luke controlled the plotting and the blocking.

To those with eyes to see and ears to hear, Matthew's and Luke's infancy narratives constitute a dramatic, not inert, story that fits into the larger plot of Incarnation. If they first invite historical study and attention to literary nuance, they next call for a decision about their meaning and claims. While rendering them as inert, fairy-tale reminiscences of another age is one option, a road often taken, another is to experience them as the authorizing documents for authentic, momentous, historic celebrations of Christmas. As the Bible itself became an object of material culture, its stories could become more or less gripping museum pieces. But it is also possible that the biblical drama reaches out from glassed-in dioramas, across time and space, gripping the modern hearer with excitement and astonishing claims. Christmas is the best site for this experience.

2

The Human Play of Christmas

How might this goodness draw our souls above
Which drew down God with such attractive Love.
—William Alabaster

At the beginning of the twentieth century, Albert Schweitzer traced the "quest for the historical Jesus." He, and many after him, concluded that every age casts its own Christ, that the Jesus embedded in the pages of the New Testament travels well and far and is reborn in a thousand new locales. If the ambitious plot of Incarnation even *requires* a divine protagonist who does not remain fixed in one sacred time, it is equally true of the human play of Christmas that the dramatis personae who respond to the divine initiative are constantly evolving. Like medieval mystery plays staged on the streets, the Christmas cast rolls from town to town, carrying the Child with them. Pliable characters put through their paces are evoked by ever-changing audiences and directors.

Mary and Joseph and all the rest are permanent legacies of the Christmas festival and as essential as Hamlet to Western self-understanding. Close acquaintance with them is part of cultural literacy, but there is more to them than that. They seem to have escaped their original conveyance and hitched rides around the world. It is said the Wise Men's bones (as relics with symbolic import) traveled far more than they themselves ever did. It is a wonder to trace the uncertain migrations of Incarnation, as Christmas actors on a thousand new stages exercise unpredictable agency in the play of religious and secular culture. This seems to be inevitable in a divine-human venture such as the Christmas story. To overstep, to go beyond the first stage directions may be the dramatic unfolding of the divine plan or a transgression that displays the poignancy and risk of Incarnation—both of them central themes in this book.

The play itself, if it is to be more than a beloved chestnut, must achieve a grip on ever new audiences. If contemporary talk about the "narrative quality of human experience" is true, the largest investment in the drama of Christmas comes when the characters in the audience rush the stage, unable to resist the lure to embrace the leading characters and to ask what it was like to accept a role in a divine play.

The Christmas story is a thick plot. The reach of Incarnation means not only the belief-ful appropriation of Christ the protagonist but the sense that an entire territory is hallowed, enchanted, and shaken by God on the ground. While early Christianity came to confess that Jesus Christ is fully divine and fully human, it was in the lives of the biblical characters that the proximities of Incarnation and the terror and hope of divine-human interaction were especially felt. A human life troubled by God becomes an edifying text and then a compelling invitation. In the modern world especially, so removed from a time when the sky hung low, the biblical characters lend a worldly realism to stories that might otherwise evaporate into fanciful mystery or distill as merely intellectual ideas. The Incarnation seems truer, its course more promising, if God keeps taking up habitation in the evolution of Christmas characters and audiences. As a way of turning staid drama into personal engagement, the modern movement of radical theater tried calling the audience onto the stage and inserting them into the play. In Christian Europe, artists and patrons for a very long time were painting themselves into manger scenes, and librettists were giving poignant lines to contemporary hearers of oratorio narratives. The idea was to rescue sacred story from inert nostalgia and reinvest agency in a passive audience of hearers and onlookers.

Peasants in Latin America talked themselves into the Infancy narratives, identifying with shepherds overcome by good news, identifying their ruthless dictator with Herod, and naming the United States as the distant power of empire. The American colonists similarly wrote themselves into the exodus story, making America the promised land, the Old World the oppressor Egypt, and taking for themselves the starring roles of the new children of Israel led by God to a land of milk and honey. Later, black slaves decoded the same exodus story and sang spirituals in which God gave them long-hoped-for roles to play.

But since the European Enlightenment, we are accustomed to being skeptical about sacred texts and to being suspicious of their leading characters, perhaps channeling them not as real people but as fanciful legends no longer inviting belief or credulity. Yet now in our own time, we see new tellings and decodings, for example, of a passionate Jesus and Mary Magdalene. What does the current taste for these reconstructions mean? Is the narrative power of experience, or the longing for engagement with mystery, reasserting itself?

The constant flux of the characters in Matthew and Luke resembles the course of Christmas itself, in its elastic response to new cultural inquiries or demands. But the place to begin, as compelling as their trajectories over time may be, is with their memorable roles in the original story.

I Sing of a Maiden

. . . child, it lies
Within your power of choosing to
Conceive the child who chooses you.
—W. H. Auden
"For the Time Being: A Christmas Oratorio"

And many children—God give them grace
Bringing tall candles to light Mary's face.
— Ruth Sawyer, "Christmas Morn"

In Matthew's account of the birth of the Messiah, Mary appears as the betrothed of Joseph, pregnant by the Holy Spirit as foretold by Isaiah and giving birth after the angel counsels Joseph to stand by her. She is present with the child when the magi arrive to pay homage. As refugees from King Herod's wrath, she and Joseph and the child flee to Egypt. For the most part, the just Joseph is the leading figure in the story.

Mary, by contrast, is the leading character in Luke's story. In one of the most famous scenes in the New Testament, the angel Gabriel appears to the Virgin Mary, exclaiming: "Greetings, favored one! The Lord is with you" (Luke 1:28). Then the announcement: "Do not be afraid, Mary, for you have found favor with God. And now, you will conceive in your womb and bear a son, and you will name him Jesus. He will be great, and will be called the Son of the Most High" (1:30-32). Then the expected exchange in which Mary asks how this could be possible, given her virginity, and Gabriel explains that the Holy Spirit will come upon her (1:34-35). Mary's believing response establishes the pattern for divine initiative and human consent: "Here am I, the servant of the Lord; let it be with me according to your word" (1:38). Subsequently, Mary visits Elizabeth, pregnant with John the Baptist, and her cousin exclaims: "Blessed are you among women, and blessed is the fruit of your womb" (1:42). Gabriel's greeting and Elizabeth's exclamation give the Catholic rosary its opening lines: "Hail Mary, full of grace, Blessed are you among women and blessed is the fruit of your womb." Mary sings a song of praise, the *Magnificat,* to Elizabeth (1:46-55).

Luke's second chapter finds Mary and Joseph arriving in Bethlehem, compelled by an imperial census. There she gives birth to Jesus, lays him in a manger, and shepherds come to see. Mary treasures the shepherds' words and ponders their meaning. Mary and Joseph present Jesus for circumcision eight days later, and subsequently she presents herself for purification in the temple. There an old holy man named Simeon foretells that the child will play a great role in the plan of God but that a sword will pierce his mother's soul too (2:35). When Jesus is twelve years old, his parents take him to Jerusalem for Passover, he becomes separated from his parents, and when they finally find him, Mary admonishes: "Child, why have you treated us like this? Look, your father and I have been searching for you in great anxiety" (2:48). After that, Mary is scarcely heard from again in the Gospels, though she is present at the crucifixion of her son.

Mary is the female name pronounced most often in the Western world and portrayed in art and music more than any other woman. That her measure has risen far beyond the biblical sources demonstrates how sacred texts work out among ever new hearers, and also raises, especially for Protestants, questions about the authority of postbiblical traditions. The holy book of Islam, the Qur'an, has a special chapter on Mary and makes of her one of Islam's four perfect women. Characterizations of Mary grew through an interplay of legends, theological arguments, ecclesiastical assertions, artistic representations, and pious devotions. Each age creates or discovers a Mary of its own. Eventually the story of Mary, like that of Christ, would be written "from above," and Roman Catholicism would render her the ideal woman and ultimately make infallible doctrines of her immaculate conception and her assumption into heaven. But in the first Christmas stories, she appears "from below."

The Bible is replete with accounts of divine initiative descending to invite and inspire. Mary says yes to the divine invitation, accepts a role in a great play, assumes responsibility for a change in the course of human events. Like any devout Jew, she would have believed in divine providence, even if she was too humble to imagine a special place for her in it. But when the angel proposed, she offered her will as a sacrifice to the Most High.

In Catholic Christianity, Mary touches all the great events in the life of Christ. Fifteen mysteries are conjured while tolling the beads of the rosary. The five joyful mysteries are the annunciation, visitation, nativity, presentation, and finding in the temple. The sorrowful mysteries are Jesus' agony in the garden, the scourging at the pillar, crowning with thorns, carrying of the cross, and crucifixion. The glorious mysteries are the resurrection of Christ, the ascension, the decent of the Holy Spirit, the assumption of Mary, and her crowning in heaven.

The "annunciation" stands for the engagement between Mary and the angel Gabriel. This scene is the most prominent Marian theme in Christian art. Luke is spare, and he does not say whether Mary's interaction with the angel was complicated. Mary, who gently asks how such things could be possible and then offers her consent, opens the Christian future not to passivity but agency. When God proposes, humans can say yes or no. Mary becomes the paradigm of how grace (and the Incarnation itself) always works, respecting human freedom and integrity and therefore also risking disobedience. Mary turns the key to human salvation.

Augustine likened the virgin birth to light passing through glass without breaking it. That analogy, a child entering Mary's womb without puncturing her hymen, becomes more powerful when depicted in stained glass: the light not only did not break the glass but transformed itself into richly colored patterns without breaking the ray. Those who stand and look believe this is the way of God.

Christian theologians have pondered what transpires when God and believer meet, whether God comes as the consummation of the religious quest or divine initiative is exercised in utter discontinuity with human striving. At least for Catholics (Protestants hardly think of her), Mary has come to be the perfect co-laborer and collaborator with God. Modeling every believer's yes, Mary goes beyond that to mutual participation in new creation. After that, it is her baby—even if hers is the womb and the lap and the breast—who is the meaning of Christmas. This "offering of consent" has become a significant mark of contemporary sacramental theology, whether of baptism, Eucharist, or marriage (even dying). Mary is the sacramental prototype who offers consent at every site of the holy.

Protestants are likely to emphasize that Matthew and Luke give Mary a modest role in their opening chapters and scarcely mention her again. But from those meager sources has come an ever louder amplification. In the second-century apocryphal Gospel of James, there appears a much-embellished infancy narrative that provides material for the Marian legends that grew in the early church and became popular artistic renditions in the Middle Ages. Already in that century, Christian thinkers like Irenaeus saw in her the Second Eve, through whom humanity achieves a new creation: "Just as it was through a virgin who disobeyed that mankind was stricken and fell and died, so too it was through the Virgin who obeyed the word of God that mankind, resuscitated by life, received life . . . . And Eve had to be restored in Mary, so that a virgin, by becoming the advocate of a virgin, should undo and destroy virginal disobedience by virginal obedience." In the fifth century, Mary acquired the magisterial title *theotokos* (God-bearer) as a way of asserting the full divinity of Jesus. She gave birth to the one who is God. The Greek Orthodox Church chanted her glories:

> Hail, thou, the restoration of the fallen Adam;
> Hail, thou, the redemption of the tears of Eve.
> Hail, heavenly ladder by which God came down;
> Hail, bridge leading from earth to heaven . . .
> Hail, land of promise;
> Hail, thou from whom flows forth milk and honey.
> Hail, space for the uncontained God;
> Hail, door of solemn mystery.

In the Middle Ages, mystical theologians like Bernard of Clairvaux stirred hearts and minds with pinnacles of Marian devotions. No doubt medieval traditions of courtly love came together with Christian theology in the passionate adoration of the untouchable virgin. Ladymasses and other votive services proliferated in daily life across Europe. During the Protestant Reformation, Luther and Calvin were still able to see Mary as a model of faith, of total and trusting self-surrender of mind and body to God. She was the peasant girl snatched by the initiative of God from her ordinary life to take her great and historic part in the drama of salvation. Queen Elizabeth I understood the half-mystical power of her own virginity, celebrated by poets like Spenser and Raleigh, and how it inspired the loyalty of a newly Protestant people who still venerated the Virgin Mary.

The great age of modern Marian apparitions ran from Lourdes, France, in 1858 to Fatima, Portugal, in 1917. In the middle of the nineteenth century, the pope made official dogma the Immaculate Conception of Mary (that she was not born in sin), perhaps to shore up the authority of the papacy, since Mary's sinlessness had been a staple of popular piety for centuries. By the middle of the twentieth century, another pope was decreeing the dogma of her Bodily Assumption into heaven. The Second Vatican Council of the Roman Catholic Church, however, exercised considerable restraint and appended a declaration on Mary to its teaching on the nature of the church, rather than making an independent statement on her, disappointing conservatives who were hoping to see her pronounced the co-mediatrix of grace.

Mary and the virgin birth of Christ serve to guard the paradox and mystery of Christmas. Mystery and metaphor appeal to poets. John Donne calls Mary "Thy Maker's maker, and thy Father's mother" and exclaims:

> Thou hast light in dark, and shut'st in little room,
> Immensity cloistered in thy dear womb.

And William Butler Yeats has the mother of God say:

> The terror of all terrors that I bore
> The Heaven in my womb.

Down-to-earth modern women try to imagine a peasant girl balancing maternal obligations with divine agendas. In "The Annunciation," found in *New Collected Poems* (Carcanet), Elizabeth Jennings writes:

> So from her ecstasy she moves
> And turns to human things at last
> (Announcing angels set aside).
> It is a human child she loves
> Though a god stirs beneath her breast
> And great salvations grip her side.

Luke says that Mary "kept all these things and pondered them in her heart." Yeats has Mary musing:

What is this flesh I purchased with my pains,
This fallen star my milk sustains,
This love that makes my heart's blood stop
Or strikes a sudden chill into my bones
And bids my hair stand up?

Accoutrements of material culture accumulated around Mary. She was seen as the spotless rose, and that became one of her images. From the twelfth century came the rosary, a string of beads to help keep track of prayers. Amidst remembrances of the mysteries of Jesus' life are endlessly repeated the words: "Hail Mary, full of grace, the Lord is with thee. Blessed art thou among women and blessed is the fruit of thy womb, Jesus." Protestants have a hard time remembering that these words are biblical.

Powerful symbols give rise to contested meanings. Not everyone agrees on the proper postures of faith. Different people in different situations for different reasons lay claim to the Virgin Mary. The best known example in the Americas is the Virgin of Guadalupe, commemorated on December 12. It cannot be accidental that the Virgin appeared to a Mexican Indian (not a European colonizer) in 1531, that the significance of this apparition was at first denied by the Spanish colonial church, that it nevertheless became an irresistible symbol, and that this unique Mexican Virgin Mary came to symbolize the whole of Mexico coming to terms with its native peoples and its colonizers, body and soul, a kind of unofficial flag for Mexicans. In a famous painting found on the cloak of Juan Diego, to whom the apparition came, Mary is depicted as an indigenous native, head bowed in prayer, and pregnant with the Word of God. Mary becomes a sign of the blending of Aztec and European culture, of God's identification with the poor and powerless, and of the coming of the gospel to the new world. Mary exceeds Christ himself in the altars and *retablos* dedicated to her in Mexican churches.

Perhaps Mary, less pronounced a personality and not creedaly defined like her son, more readily lends herself to new constructions and reconstructions. To some at least, the Virgin speaks for all the lowly, those on the outside, at the bottom, colonized, suppressed, outside the halls of power. Common people in every time, perhaps more than theologians, identify with her. Mary also makes her appearance in North America. The basilica of the national shrine of the Immaculate Conception in Washington, D.C., succeeded in making Mary an American citizen and sanctioning Catholic patriotism and loyalty to the nation in a time when some Protestants still doubted it.

Not everyone is able to find spiritual empowerment in the figure of Mary. Christian feminists claim that sin (Eve) or holy virginity (Mary) are too narrow a range of choices for modern women. A theology that makes Mary high often seems to make women low. Catholic women notice that their roles in the church are most constrained by those who practice Marian piety the most—a male, clerical, and ascetic culture and theology. By the Middle Ages, mystical theologians took the image of the enclosed garden (*hortus conclusus*) from the Song of Solomon and made it a powerful symbolic affirmation of Mary's virginity—and the proper enclosure and protection of all women. Mary on a pedestal does not please everyone. Some moderns would say Mary suffers from excessive adulation, from too much affection of the pious.

Joseph, Dearest Joseph, Mine

Gladly, dear one, lady mine,
I will rock this child of thine . . .

In Matthew, Joseph is the just and pious Israelite who heeds the angel's admonitions and plays his strong and dutiful role in God's plan. He embraces Mary when he might have shunned her for her shameful pregnancy. He leads his refugee family to Egypt to escape Herod's troops. Finally, he returns with his family to Israel and makes their home in Nazareth. Directed repeatedly by angels, Joseph is the protagonist who is the human agent carrying the story along. For Luke, Joseph is more of an afterthought. He happens to be engaged to the leading character, Mary. He takes Mary to Bethlehem for the census, he is present at the baby's birth and the shepherds' visit. He is amazed at Simeon's prophecies regarding his child. He, with Mary, takes Jesus to Jerusalem for Passover. Nothing more is said of Joseph.

To preserve and honor Mary's role as "bearer of God," early Christian traditions tended to render Joseph old and, ultimately, irrelevant. In much Christian art, he is off to the side and in the shadows, sometimes asleep. In the second-century apocryphal Gospel of James, Joseph is having doubts about the child's paternity. In medieval mystery plays Joseph sometimes becomes a comic cuckold whose jealous anger gives way to penitence when an angel appears to chasten him. In other plays he gets his own music to accompany his role. This is the fourteenth-century German carol "Resonet in laudibus," a cradle-rocking song that becomes "Joseph, dearest Joseph, mine." The carol serves the parental drama around the child. Later, the Joseph song appeared at weddings as well to depict a loving family relationship and an archetypal Christian marriage.

Less kind to Joseph is the Cherry Tree carol, which makes him grudging, resentful, and even mean. When pregnant Mary asks, "Pluck me a cherry, Joseph, they run so in my mind," Joseph responds, "Let him pluck thee a cherry that brought thee with child." Then immediately the unborn Christ commands the cherry tree to bend down to offer fruit to his mother.

The development of holy family devotions in the fifteenth century helped to rehabilitate Joseph. He became a responsible husband and father tending animals and a vigorous worker earning a living and supporting his family. Jean Gerson, chancellor of the University of Paris, became an advocate of Joseph's cause when he proposed to the Council of Constance a feast day in Joseph's honor. Curiously, Gerson thought that Mary's perpetual virginity would be more impressive if she were married to a significant and virile man and not an old, impotent one.

Some modern Roman Catholic parishes name themselves "Saint Joseph the Worker," and he is the industrious and loyal carpenter in occasional stained glass windows, but otherwise the Christian imagination has mostly consented to his decline. Why was Joseph so much less usable than Mary, in spite of his prominent role in Matthew's telling? Perhaps the early insistence on Mary's perpetual virginity, a surprising and very non-Jewish privileging of sexual asceticism, became a gratuitous insult to Joseph, from which he has never quite recovered. In an age when fathers are often forgotten, or absent, or beside the point, when the men's movement craves dignity and purpose, it would seem time to recover the Joseph of Matthew's Christmas story, as the patron saint of male commitment. But it is difficult for other than celibate men to honor someone who was merely loyal, loving, and obedient, someone dimmed by his wife's glory, someone who yielded to the action of God but lost his own sexual agency.

Jesus, Jesus, Rest Your Head

> The same you saw in heavenly seat,
> Is he that now sucks Mary's teat.
>
> —Robert Southwell, *New Heaven, New War*

The Christ Child gives the culture of Christmas its gravitas, if also its sweetness. Viewed as Christology "from above," the divine baby is the evidence for a genuinely human Incarnation and the authorization for the sacred canopy erected over the festival stage of Christmas. But "from below" the helpless infant is in need of human nourishment and care. The simple baby carries heavy meanings—for Saint Francis the motivation for the believers' attentiveness to their God, for Luther the proof that God really meant a self-emptying descent, for the Romantics the proof that every human baby trails divinity.

Early Byzantine iconography, enthralled with a divine baby and with a mother as the bearer of God, had presented a stiff royal personage in the guise of a baby. But Saint Francis of Assisi made him a helpless infant dependant on the ministrations of pious adults. Under the influence of Franciscan and Cistercian piety, the baby evolved from a miniature adult to the humble child (when God first sucked on a human breast) in the manger and needing the care of Christian believers. Renaissance artists did not blush to paint in male genitals, in some cases startlingly erect. Vivid depictions of the circumcision of the baby at eight days were sometimes benign and sometimes, it would seem, anti-Semitic. A 1450 panel from the Frauenkirche in Nuremberg terrifies the viewer with an oversized knife, a child's straining pose, the expression of anxious parents, and the crowding close of three menacing men seemingly engaged in ritual torture.

As a human baby, the Christ Child contributes to the domestication of Christmas in homely and idyllic settings, as G. K. Chesterton imagines it in "A Christmas Carol":

> The Christ-child stood at Mary's knee,
> His hair was like a crown
> And all the flowers looked up at Him,
> And all the stars looked down.

Luther made theological hay from God-as-a-baby. It was the best evidence that God descended to the lowest human level; one could know that God would not put on airs with humble people in need of grace. Across the Christian traditions, poets, hymnwriters, and theologians remarked on the coincidence of opposites: God in a baby.

Romantic poets were determined to see divinity in *any* child and to authorize baby talk. Wordsworth worried that, as we grow up, we lose this consciousness. Every child at Christmas is a stand-in for Christ, and Christ for every child. Somewhat cloyingly, Francis Thompson, in his poem "Little Jesus," imagines himself a baby and carries on an extended conversation, baby-to-baby, with Jesus. Thompson's point is that every believer is like a child, hoping that Christ as the Baby Jesus will recognize that.

Hark! The Herald Angels

> Angels, from the realms of glory,
> Wing your flight o'er all the earth;
> Ye who sang Creation's story
> Now proclaim Messiah's birth!

In Matthew, angels three times coach Joseph on his role in God's plot (1:20; 2:13; 2:19). In Luke, an angel informs Zechariah the priest that his wife will have a baby to be named John, who will be a great prophet (1:11-17). When Zechariah demands proof, the angel, now revealed as Gabriel, curses him with muteness for doubting God (1:18-20). Most famously, Gabriel appears to Mary to announce that she will give birth to the Messiah, the angel and Mary converse, and she humbly accepts her role (1:26-38). Over the fields of Bethlehem, coincidental with the birth of Jesus, an angel appears to tell the shepherds, and then an entire heavenly host sings: "Glory to God in the highest heaven, and on earth peace among those whom he favors" (2:9-14).

Biblical angels once registered the weight of God's glory, messengers of serious purpose who strike terror or obedience in human hearts. In the modern period, angels-lite bring a pleasant whiff of spirituality to otherwise post-religious festivities. Like all the other characters of Christmas, angels have left behind their roles in biblical texts to accept new positions as the culture requires.

In the Old Testament, any appearance of a divine intermediary became holy ground, and humans took off their shoes in the presence of theophany. The Hebrew root word for God's glory means heaviness. The angelic mission at the beginning of the New Testament is to make Christmas weigh in the human imagination. The angel Gabriel invites Mary's consent to the movement of God inside her and coaches Joseph on his role in God's plan. Angels appear over Bethlehem's fields to express astonishment at the event. Martin Luther wondered if the angels were jealous that God became one of us instead of one of them. When the adult Jesus, as an inauguration of his public ministry, goes into the wilderness to face the powers that claim the world, angels accompany him (Mark 1:12-13, and parallels). They are present again in the garden of Gethsemane, as Jesus prepares to face Good Friday (Luke 22:43, variant reading). They are the first witnesses to Easter (Mark 16:5-7 and parallels). Anticipating the worship life of the church, the New Testament closes with angels singing of the lamb who was slain who reigns over all (Revelation 5:11-12; 7:11-12).

Sometimes in the Western traditions, angels are meant to persuade us that heaven could be enjoyable, its company lively, its music of the highest quality. Christian painters like Fra Angelico brought celestial beings down to earth, gently, and incited Christians up to heaven. Both heaven and earth, rising and descending forces, are available to the pious imagination. In a later age dying for lack of metaphor, angels answer the call.

Too often. The turn of the third millennium finds Western culture choking on Renaissance cherubs. Angels star in television dramas. The Romantics feared that the decline of angels would lead humans to miss a many-splendored universe. Moderns have a different problem.

Factory-made angels do not imitate biblical prototypes, but they may provide minimal doses of spirituality for those whose intake does not regularly include religion. It is not beyond the elastic culture of Christmas to re-enchant the world in collectible yearly editions. But biblical angels came not to simplify lives but to complexify them. Once, an angel employed a hot coal to purify the prophet Isaiah's tongue so that it could dare to speak the word of the Lord. After an all-night struggle of a dangerous kind, an angel threw the patriarch Jacob's hip out of joint, where today one would expect a gentle massage. Like Santa Claus, modern Christmas angels encourage shoppers in their errant missions and halo jobs well done. Allegedly, angels designate the location where the glory of God touches down, so today they appear as evidence of the sacred beyond usual sites, including finding parking places.

Let Heaven and Nature Sing

Shine forth, and let your light restore
Earth's own true loveliness once more.
—Charles Coffin, "On Jordan's Bank"

Modern children who have ever seen a live manger scene never forget it. The early American caroler William Billings boldly sings: "The oxen are near him and blow on your God." Saint Francis preached to the animals and treated them like brothers and sisters. When one first hears a French carol sing of rushing wings, it reminds of angels, but no, it means the birds of the air:

Whence comes this rush of wings afar
Following straight the Nowell star?
Birds from the woods in wondrous flight
Bethlehem seek this holy night.

The magi are drawn to a special star; to those who can see, the night sky reveals a change in the universe. The claim of Christmas is that heaven and earth are brought together again. Matter is touched by spirit, and the earth becomes a sacrament of divine presence, not merely the dreary place of sin. The Incarnation means the enchantment of all creatures.

The Christmas rose and the branch of Jesse are well-known metaphors for nature mysteriously reborn at Christmas. Isaiah had prophesied that from the stump of Jesse, the apparent dead end of the Davidic line when Israel went into exile, new life would one day emerge. The branch, the new life, became a rose ever blooming. The holly and the ivy are metaphors for the Virgin Mary and for the passion of Christ, if also for male and female. Finally, there is the obvious—the winter solstice. Of course Christmas has something to do with bleak December, with the dying of the light.

Most famously, the hallowing of nature is expressed in a speech in Shakespeare's *Hamlet:*

> Some say, that ever 'gainst that season comes
> Wherein our Saviour's birth is celebrated,
> The bird of dawning singeth all night long:
> And then, they say, no spirit dare stir abroad;
> The nights are wholesome; then no planets strike,
> No fairy takes, nor witch hath power to charm;
> So hallow'd and so gracious is the time.

Shepherds, Why This Jubilee?

> Shepherds, why this jubilee?
> Why these joyous strains prolong?
> What the gladsome tidings be
> Which inspire your heavenly song?

There are no shepherds in Matthew's account, but Luke makes them the first witnesses to the Christmas miracle. They hear the angels' proclamation, they go to see for themselves, and they praise God and tell everyone (Luke 2:20). Children of the modern age dress in ridiculous bathrobes and play the part of shepherds in Sunday school Christmas pageants throughout the land. Of all the characters of Christmas one might wish to meet, the shepherds seem the most approachable. Christmas pageants, in fact, reach back to the Middle Ages. As liturgy was giving rise to drama, an early Easter play gave its lines to Christmas. Once angels at the tomb asked "Whom do you seek": now the question is put to Christmas purpose. As a medieval congregation on Christmas morning imagines shepherds arriving at the manger in search of the infant Christ, two deacons get the first lines ever in a church Christmas play: "You shepherds, whom are you looking for in the crib, tell us?" Cantors respond: "The Savior Christ the Lord, the infant wrapped in tatters, as the angel told us."

When Christmas plays leave the sanctuary of the church, people want ever more. Because holy day and holiday are birds of a feather, shepherds' plays performed in the squares outside cathedrals are soon turning to bawdy humor. In a fifteenth-century English play, the newborn is actually a lamb stolen by a shifty shepherd and disguised so that the others who come looking will not find it. The thief says to his wife: "Get ready, and I shall say you were delivered of a boy-child this night." The shepherds scrutinize, the wife plays her part, the thief dissembles. Eventually, one of the suspicious shepherds wants to give a small gift to the child, lifts up his cloth to give him a kiss, and discovers that the baby looks remarkably like their lost sheep. After an argument over the baby's features, an angel appears and the play turns to the proclamation of the meaning of Christmas.

Sheep and shepherds were familiar images of Israel and of God in the Old Testament. Sheep were affectionate, defenseless, and in constant need of care and supervision. So Israel said: "The Lord is my shepherd, I shall not want." Religious leaders were expected to be good shepherds, though they often were not. The Gospel of John proclaims Jesus as the ultimate Good Shepherd. But in first-century Palestine, shepherds got no respect. Now mostly quaint, the original shepherds were unlikely candidates for epiphany. Unshaven and drinking hard, shepherds starred among the thieving and cheating professions; they could not hold office or be admitted as witnesses in court. Just because of who they were, they are important to Luke, who always makes heroes of the lowly, the marginalized, the foreigner, and women. God was sublimely ironical to call shepherds, who could not be trusted, as the first witnesses to the Incarnation.

We Three Kings of Orient Are

> The eastern sages saw from far
> And followed on his guiding star;
> By light their way to Light they trod,
> And by their gifts confessed their God.
>
> —Sedulius

Luke gives us no magi, but Matthew makes them register the cosmic significance of Jesus' birth (Matthew 2:1-12). They appear as astrologers who have noticed a new star and come to Jerusalem to see what the birth of a new king portends. As the court arouses and King Herod plots, the wise men move quickly to Bethlehem, present royal gifts to the child, and, warned by God, return to their origins by another route.

The magi are the most mysterious characters in the Christmas story and the ones most susceptible to imaginative expansion. The wise men were elevated to royalty based on Matthew's implicit citation of Psalm 72:10-11, where kings bring tribute to Jerusalem. Then they were three, since they brought three gifts, but the early traditions ranged from two to four to twelve. Once named and representative of the races, one of them became black. In an Armenian myth, the wise men are the three sons of Noah, raised from the dead to represent all humankind worshiping the Christ who is the second Adam. Their gifts became metaphors of the child's kingship, divinity, and burial.

Around 200 C.E., images of the magi appear in the catacombs, three filmy figures in a row leading to Madonna and child. They represent the community of the faithful coming before the throne of God. As magi saw Christ at his first coming, those buried here will see him in his second coming. By 547, in the Church of San Vitale in Ravenna, the magi are imaged on the hem of Queen Theodora's dress, a trimming of royalty. A decade later in the

Church of Saint Apollinara Nuovo in Ravenna, they are much more elaborate, stylishly dressed, larger in scale, rich, and prominent in their own right. They resemble the kings who came to King Solomon's court bearing gifts, recounted in 1 Kings 10:1-2. With passing centuries they became liturgical stars throughout Christianity, their stories ever more elaborate. They were called to represent the whole world honoring Christ and so were assigned origins in Asia, Africa, and Europe.

Of course, the magi needed to acquire names. A medieval calendar of saints has them meeting one last time in 54 C.E. to celebrate Christmas; thereupon, after mass, they died: Melchior on January 1, Balthazar on January 6, and Gaspar on January 11. Long ago their bones were carried in imperial procession in Constantinople, to sanctify the emperors' rule. The Emperor Zeno in 490 had brought them there from Persia. Then they went west to Milan because of the Muslim threat. A bell tower there still bears a star, not a cross, in their honor. In 1162, as part of the booty from a ravaged Italy, Emperor Frederick Barbarossa brought them to Cologne, where they became the "Three Kings of Cologne," entombed in a marvelous golden and bejeweled casket and the city's most famous relic by far, that still is seen and marveled over today. In 1906, a few bones were returned to Milan in a gesture of good will. But the great reliquary in Cologne, begun in 1181 and completed in 1200, summoned pilgrims from everywhere. Guessing the commercial value of the magi's gifts even drove interest in trade, of which they became emblems. World travelers, Matthew's magi have gone forth in the company of Byzantine emperors, German kings, Medici bankers, and South American chieftains. They behold and proclaim the utter universality of Christ.

In the appropriation of the church, the magi are the prototypical pilgrims, and their relics traveled even more than they did. Their ever-changing characters are examples of how believers and other interested parties appropriate the dramatis personae of a great story and take them, for their own purposes, to places they never went before. The magi far outstrip the shepherds in the imagination of later ages. Reportedly their bodies were still incorrupt when brought to Cologne. (After the Reformation the shepherds became more popular among Protestants, partly because they were less tainted with relic worship and Catholic piety.)

In the evolution of medieval liturgies into medieval drama, the *Office of the Star* (the three kings' play) was the most popular. The drama was inserted at the moment when the gifts of bread and wine are brought forward in procession at the high point of the Mass. Priests dressed as wise men would bring three gifts, led forward by an often clumsily staged star. The kings kneeling at the manger suggest the congregation kneeling before the sacred host, and their gifts parallel the gifts of bread and wine. More than almost any other biblical narrative, these scenes were endlessly decked out. Replayed before an adoring populace, their roles became the quintessential medieval story: pilgrims on a journey. Somewhat surprising to moderns, it was envisioned that the magi each set out from different locales. On the way, they were deeply engaged in discussions with their servants: What would be the perfect gift? In one play, the wise men do not meet until just two miles from Jerusalem. The star is briefly lost in the fog. When the wise men finally come together, at a kind of pilgrim fork, they overflow with their individual stories, comparing notes as it were. They trade introductions, reasons, motives, allegorical insights. As they arrive in Jerusalem there is time for theological disputes. In some plays they meet the shepherds on their way back to their fields. The journey home, at last, is easier because they bask in the full light of faith.

If the church learned how to render the magi for holy purposes, the world soon enough turned them to secular ends. One could write a political-sociological-economic history in which the magi legitimate the divine right of kings or the orders, customs, and structures of society and culture, just as Matthew had made them effective witnesses to the Christ. Even up to the present, the star above the crèche and the magi following it transform social and political universes into astral (heavenly) terms.

The figures of this world jockey for position at the manger in order to mimic in the world of religion the political arrangements of societies. For a long time, both Byzantine and Western monarchs played themselves as magi. Charlemagne (and his successors) certainly processed down the aisle, past art dominated by magi scenes, and arrived at the very crib. It is hard to imagine they did not think of themselves as magi. From the eleventh century the magi were used to legitimize crusades: Western kings, Gentiles, were commissioned to return to rescue Jerusalem from latter-day Herods. The magi's bones needed to go from Constantinople to Milan, the last seat of the old Roman empire in the West, and then on to Cologne as power shifted north. Cologne would become the first pilgrimage goal of each new Holy Roman Emperor. Royal coronations and then the adoration of Jesus by these newly-crowned kings-as-magi would become two sides of the same coin. The magi crowned Jesus, and now the Christ of Christendom inversely crowns its kings. From the fifteenth century and the age of colonialism, the traversals of the magi become the lens through which European conquerors make sense of a new world, a new age of travel, adoration, and appropriation. As gift-bearers, the magi of course bless commerce and the merchant class, and today's pilgrim as consumer.

As needed, the magi can morph from kings to wise men. As wise men, they stand in for exoticism, the occult, the legendary Old Testment priest Melchizidek (Genesis 14), and the mysteries of the ancient world. Once, and again, they offer almost magical protection. It is said that when the Persians invaded Palestine and took Bethlehem in 614 C.E., they found magi among the mosaics dressed just like them and spared the whole basilica. In early modern Europe, as the political significance of the magi came to an end, they came to play other roles. They are ageless beings who come to re-enchant the world. They hint of a wisdom beyond urban life. Astrology, whenever it appears, is a kind of science in service of the sacred. As with other characters in the manger scene, the magi, like dolls, can be dressed, arranged, and moved around to fit human fancy.

Herod and the Holy Innocents

All hail, ye infant martyr flowers,
Cut off in life's first dawning hours.

—Prudentius

Luke's infancy narrative is sunnier than Matthew's. Juxtaposed with Matthew's delightful story of the wise men's visit is its aftermath: King Herod, crazy with jealousy over a newborn king of the Jews, slaughters all the babies in Bethlehem under age two. Because what liberation theology calls Matthew's "dangerous memory" goes unheeded today and because Christmas shoppers cannot imagine that Herod still rages, Matthew's awful story (Matthew 2:16-18) is indispensable to biblical realism. On December 28, the festival of the Holy Innocents is on the Christian calendar—but celebrated by almost no one today. The tragedy in Matthew's drama is revealed in the heart-wrenching cries of the mothers of Bethlehem as they plead with and then curse the slaying soldiers. The holy innocents cast a backward shadow over Christmas, and they are meant to. Jesus was born under the sign of state power. Matthew wants his readers to see that as the baby grows up, his claims provoke a crisis. He pays for this with his life. But in the view of Christian theology, he takes death, even of these babies, up into the life of God. The carrying capacity of Matthew's account is an interesting contrast to a sentimentalized baby or infantilized adults.

Possibly the earliest stage direction in European drama is "Here Herod rages." The drama in the mystery plays of Matthew's story comes out in the grotesque dialogue between Herod and his soldiers and at the heart-wrenching moment when the mothers of Bethlehem, arguing and screaming at the soldiers who are killing their babies, break into dialect to express hopeless rage or quietly sing the Coventry Carol, a song originally connected to a medieval play:

> Herod the king, in his raging,
> Charged he hath this day
> His men of might in his own sight
> All young children to slay.

Although Herod's evil and the babies' innocence and their mothers' grief once tantalized the European imagination, including for their melodramatic potential, they play hardly any role today. Matthew's ominous ingredient is a litmus test for the realism of contemporary celebrations.

Part Two

Theater of Incarnation

The Church as Festival House

O come, all you faithful, joyful and triumphant.

On Christmas Day in London, 1628, the dean of St. Paul's Cathedral, the metaphysical poet John Donne, was preaching. "Make good your Christmas-day, that Christ by a worthy receiving of the Sacrament be born in you; and he that died for you will live with you all the year and all the years of your lives; and inspire into you and receive from you at the last gasp this blessed acclamation, 'Lord now lettest thou thy servant depart in peace.'" Donne was setting the festival of Christmas within the sacramental life of the church. The apostle Paul and his followers had written that Christ's body born in Bethlehem can still be located on earth: the church is the continuing extension of the Incarnation (1 Corinthians 12:27; Romans 12:5; Ephesians 1:23; Colossians 1:18). That Christ is continuously reborn in the lived experiences and rituals of Christianity is Donne's point. Centuries of festal days have laid down rich accumulations of Christian culture that are the incarnational imprint on the Western tradition and the church's own birthright and legacy.

Christmas as the great festival of an Incarnation proclaimed in sacred texts, the church as its primal festival house, and the world itself as the eventual stage for the cultural performance of Christmas are the themes in this book. In this section, the spotlight is on the church as the first great festival house of Incarnation. A focus on the church and the history of its festive celebrations is an indispensable "way into" Christmas that takes its full measure and keeps casual observers from too quickly leaving the scene asking: Is that all there is?

Christmas, a multi-coursed event that everyone can sample, is a significantly different experience within lived Christianity, which proposes to offer a full feasting to those who seek it. The church's claim to be the proper host of Christmas is easily missed amidst the aggressive commodification of the culture of Christmas, where sufficient imagination and effort is required to move beyond the advertised sales. Christmas-lite is the cultural default. When college music departments host "Carol Dinners" as fundraisers, they must expend great energy and preparation to offer the public a taste of authentic Christmas from another time. Similarly, Shakespearean dramaturges labor to duplicate the experience of the original Globe Theatre for modern playgoers. The early music movement that arose in the last century attempted to recover the "performance practices" of earlier times—how a trill was played, the bowing of a string instrument during a particular musical period, how much vibrato was allowed in a soprano's voice, how many singers were employed in Handel's first performance of *Messiah*, how the "original instruments" sounded.

If it is difficult to recover what was heard, it is far more so to imagine the hearers themselves, whose mindsets were so different from those of contemporary audiences. Museum guides know that an understanding of past religious art requires a retrieval of knowledge lost and an unlearning of modern assumptions. A revival of the "audience practices" of historic Christmases would be fruitful for those who seek the full panoply of Christmas today. Of course, neither concert halls nor museums were the seminal festival sites. The church was the original theater for the performance of Christmas, just as for Bach's sacred music and for much Christian art.

The performance and celebration of Christmas is not unlike a theatrical event, and indeed there are historic links between religious ritual and theater. When early Christianity went public, it did not adopt the architecture of classical temples, where only the gods reside, with no room for the presence of large numbers of humans. The church took the Roman basilica, rotated it ninety degrees, and filled it with people, all entering at the west end and pointing themselves toward the divine images at an ever-more-elaborate east end. Christmas became a kind of sacred theater, reprised every year. Just as every institution (or nation) is brought to life by a gripping primal narrative, the church believed it was called to perform Christmas convincingly in the presence of God and the world. Early Christianity tried to heed a persistent New Testament admonition to be well-rehearsed, as when Jesus portrays foolish attendants at a wedding who are not prepared for the groom's arrival (Matthew 25:1-13) or when Saint Paul admonishes his readers to wake up, lay aside works of darkness, and clothe themselves with Christ (Romans 13:11-14).

Christmas became Christianity's opportunity to do the play, to attract new audiences, to stage the story in fresh ways. As was the case in the evolution of theater, however, churchly drama moved from inside ecclesiastical buildings out to the square in front of them and then to rolling carts on the streets, and Christmas as a holy day staged in church soon began the long migration to Christmas as a holiday on a world stage, the subject of the third section of this book. In Christianity, as in all religions, the way of great festivals and their pilgrims and props becomes the way of God in the world.

Envisioning the church as a performance troupe or festival house suggests the agenda for a successful season. The next five chapters portray what is required as the church engages in its annual performance of Christmas. Today, as in every age, performance on stage requires the suspension of disbelief by the audience. Modern performances of Christmas as a religious festival require that playgoers immersed in a consumer culture outside the building enter the theater that is the church and suspend their incredulity during a staging of alternative realities. As we shall see, every dimension of the Christmas "performance practice" of lived

Christianity is troubled. Altogether, this constitutes the crisis of Christmas as holy day in the modern world.

Early on, the church began to structure its performance season (worship life) into a Christian Year. Annually, the liturgical calendar rehearses and reenacts the birth, ministry, passion, and resurrection of Christ in the ritual sequences from Advent through Epiphany, Lent, Easter, and Pentecost. Around the Christian Year, an entire Christian civilization grew up (chapter 3).

The church would become both an ordered institution and an unwieldy and diverse collection of believers. This mirrors the uneasy course of Incarnation as a divine-human venture. The objective faith of the church becomes, in not entirely controllable or predictable ways, the subjective faith of individual believers. Pilgrimage became a root metaphor for the church's journey from earth to heaven, and the posture of the pilgrim came to define the ideal state of the individual believer approaching a great festival. Because pilgrimage has historically been connected to sacred sites and days, pilgrimage also provides a useful window for glimpsing how people in all times, believers and onlookers, interact with a holy day and holiday like Christmas. This interaction is what religion actually looks like in the world (chapter 4).

Already in the fourth century, the Christian manger scene became a significant prop in the church's staging of Christmas as an abundance of material culture piled up in the wings. When Saint Francis constructed a live manger scene in a humble outdoor setting, he set in motion not only a new kind of Christian piety but also accelerated the migration of Christian symbols and props beyond religious precincts. As manger scenes moved from church to home, to public square and to market, they acquired new meanings and lives of their own. A manger scene as household shrine is a festival theater in miniature and under vernacular control. A manger scene in the public square demonstrates the carrying capacity of material culture but also the provocation of contested meanings in a pluralistic society (chapter 5).

When early Christianity attempted to define the significance of Jesus Christ for the world as well as his meaning for the life of the church and its religious festivals, it depended on theology. Theologians became dramaturges who prepared the Christian audience for the play and fit the play into a larger endeavor that aspires to render Christian belief and practice adequate and compelling to human experience. This account of Christmas places theologies of Incarnation among the humanities and arts that came to amplify churchly celebration and to constitute the Christian culture of Christmas. Theology's studio is not only the church but also the academy and contemporary culture and society, including today the constituency of all those marginalized by or from religious festival. As Christmas played to an ever widening audience, theologians were required to imagine fresh stagings and to interact with new audiences (chapter 6).

But sometimes there were second thoughts about Incarnation. A long tradition arose to question whether Christmas should be staged at all. It was easy to lament the downward slide of Incarnation, the precipitous descent of God into every matter. Naysayers seek doctrines that hem God's rash risks while getting a head start on scolding pilgrims for their predictable abuses. One idea is to confine the festival site to the human heart, to avert the fall from holy mountain to golden calf and protect the Incarnation from profane encroachments. Another, lately, is to reimagine the festival with new hosts and guests. Christian theology is replete with paradox, so it was not unexpected that a determined no be juxtaposed with every jubilant yes to Christmas. When the early church first set Christmas at the very time long given to Roman celebrations, it took a deliberate risk. Would the church sanctify pre-Christian celebrations, or would the long reach of pagan roots undo the attempts at Christianization? The modern Christmas sees theologians measuring the distortions of consumerism in religious and cultural life, while economic theorists analyze the commodification of culture and the reduction of religion to market values (chapter 7).

3

Christian Worship as Theater

No love that in a family dwells
No caroling in frosty air
Nor all the steeple-shaking bells
Can with this simple truth compare—
That God was man in Palestine
And lives today in Bread and Wine.

—John Betjeman, "Christmas"

Sudden as sweet
Come the unexpected feet.
All joy is young and new all art,
And he, too, whom we have by heart.

—Alice Meynell, "Unto Us a Son Is Given"

Public Worship as Performance

Ordering and ornamenting time are historic tasks of culture, and religion often takes the lead in creating seasonal and life-cycle rituals. Mindful of the Old Testament's exclamation, "Thou crownest the year with Thy goodness" (Psalm 65:11), early Christianity gradually structured its praise and thanksgiving into a year of worship, creating recurring sacred times within cyclical secular times. Certain days and times of the year, ordinary time, are made holy through the religious culture of the calendar. This is how Christmas came originally to be celebrated.

The Julian calendar of 46 B.C.E. had named December 25 the shortest day of the year. The Roman Emperor Marcus Aurelius in 274 C.E. proclaimed *dies natalis invicti solis*, the birthday of the invincible sun, which came to be celebrated at the winter solstice. The Old Testament prophet Malachi had written, "The sun of righteousness shall arise" (4:20), so it was not incongruous when, as a counterweight to Roman civic religion, Christianity in the fourth century chose to celebrate Christ's birthday on that same day in Rome. The church was making a risky compromise with, or attempting a daring co-optation of, secular culture. In 354 C.E., the Roman bishop Liberius officially set December 25 as the festival of Christmas. Ancient Israel too had attempted to overlay pagan festivals and times. Following this example, the New Testament infancy narratives convert cosmic time into sacred history and set the birth of Jesus on a world stage previously dominated by Herod and Caesar Augustus. If everything is to be claimed for God, as biblical monotheism admonishes, the calendar of everyday life cannot remain neutral or unencumbered. Time would vie with space for the elaboration of salvation. Christianity would make the entire year a theater of operations in which the deeds of God would be set in the junctures where temporal and spiritual come to grips. The practice of an encumbered year would become both a lively art and an adopted spiritual discipline, much more than a passing notice.

Of course Christmas and solstice are related. (This is not an embarrassing secret discovered by college sophomores.) Not only ancient Greece and Rome but pre-Christian northern Europe sensed the presence of the gods in the turning of the seasons and responded with awe and careful attention. In the religious rituals of December meant to assuage separation anxieties about the decline of light, humans stopped working in order to pay special attention. They waited, they hoped, they danced, they lit fires, and they hauled the sun back. Sometimes they removed wheels from their carts, festooned them with greens, and brought them indoors. Now Advent wreaths remember those wheels, and Christmas announces the arrival of a permanent light in the world.

Early on, to contextualize its worship and liturgy and to set them on a larger stage, the church structured its faith and life into a *Christian year,* which season after season is meant to reproduce the coming of God into human life. This process began with the every-Sunday celebration of Easter, as both the New Testament and the earliest liturgies show, then moved backward to Christ's suffering and death, then still further back to his birth. As Christmas and Easter became pinnacles of worship, Advent and Lent, respectively, were added as periods to prepare for and intensify their celebrations. A Christian culture of the calendar was born. Devotional writers then and now propose that to live each liturgical season as a spiritual discipline is to conceive the daily life of Christian faith as an entire work of art. The whole year is experienced as a sacramental journey, the Christian pilgrimage through the world distilled into three great festival seasons—Christmas, Easter, and Pentecost, running from December through May.

In this book's notice of the material culture of Christmas, the church year as a ritually structured and aesthetically stylized journey through earthly life turns out—perhaps unexpectedly to the modern temperament—to be as important and concrete an expression of Christian culture as painting or music. Indeed, it was seen as a sacred architecture of time, a completed construction of the Christian life meant for earthly habitation, and eventually a great edifice in the public consciousness attracting every kind of visitor and every kind of art and commerce. When early Christian worship finally went public, after the conversion of Constantine in the fourth century and the installation of Christianity as the state religion, all the resources of the new patrons of the church were devoted to the arts of the liturgical year. The Roman basilica structure was converted into the Christian church. Its long aisle, the nave, culminated in a *platea,* a great open chancel that seemed to invite dramatic rites and artistic presentation. An entire Christian world, replete with power and vitality, came to display itself here, and then in the public space outside.

Artistically, Christmas is best known today through its music, from humble carols to monuments by Bach and Handel. But in earlier times the visual arts, including architecture, stained glass, sculpture, and painting, were equally important. Nor was it long before an implicitly dramatic liturgy turned to more explicit drama and ultimately to street theater. Sacred arts moved from cathedral to market square and certainly linger in contemporary celebration. Through the "troping" of the liturgy, adding endless creative energies to final notes and syllables, new artistic energies poured into the church to elaborate the art of Gregorian chant.

The third century already saw the enactments of devotion around the true manger. The dramatic dimensions of the Christmas story—the appearance of angels to Mary and to shepherds, the search for room in the inn, the pilgrimage of the magi, the wrath of Herod—would, centuries later, eventuate in the first Christian plays. The immediate and recurring significance of the liturgy opened the way for seeing Christian worship as a theater for the reenactment of Christ's birth, life, death, and resurrection.

The first plays were in Latin, performed by a variety of religious staff moving about the building, with the sanctuary the central dramatic site. More actors, staging, and costumes were added. Given the illiteracy of much of the congregation, great importance was attached to symbols and visual signs, costumes, emblems, ceremonies, processions, and the dramatic tenor of daily life. Under the influences of religion, recreation, and commerce, these music-dramas went public, first to the open space in front of the great west entrances of the cathedrals, then in processions throughout the town, and eventually to fixed theater spaces. Driving religious drama ever outward was the natural desire of playwrights and audiences for an increase in scope, enrichments, content, and use of everyday language. The evolution of Christmas celebration runs from the liturgy to small dramas, from clerical to lay actors, from church to public sites, from Latin to the vernacular.

Christmas as a performance season begins around December 1, as the four Sundays of Advent prepare for the climax of Christmas Eve and Christmas Day. The Christmas season comes to a conclusion on Twelfth Night, January 6, after which follow Epiphany's attendant Sundays until the beginning of Lent on Ash Wednesday. By then Jesus has, in the lectionary readings, grown up, accepted baptism from John, turned water into wine, called disciples to himself, manifested divine glory, and is moving toward death and resurrection. By the end of the Middle Ages, nine festivals were occurring between November 11, St. Martin's Day, and February 2, the Presentation of our Lord and the Purification of Mary (Candlemas).

The church year is intended to nurture and delight through the familiarity of annually repeated stories and events. Year after year, Christians who follow it are provided the familiar constancy of repeated stories from Scripture encountered amidst changing life experiences and circumstances. Of course, many Protestants do not follow a Christian year, and for them Christmas in particular has often been a family celebration, though increasingly almost all Christian churches are offering Christmas Eve services. But many Protestants are more likely to stimulate spiritual growth and awareness through applied preaching or small group fellowship or daily Bible reading than through a regularized calendar of major festivals.

Especially in Roman Catholic and Orthodox thought, but also among Lutherans and Anglicans, the Christian Year is intended to be a planned running into mystery, a storing of grace for every season. For all Christians, however, worship is understood to mimic the dramatic patterns of divine initiative and human response, already evident in the Hebrew Bible and displayed again in the Christmas stories found in Matthew and Luke. In Old Testament thought, God first chooses a people and then, in turn, God is "enthroned on the praises of Israel." Early Christianity created the formula *lex orandi lex credendi* (the pattern of worship precedes what is confessed in doctrines). This seemed to mean that if the community gets its worship life right, everything else will follow.

Protestant Reservations

Historic legacies can be splendid gifts, ambiguous bequests, even unwelcome burdens. There is a long tradition, whether among Catholic mystics or Protestant reformers, of being hesitant, suspicious, or openly critical of formal liturgies, though not of public worship itself. To those who made Jerusalem temple worship normative while neglecting other dimensions of religious life, the Hebrew prophets insisted that God desires works of mercy more than ritual. In the New Testament Gospel of John, Jesus calls for a worship in spirit and in truth (4:23), and in the book of Acts, Stephen, about to be stoned as the first Christian martyr, challenges the crowd's attachment to the formal traditions of Jerusalem worship: "God does not dwell in temples made with hands" (Acts 7:48).

In the sixteenth century, Martin Luther, though a conservative reformer who cherished historic Christian traditions, laid out an early Protestant position: "Of what benefit to your neighbor are the many candles and much incense? Of what benefit to him is the much chanting, the singing of vigils and masses? Do you think that God wants to be served with the sound of bells, the smoke of candles, the glitter of gold and such fancies? He has commanded none of these, but if you see your neighbor going astray, sinning, or suffering in body or soul, you are to leave everything else and at once help him with words of comfort and prayer. Thus has Christ done to you and given you an example for you to follow."

Later Protestants, pioneering nonliturgical Christian traditions and rejecting much of the past, would insist that a vibrant fellowship is an attractive alternative to a too-frequently moribund formal worship. Believers themselves would be the temple of the Holy Spirit. Early Methodists, for example, and the frontier religion that followed them, spurned formalized worship and threw their energies into making of their gatherings a living edifice fit to communicate the warmth and passion of their faith. Lay preaching, lively fellowship, and fervent hymn singing, they believed, would create a more powerful Christmas celebration than any high church liturgy. In effect, then, the many Christian denominations are offering *widely varying performances of the same Christian classic*, each a unique and tradition-rich interpretation. A history of struggle over appropriate worship, over what is likely to please God the most, still backdrops modern Christian celebrations of Christmas. By no means do all Christians agree on how God's play is to be performed.

Can Liturgy Save Christmas?

Some would claim that Christmas ritualized and performed in the historic liturgies of Christianity is the only Christmas that can survive as a religious festival amidst the ever more aggressive encroachments of commodified culture and the subjection of human festival to the forces of consumerism. In a word, liturgy alone can save Christmas in the modern world. But what are the chances?

Scholars who study the long, even prehistoric, link between ritual and drama, religion and theater, wonder whether it has been permanently broken in the modern world. Long ago, the seven arts of history, poetry, comedy, tragedy, music, dance, and astronomy were all aspects of religious activity. Historians of theater, dance, and other arts write wistfully of these ancient connections, and some contemporary performers attempt to reestablish them.

But although there are fruitful collaborations between anthropologists and theater professionals, although investigations of ritual action are now pursued all the way back to animal behaviors, although many artists understand themselves to be on spiritual quests of one kind or another, on-the-street connections between religion and secular drama rarely occur. The continuous exchange between religion and culture, church and society, holy day and holiday continues, of course. May one hopefully conclude that Christmas as a religious holiday has in fact morphed into the street dramas of every December? Is this, then, the subtle triumph of religion in the world or its ultimate degradation—the tragic confirmation of the risk of Incarnation? Has the contest for December rewarded the church's risky venture or confirmed the long reach of a pre-Christian past?

The church is one of the few places left in modern societies where adults can still have a story read to them. There is a point to this. While the arts and ritual can excite, they also calm and focus. It is commonplace to notice and perhaps to lament that the Christmas story is fraying in the world while seasonal festivity overwhelms. Advice columnists report that the minions of holiday are exhausted, overspent, grim, depressed, and possibly without hope for times and places of respite and renewal. Each year brings news of a December chock full of stories of regret and excess, of running everywhere and getting nowhere, and no one can think what to do about it. Religion, naturally, aspires to get holy day right, even without condemning and indeed fully participating in holiday festivity. Those bent on "keeping Christ in Christmas," when they are not merely sour prohibitionists, argue that Christmas worship is the best hope of getting the season right.

All communal worship may be thought of as ritual. It is said that ritual is a "way of paying attention." In Italian folklore, Befana was so distracted by everyday life that she delayed setting out for Bethlehem, never saw the star, and was doomed to wander forever. Always she would leave gifts, hoping somewhere, sometime, somehow, to encounter the Christ child. Modern reformers of Christmas propose worshipful observance as the best antidote to that modern form of preoccupation that defaults to holiday busyness and, like Befana, misses the experience.

But sociologists and anthropologists see modern societies as not conducive to a rich ritual (and communal) life. The sociologist Max Weber diagnosed the modern "disenchantment of the world." Bureaucratic rationalization leaves little room for the validity of ritual, the market cannot measure its value, and unencumbered individualism does not readily immerse itself in meanings only accessible in community. After a "medieval synthesis" in which worship, music, image, culture, and community came together in an organic whole, the Renaissance and especially the Enlightenment seemed to break them apart. Disaggregated meanings no longer gather under the sacred canopy of religion. Ritual requires a social imagination and "social capital," now in decline or total eclipse. In such infertile ground, the religious ritualization of a major festival becomes vulnerable. Holy day, abducted from earlier roots, is susceptible to powerful economic forces that overgrow its meaning.

It is an open question whether effective Christian ritualization can retrieve Christmas as a uniquely religious festival and continue to imagine performances compelling to the modern world. Enthusiasts for religious ritual, with some scholarly support, remain hopeful. In all cultures, anthropologists report, ritual life offers an aesthetically rich and spiritually satisfying means to display and experience life as fully human. A lifetime of church years, for example, yields a vast repertoire for displaying the breadth of human response to God. *In ritual, worshipers pass through the festival of Christmas, and an entire Christian culture passes through the worshipers.*

Christmas worship intends to convey heartfelt and active participation, the depth dimension of human existence expressed in evocative symbols and a shared faith that is not either emotional or intellectual but both, fully integrating the affections with the mind. Liturgical worship is not reducible to the emotional jag of individualistic piety and star preachers nor to a cerebral format that exhausts itself in a didactic style that renders the community only an audience. Creative artists of worship understand the freshman-English admonition "show, don't tell." Martin Luther said that worship pauses our lives to let Christ do us good. Words and sacrament, spirit and matter, inner piety and extrinsic art are stereophonic stimulation of both sides of the brain, a full sensory participation far exceeding intellectual understanding or explanation.

In a manner Thoreau would recognize, theorists and practitioners of liturgy are determined to make the liturgies of Christmas a disturbing and empowering counterculture. In this attempt, Advent is a spiritual discipline enabling the attention that must be paid, an antidote to the powerful narcotic of the market. When every season of the year is homogenized into commerce, when shopping cannot be interrupted, society loses touch with former times and cannot find the way to hope for radically new times. The peace and nourishment of Walden Pond is missing. The practice of a sacred calendar becomes a mode of resistance to the relentless claims of the everyday. To number the days until Christmas as holy becomes a subversive enterprise. The Advent-Christmas-Epiphany season, like the Old Testament Sabbath, aspires to return to the great rhythms of creation and salvation. To reclaim the Christian year is to be reconstituted by an alternative narrative of human life. To take a parallel instance, Jews do not keep the Sabbath, the Sabbath keeps Jews. The idea of Christmas liturgies is to set worshipers free from bondage to the ephemeral—and to themselves.

It may seem that the odds are against successful performance of this holy day. Finally, artistically enriched and morally imagined liturgies speak for themselves—or do not. It is well known that some who cannot respond to Christmas piously can do so aesthetically. Worship with all the arts elaborating the Incarnation leaves profound and luminous experiences in the lives of many. Even the distracted, the ironical, or the dubious are sometimes drawn to the mysteries of sacred places. In the "staged heaven" of Orthodox Christianity, for example, one kisses icons, a profoundly different practice from glancing casually at religious art in a museum or overhearing carols while riding the escalators. The idea of liturgy is to be lifted beyond one's restricted and often idiosyncratic self into a fuller and communal vision of religion, in earth and heaven.

This is the rationale and ambition for church year and liturgy. But what does Christmas worship look like, sound like, feel like? In the next section is described an idyllic Christmas Eve service, a once-and-future celebration.

Staging Christmas Eve

The proliferation of Dickens villages that feed the collectibles trade suggests that Americans would like to imagine themselves in quaint small towns, in settings they can properly arrange to fit their dreams. From front yards and town squares spectacularly lit, from homes where the last door in the Advent calendar has been opened and the last chocolate gobbled, people make their way to worship. The path from the church parking lot is lined with evergreens and simple candles set in paper bags, according to the directions in *Sunset* magazine. Choirs are rehearsing, brass blowing, children nearly behaving. Old-timers who know to come early are trying to reserve seats with their purses and coats, while strangers look for a place, and the overflow is replete with modern Madonnas and their children. To the now-worn Advent wreath is added a white Christ candle, and the great tree with its ancient icons, lovingly crafted by the women's guild, is about to be lit. Every art has been invited: exultations in homemade stained glass, spectacular banners carried, unsteadily, in procession, hints of Bach or Handel if the choir has been ambitious, colorful altar hangings turning from Advent blue to Christmas white and gold, manger scenes awaiting the placement of their star character, poinsettias unnumbered (later to be delivered to shut-ins), and special creations of Christmas art hung high.

A hush comes over the congregation as opening devotions at the manger scene begin, in patterns that go back to fourth-century Christianity. Catholics and Protestants have been rocking the baby and singing carols to it for centuries. Today's manger scenes are marked with every culture and ethnicity. Throughout Advent the scene has been slowly populating, to signal for children and adults what all is on the way. Now the tableau, made up of the congregation's children, their parents avidly flashing cameras and video-recording, forms in front of the congregation. All in their finest dress, the lucky children play Mary and Joseph, and as many other characters as possible, and everyone waits the arrival of the baby, while singing "Away in a manger, no crib for his bed, the little Lord Jesus laid down his sweet head; the stars in the sky looked down where he lay, the little Lord Jesus asleep on the hay." The baby mysteriously appears, though not as in the Middle Ages—sliding down a wire.

Then it's time for the big procession, ritual on the move and signaling threshold-crossing into sacred time and place. Trumpets and bell-choirs alert the congregation, banners fly, the cross is carried at the head of the procession, acolytes come to light the candles, choirs of adults and children lead the singing, the organ sounds, and all sing,

> O come, all ye faithful, joyful and triumphant!
> O come ye, o come ye to Bethlehem;
> Come and behold him, born the king of angels:
> O come, let us adore him, O come, let us adore him,
> O come, let us adore him, Christ the Lord!

The *Gloria in excelsis Deo* has not been sung for the entire Advent season, as a kind of holding-back discipline, but now the congregation once again, in an elaborate treatment arranged for Christmas Eve, joins the angels in singing this standard exclamation of liturgical worship, "Glory to God in the highest, and peace to God's people on earth." A favorite prayer from the ancient church, just for this night, is prayed by all: "Almighty God, you made this holy night shine with the brightness of the true Light. Grant that here on earth we may walk in the light of Jesus' presence and in the last day wake to the brightness of his glory; through your only Son, Jesus Christ our Lord, who lives and reigns with you and the Holy Spirit, one God, now and forever."

Just as the earliest performances of Christmas were born in the hearing and reading of stories from Scripture, many modern Christians arrange to hear three Bible readings. The Old Testament reading from Isaiah, once written to celebrate a royal birth or coronation, now foretells that God will raise up one who will be "wonderful counselor, mighty God, prince of peace." A New Testament reading from Titus sounds, as it would have to late first-century ears, like an imperial proclamation: "The grace of God has appeared, bringing salvation to all."

A special procession now moves the ritual along again, as acolytes, cross-bearer, and ministers mark the drama when the Gospel is to be read. Alleluia verses sound, and the entire congregation turns toward the reader. It may be that a special, even bejeweled Gospel-book of red and gold is held high as its own kind of incarnate Word, the single most treasured object of Christian material culture. This year the congregation, many unaccustomed to smells and bells, has been prepared to notice the fragrance of incense to accompany the reading and to think of the magi. Of course, it is Luke's infancy narrative that is read (from which the magi are absent), the most famous words in the New Testament. The ruler of the Roman world is eclipsed by the arrival of a newborn child who brings good news to all the peoples. Angels sing, shepherds follow, Mary ponders. While this narrative can be read at home or recited along with Charlie Brown, in the formal worship of the church it achieves incantatory power. Fully to register the occasion, all lights are dimmed after the Gospel has been read, and candles are lit from minister to acolyte to the worshiper standing at the end of each row, everyone having learned how to tip their unlighted candle to receive the flame from their neighbor's erect lighted candle. All sing "Silent night, Holy night!" as grandmas cry, children hush in delight, and everyone wishes it might be so.

At this point, everyone who has invited their neighbors or dragged along adult children is hoping the sermon will not disappoint. The modern preacher aspires to move well beyond the old three-point conceptual edifice built of shaky intellectual arguments with a couple of *Reader's Digest* stories sprinkled on. Now the sermon is an extended narrative with plot, characters, and emotion, meant to draw the hearer into a synergy of divine direction and human response. The word of the sermon prefigures the Sacrament of the Eucharist, as the senses bring Christian proclamation to life. Like Jesus' parables, the sermon seeks to draw the listener in through familiar settings, only to upset contemporary equilibrium, analyze the dilemmas in human existence, and propose resolution, which is what the Gospel amounts to. Finally, there are deft suggestions as to the consequences that flow from transformation in Christ.

The central themes of Christmas worship are well expressed in verses from Luther's hymn for Christmas day:

> God's Son to whom the heavens bow,
> Cradled by a virgin now,
> We listen for your infant voice
> While angels in your heaven rejoice.
> Hallelujah!
>
> A little child, you came our guest,
> All the weary to give rest!
> Forlorn and lowly was your birth
> That we might rise to heaven from earth.
> Hallelujah!

Since the fourth century, the church has publicly confessed its faith with words from the Nicene Creed, hammered out over centuries to bear the weight of believers' experience of the incarnate Christ. Contextualizing Christmas celebration in the history of God and the long traditions of Christianity, it invites individual believers to fall in line with a mighty train of confessors across the ages.

When Catholics invented the "passing of the peace" in the 1960s, it was not to universal acclaim. Now almost all Christians find an opportunity for handshakes, hugs, and even kisses, as the gathered and somewhat straight-jacketed community flood out of fixed pews and dance their way to their neighbor, so that shoppers at Walmart and Bloomingdales, respectively, embrace, as at no other time. Ideally, considerable turmoil ensues, and order does not reassert itself too swiftly.

More ritual movement is occasioned when the "gifts of the people" are brought forth to be made holy, just as the gifts of nature, bread and wine, are also brought to the altar to become the body and blood of Christ, and as the magi once brought their gifts. This is meant to be an incarnational extravaganza, for those with wild imaginations. All creation becomes holy gifts for holy people, and the peoples' gifts of money go for the spread of the gospel and ministry to the poor.

A special Christmas prayer gets the congregation ready for the Eucharist: "It is indeed right and salutary that we should at all times and in all places offer thanks and praise to you, O Lord, holy Father, through Christ our Lord. In the wonder and mystery of the Word made flesh you have opened the eyes of faith to a new and radiant vision of your glory; that, beholding the God made visible, we may be drawn to love the God whom we cannot see. And so, with the church on earth and the hosts of heaven, we praise your name and join their unending hymn." The hymn that follows is the so-called Sanctus, full of holy holies. "Holy, holy, holy Lord, God of power and might: Heaven and earth are full of your glory. Hosanna. Hosanna. Hosanna in the highest. Blessed is he who comes in the name of the Lord. Hosanna in the highest."

Simple or elaborate prayers set Jesus' "words of institution" at the Last Supper into the entire history of salvation. The words from the New Testament are intoned: "In the night in which he was betrayed, our Lord Jesus took bread, and gave thanks; broke it, and gave it to his disciples, saying: Take and eat; this is my body, given for you. Do this for the remembrance of me. Again, after supper, he took the cup, gave thanks, and gave it for all to drink, saying: This cup is the new covenant in my blood, shed for you and for all people for the forgiveness of sin. Do this for the remembrance of me. For as often as we eat of this bread and drink from this cup, we proclaim the Lord's death until he comes."

These days it is common to pray the Lord's Prayer, which Luther called the greatest martyr in the Christian religion, in words of modern English that disturb the tongue and, maybe, the mind. Then the best opportunity for the ritual to move happens. Everyone is invited to come forward and mysteriously receive the very body and blood of Christ. The idea is a ritual passage for everyone that reenacts Jesus' own passage through death into new life. The juxtaposition of Christmas, Good Friday, and Easter is deliberate. As people move forward, many sing "Lamb of God, you take away the sin of the world; have mercy upon us." Then, as the Eucharist progresses, all sing:

> Let all mortal flesh keep silence
> And with fear and trembling stand;
> Ponder nothing earthly-minded
> For with blessing in his hand
> Christ our God to earth descending
> Comes our homage to demand.
>
> King of kings, yet born of Mary
> As of old on earth he stood,
> Lord of lords in human vesture,
> In the body and the blood,
> He will give to all the faithful
> His own self for heavenly food.

Then it's all over, and people sing lustily, perhaps also anticipating presents to be opened or live manger scenes to be visited or quarrels over the sermon to ensue:

> Joy to the world, the Lord is come!
> Let earth receive its King;
> Let every heart prepare him room
> And heaven and nature sing,
> And heaven and nature sing,
> And heaven, and heaven and nature sing.

4

Motley Crew: Pilgrims on Holiday

If someone said, on Christmas Eve,
Come; see the oxen kneel . . .
I should go with him in the gloom,
Hoping it might be so.

—Thomas Hardy, "The Oxen"

Men's empty hearts: let's ask for lodging there.

—Sir John Suckling, "Upon Christ His Birth"

Festivals and Pilgrims

Festivals draw pilgrims. The Incarnation sought human consent. The first Christmas congregation, the shepherds, were mangy. Jesus' disciples were unreliable. People seeking holy sites often detour. The hawkers and charlatans in the public square outside the great cathedral are beguiling. The Christmas story implies that God is content to draw a dubious crowd. That would be the church—simultaneously saints and sinners, as Luther always emphasized.

But a great play deserves a fitting audience. Ministers hope their congregations will become worthy of the stories they tell. Matthew and Luke, not to mention Saint Paul, wrote to shape the early Jesus movement into the body of Christ. The New Testament proclamation is about formation, not information. Still, the "Christian faith" as the objective summary of what Christians are called to believe is one thing; the homely and subjective assent that pilgrims muster is quite another. The church that stages Christmas and invites the world to its festal house is an ordered institution, but also a motley crew. Together, this is the uneven course of Incarnation as a divine-human venture.

Pilgrimage is an indispensable dimension of every world religion. Think of Muslims on their way to Mecca or Hindus heading for the Ganges. In Christianity, pilgrimage is a root metaphor for the journey from earth to heaven, and the posture of the pilgrim also defines the appropriate disposition for approaching a great festival. Over time, and in all religions, pilgrimage is connected to sacred sites and days. To see the pilgrim band is to glimpse how people in all times, believers and onlookers, interact with holy day and holiday, what Incarnation comes to in the real world. The Christmas authorized in the New Testament travels. Seekers and scallywags celebrate religious festival. That demarcation line runs through every human heart, as well.

Giving first place to divine initiative (grace), Christianity sees God as the primal pilgrim, traveling light-years from heaven's throne to Mary's womb. In the pious imagination, God comes in search of a guest house in every human soul. Mary and Joseph traveled to Bethlehem and Egypt and back, and the wise men made the first long journey in adoration of Christmas. Jesus replicates God's risky course when he takes the road from Galilee to Jerusalem, the journey that became his *via dolorosa*.

Pilgrimage is a root metaphor for Christ's direction, and his followers' redirection. Everyman is Adam, expelled from Paradise and now trying to find the way home. Early Christianity understood the Christian life as a travel narrative, a lifelong journey toward God. Festal sites are way stations.

The earliest Christian pilgrimage site was Jerusalem and its environs, advanced by Emperor Constantine in the middle of the fourth century to anchor the sacred texts of the new state religion. One of the earliest Christmas pilgrims we know about, towards the end of that century, was the Galician nun Etheria, who recorded her journey to the Holy Land. On Epiphany eve she joined worshipers processing from Jerusalem to Bethlehem and sang with them the night service at the grotto of the Holy Manger. Already in the third century, Origen had described the site of such devotions, over which a basilica was soon erected. Ancient pilgrims would enter the world of the magi through imitative gestures built into the Jerusalem liturgy. Christian pilgrimage meant to stimulate the eye of faith and awaken the power to conjure biblical events. Pilgrimage turns historic event into contemporary sacrament.

In Christian devotional practice, *pilgrimage is an attitude as well as a journey*, a disposition to seek and to find. Pilgrimage would seem to be what authentic celebration of Christmas requires—and mostly lacks. It is less going back in time than going down to depths of religious meaning, to the junction where God, who seeks the world, and humans, who seek God, embrace. The pilgrim trajects holy day in search of religious verification and spiritual adventure, all the while fully immersing in the material culture of holiday. But a mystic can travel far without even leaving home, as can a thoughtful reader. The point of pilgrimage is not the distance of the journey but the leap of imagination and the intensity of focus. Not every pilgrimage is heroic. W. H. Auden looks to Mary and Joseph as examples for everyday abilities and aspirations:

> Blessed Woman
> Excellent Man
> Redeem for the dull the
> Average Way,
> That common ungifted
> Natures may
> Believe that their normal
> Vision can
> Walk to perfection.

In India, Hindu pilgrims go to "take *darshan*" to see and to be seen by God. As in Christianity, the pilgrim views God viewing the pilgrim, an intentional reciprocity in which the seeker and the sought-after unite. The Hindu is expected to return with stories to tell and water from the Ganges to share. Pilgrims carry God back from festal celebration to everyday time.

Medieval dramatizations made Bethlehem a destination of wonder, the ideal site during a long age when pilgrimage captured the Christian imagination. In Boccacio's *Decameron*, a priest returns from the Holy Land with a feather the angel Gabriel dropped in the Virgin Mary's bedroom. Abbot Suger described the extreme congestion on the great feast days when pilgrims could scarcely move at the great cathedral of Saint-Denis. Occasionally, nearly faint women would need to be hoisted up by pious men and passed over the heads of the crowd as they screamed out as if in labor. Perhaps modern Christmas shoppers know this experience.

The pilgrim requires traveler's aid. This was the ministry of Saint Christopher. His legend has him aspiring to serve the most powerful man on earth, presumably some king. But a hermit diverts him to a higher service by telling him to wait patiently at the bank of a river, occupying himself carrying travelers to the other side. One night he carries a little child, who, growing heavier and heavier, tells him he is bearing the weight of the world on his shoulders, thereby revealing himself to be the Christ. Christopher ("Christ-bearer") is usually depicted with one foot in the water and the other on the shore, with Christ on his shoulder. The Christian pilgrim forges the streams of the world, longing for the far side.

Christmas carols sing of pilgrimage. An English carol, "I saw three ships come sailing in," depicts Christ and his lady sailing in on Christmas Day in the morning: "Pray whither sailed those ships all three/ O, they sailed into Bethlehem." A fifteenth-century German carol brings together the Mediterranean journeying of the relics of the magi to Cologne, the splendor of whose final voyage had remained vivid in European folk memory, a long German tradition of symbolic ships, and of course the notion of Mary/the church on a pilgrimage through the world with Christ himself as their cargo:

There comes a ship a-sailing
With angels flying fast;
She bears a splendid cargo
And has a mighty mast.

This ship is fully laden,
Right to her highest board;
She bears the Son from heaven,
God's high eternal word.

And that ship's name is Mary,
Of flowers the rose is she,
And brings to us her baby
From sin to set us free.

The ship made in this fashion,
In which such store was cast
Her sail is love's sweet passion
The Holy Ghost her mast.

—Percy Dearmer (translator)

In the New Testament, sacred site gives way to sacred person. Christ is present in the church, and the church is the body of Christ—in terms that do not require travel, because the road to the real Jerusalem runs through the heart and into the setting of worship. The sacred geography of the Old Testament became, momentarily, dispensable. But it would not be long before European Christianity generated innumerable sacred sites, together with a vast material culture of Christmas. This may have stemmed from a relentless incarnational attachment to holy place, holy person, holy time, and holy material, or to Christianity's adaptation to pre-Christian preoccupations with a sacred earth with sacred seasons. Modern Europe has six thousand pilgrimage sites that generate sixty to seventy million religiously motivated visits each year. Humans seek the blessing of proximity, as skaters do in front of the Christmas tree at Rockefeller Center in December.

In every age, seekers of all kinds and for all things find their ways. Medieval roads were crowded with gullible believers on their way to relics of dubious provenance, and shrines grew rich from suffering humanity. It was also easier to sin freely when far from home, and to detour gladly to the extravagances of holiday. Saints Anselm and Bernard tried to forbid monastic pilgrimage and impose "stability" as a needed monastic virtue, along with poverty, chastity, and obedience. They admonished monks to confine their travels to their hearts. But nobles would write their names on the very walls of the Church of the Holy Sepulcher or on the slab that covers the tomb of the Lord. One pilgrimage guide book offered the phrase "Woman, may I sleep with you," in Greek, Slavonic, Arabic, and Jewish speech.

"Lived religion," in contrast to theological formulation, is always messy, just like the celebration of Christmas. The metaphor of pilgrimage is a useful window on how religion actually works itself out in the world. The fervent piety of all who respond to divine initiative or set out on sacred quests jostles against the bewildering transgressions of holy day by holiday—often in the same person. Anthropologists have learned to observe closely the great rituals of cultural performance as a way of discovering what matters in society, becoming aware of all the currents that rush beneath the surface.

If Christmas, in one way or another, invites the response of pilgrimage, that metaphor suggests leading and misleading, finding one's way and getting lost, matter and spirit, main streets and dead-ends. Of all the Christian festivals, Christmas is the one that thoroughly mixes the divine in the crucible of this world, intentionally blending sacred and secular and thereby also attracting detour and diversion. Christian theologians, and Plato before them, have always worried about excessive entanglements with matter. Religious communities therefore have made careful preparations for pilgrimage, as Advent specifically prepares for the perils of Christmas. Special liturgies with the prayers and good wishes of the church commissioned medieval pilgrims. They marked their clothing with a red cross and carried staff and scrip, symbols of their endeavor. Yes, they collected souvenirs to show where they had been, to prove they arrived. (In some ways, they were not unlike modern rock fans who wear T-shirts that feature their band's concert tour.) Sometimes they practiced forty days of sexual abstinence before setting out, an unlikely choice today. No matter the definitions and directions of ecclesiastical authorities, or even the normative constructions of the Bible itself, individual pilgrims at festival blur the boundaries of holy day and holiday, because they live in both worlds, because those lines run through their own consciousness.

Pilgrimage as the Ideal Way

Even with its undeniable foot in holiday, pilgrimage is never less than (if also more than) an idealized devotional posture suitable for holy day, a challenge to set out on journeys, real or imagined, that cross thresholds and achieve transcendent meaning. A pilgrimage at Christmas would search for out-of-the-way routes that run away from December every-days. Hopeful Christians say that on Christmas Eve all roads lead to Bethlehem. "O little town of Bethlehem, how still we see thee lie." In the Festival of Nine Lessons and Carols at King's College, Cambridge, seen on television or heard on countless recordings, worshipers are entreated each year to go the distance: "Beloved in Christ, in this Christmastide, let it be our care and delight to hear again the message of the angels, and in heart and mind to go even unto Bethlehem, and see this thing which is come to pass, and the babe lying in a manger."

Jung and New Age devotees who look to him for inspiration encourage mythic journeys as the best way to uncover the meaning of life. Dante, the paragon of Christian culture, began the *Divine Comedy:* "In the mid-path of my life, I woke to find myself in a dark wood." Being lost in the forest is said to be the emotional and spiritual landscape of modern life. Quests for the grail search for something that is wanting. In that myth, the king's wounds will not heal, the realm remains a wasteland, and no one seems to know why. In Jung's analysis, the journey of adventure is an invitation to the pilgrim-as-hero. Pilgrimage becomes the locus of transformation, a threshold across old horizons and concepts, a passage of dying and rebirth. It becomes possible to experience a synchronicity of the subjective world and outer events. But in Jungian thought epiphanies come only to those who search diligently and ask the right questions.

As Chaucer did, it is not hard to imagine a group of potential pilgrims today. Perhaps they are sitting around a table in

November wondering what to do about Christmas. There are pointed discussions about who "ruined Christmas" last year and who is likely to do so this year. What about lonely people for whom Christmas seems to accelerate depression? Can the kitsch on every corner this year be so over the top that it makes one smile? Someone remembers a caroling party where no one actually believed the words but increased the eggnog intake to cloud the loss. Pointless, excessive shopping extravaganzas lie, dreaded, ahead for everyone, and most of the people on the list have everything they need. A thousand-dollar gift to the Heifer Project did not much impress the children last year, in whose name it was given. Adult children home for the holiday will not be able to decide between going to church on Christmas Eve to please their parents or staying home to make a stand on behalf of their independence. The relatives' arrival and contributions for Christmas Dinner will again be uneven and inconsistent. People who bring rock music to play during the festival dinner because carols are passé will once again prove themselves tiresome. The children's program at church will seem under-rehearsed. Out-of-town guests taken to Christmas Eve services in hopes of impressing them back into the faith will discover that it is not one of the pastor's better years, and the choir will seem more amateurish than usual. The annual tickets to Tchaikovsky or Dickens will be overpriced, and it will not be evident that the family is deeply grateful to the one who pays for them. No one thinks long, thoughtful Christmas letters are anything but self-aggrandizement, so they have been discontinued, and most of the cards that arrive carry no personal note. At church, the clergy and the musicians will quarrel throughout the month (as in Bach's day), and at home one spouse will stew over how to pay for the other's extravagances. "Step" issues in the extended family will reappear, as each set of children scrutinizes the other. Almost everyone has an idea of what a perfect Christmas would be like; none of them agree and none comes close to being fulfilled.

As a destination of modern pilgrimage, the festival of Christmas is over-wrapped and overwrought. Any opportune moment, like a birthday or an anniversary or a graduation or a wedding, will be cluttered with the everyday, but Christmas is the apotheosis of bewildering array. As everyone longs for a peak experience as "O holy night" is sung, annual dismay is registered when the soprano or tenor manage again to slide in just under the high notes. No one can find a direct line to a perfect Christmas and a genuine religious experience. In all the centuries of Christianity, believers and hangers-on have hoped to hear the voice of God with perfect clarity, at least on Christmas Eve. The pious and the doubtful have tried to imagine eye-witnessing great events ("Oh, that we were there"), shaking hands with the characters, even finding a role for themselves in the story. Christmas, the most wonderful and the most difficult of all the holy days, stimulates the essential pilgrimage question: Can you get there from here?

In a little town on the Romantic Road in southern Germany, there is a small chapel with a world-famous altar by Tilman Riemenschneider, the greatest of German wood carvers. The pamphlet available to those who turn aside to look beckons tourists to slow down and soak up the experience. The altar, one is admonished, does not betoken the everyday reality of this world but seems to be a piece fallen down from the kingdom of God. "Every intricate detail cries out: Lift up your heart and mind! Flee your quotidian thoughts and lift your eyes heavenward." A near contemporary of Riemenschneider, Martin Luther, wrote in a hymn for Christmas:

> Your coming in the darkest night
> Makes us children of the light,
> Enabling us in realms divine
> Like all your angels bright to shine!
> Hallelujah.

Goethe admonished: What you have inherited from the past you must take pains to possess yourself. How is this done? As we have seen, Christianity—and all the religions of the world—have thought that the way of the pilgrim represents the perfect posture for approaching deep religious experiences and making the most of holy day and holiday. The pilgrim arrives, it is hoped, fully susceptible to mystery and magic. There are alternatives, of course: the way of the shopper whose over-exertions promise perfect gratitude from everyone; the way of the aesthete who buys tickets to exquisite exhibitions of beauty; the way of the bon vivant who seeks ultimate joy in perfectly matched food, wine, and guests; the way of the curmudgeon who enjoys insulting the Salvation Army bell-ringers; the way of the mother as martyr who gives all each year to her ungrateful family; the way of the tourist who, practicing celebration on the run, gives fifteen minutes to each of twenty experiences; the way of the lonely who pout for some sound from God or at least from the next-door neighbor.

Contemporary writers on the spiritual quest emphasize that any starting point for a modern pilgrimage will do. In the kitchen of a preoccupied house, for example, a mysterious invitation to set out on a mid-winter journey is opened. It is an incitement to move beyond the prevailing lament, "Is this all there is?" It requires a wager not to settle for what is on sale locally. Pilgrimage, as it has been practiced in the world religions, means to permeate the membranes between worlds, the real and the longed for, ultimate meaning and everyday life, imagination and reality, and also individual and community, performer and audience. A Christmas pilgrim, even the shopper searching for the right present and the right attitude from the recipient, hopes that once a year the world as imagined and the real world perfectly come together.

Lived religion, like holy day and holiday, is always a muddle. The motivations for pilgrimage abound: sanctity and even perfection, reconsecration, the journey to God, discipleship, amendment of life, imitation of Christ, fulfilling a vow. But also: the challenge of great difficulties, handling relics, embracing material culture, collecting souvenirs, excitement, snobbery, loneliness, curiosity, time off, even sexual adventure at the office Christmas party. There are trappings that sustain and that mislead: the prayers of the church, the power of images, alms, hospitality, profiteers, trade in trinkets, conspicuous consumption. A mountain of gifts given and received glitters at the shrine. The child beneath is as dim as a distant star. A congenial agnosticism is in the air. A quaint sign reminds the ironic that bedlam, the English name for insanity and disarray, is a contraction of Bethlehem, after the London hospital Saint Mary of Bethlehem. But retreat leaders and devotional authors promise that to every pilgrim unexpected encounters are possible and no reservations are required. Even uncertain pilgrims at dubious sites are said to receive a blessing, if only, as T. S. Eliot said, they kneel where prayer has been valid. Bethlehem, it is hoped, is a magnet to attract all the filings of human yearnings.

At the conclusion of every Passover celebration, Jews say to one another, "Next year in Jerusalem." But even participation in a perfected holy day is preceded and followed and utterly contextualized by a holiday set on a world stage. The church as the festival house for Christmas does not control the breadth of the celebration, and there is demonstrated again the risk of Incarnation.

5

Staging Incarnation: Material Culture and the Traveling Manger Scene

Away in a manger, no crib for a bed
The little Lord Jesus laid down his sweet head
The stars in the sky looked down where he lay
The little Lord Jesus, asleep on the hay.

—American

Ah dearest Jesus, holy child
Make thee a bed soft undefiled
Within my heart that it may be
A quiet chamber kept for thee.

—Martin Luther

The Evolution of a Christmas Prop

The manger scene, or crèche, is the most important prop in the staging of Christmas. If you keep your eye on it over time, you get a sense of the course of Incarnation in the world. Fourth-century pilgrimages to the primal scene in Bethlehem brought first-century biblical texts back to life. Because not many can go to Bethlehem, the manger became one of the first objects of material culture to travel, when the relics of the original were brought to Rome as objects of devotion. Through the pious imagination of Saint Francis in the twelfth century, the manger scene became the visible impetus for a long-lasting and revolutionary Franciscan piety, and soon nuns and then the laity were rocking the baby Jesus annually. When the nineteenth-century Mexican revolution was contesting the public place of Catholicism in a newly-declared secular state, the manger scene made into a home altar relocated incarnational presence from church to home. But home altars raise questions for Protestants, who worry about the propensity for idolatry in material culture and prefer to limit God's drive into the vernacular. In the late twentieth century the manger scene became a stick in the hornet's nest of church-state contests in the United States.

The manger scene cues the continuous expansion of Christmas celebrations beyond churchly settings. If the sacred texts that authorize Christmas acquire new readings, if the dramatis personae acquire the clothing of diverse times and cultures, if Christian liturgies evolve under theological and artistic pressure and opportunity, if pilgrims travel to destinations of their own choosing, it is no surprise that the central prop of Christmas, the manger scene, will find itself on stages far beyond Bethlehem or any churchly provenance. Its portability and its intrinsic capacity to hallow secular site made it a fit festival object in public squares and markets. Manger scenes can turn into high art, but they also acquire the shapes and materials of manufactured culture, and they are everywhere. Originally adjunct to the high altars of historic Christianity, they soon enough became altars of their own, set up in pious homes in quaint annual rituals and erected in public squares to put shoppers in the Christmas spirit.

Only the Gospel of Luke has a manger scene and "no room in the inn." By the third century, Christian pilgrims were flocking to see the original site of Jesus' birth. When Emperor Constantine converted to Christianity and made it the official religion during the course of the fourth century, the sacred sites of Bible times achieved increasing religious and political significance as stimulations to the formative piety of a lost age of eyewitnesses. Already in the fourth century, the manger took center stage, as an abundance of material culture began to pile up in the wings of Christmas performance, from Bethlehem to Rome. Devotions to the original manger, or cave, soon stretched across the Mediterranean. When relics of the true manger were brought to Rome in the fifth century and deposited in a special basilica devoted to Christmas, Santa Maria Majori, holy day devotions began to accumulate *ad praesepe*, around the manger. From the Latin pr*aesepe* the manger scene entered every vernacular, for example, the French *crèche* and the German *Krippe*.

When itinerant medieval actors took the Christmas play onto carts rolling through the streets, the manger scene went along. The point of theatrical staging is to lure audience imagination into the play, as the Neapolitan artisans did in ever more elaborate manger settings that they filled with characters and scenes from contemporary village life. Artists and patrons have always loved to paint or sculpt themselves into nativity sets, just as carols situated the simplest hearers in the scenery of Bethlehem. As household shrine, the manger becomes a festival theater in miniature and under local management.

If it evoked art or artifact, it was first of all meant to stimulate devotion. The manger provided spiritual and psychological proximity to the mystery of divine interaction with humans and nature. While theologians were often bent on mystical transport back to heaven, the manger scene rooted the Incarnation in a material earth. Its homely realism kept the Christmas stories from evaporating into an immaterial spirituality. When the manger scene migrated to every imaginable space, it symbolized the reach of the Incarnation, as God took up ever new habitations. There is a gentle subversiveness when the crèche escapes ecclesiastical siting and suggests that God is fond of instigating direct relations with believers and pilgrims away from churchly control.

Franciscan Piety

Most famously, Saint Francis in 1223 assembled a live manger scene in a humble outdoor setting at the edge of his village. He consecrated this natural site by preaching a sermon and holding a Christmas Mass. His first biographer, Thomas of Celano, tells how

Francis was overcome with tenderness and filled with joy, bleating like a sheep. Saint Bonaventure recounted the original story: Three years before his death Francis wanted to prepare a special celebration of the birth of Jesus, received authorization from the pope, made ready a manger, and had hay, ox, and ass brought to the place. His followers and villagers gathered that night, and the woods rang with their songs. Francis stood at the manger bathed in tears, chanted the Gospel, and then preached about the child of Bethlehem. A knight in the congregation saw, in a vision, that a little child came into the manger and roused from sleep at Francis's words. Miracles followed and then a distinctive Franciscan piety.

In the early centuries of Christianity, the Christ Child of Byzantine art had sat rigidly upright like a miniature adult ruler, looking regally at his subjects. More than anyone else, Saint Francis shifted attention from the adoration of the Christ Child in rich and elaborate tableaux to his actual humble birth, with hints of suffering and death to come. This had an enormous influence on the teaching and piety of the church and on European art. No doubt Francis saw the child through the eyes of his own vow of absolute poverty. His homely manger scene was a far cry from, and an implicit critique of, the splendor of the Roman church. Leaving the rich trappings of a privileged life behind, he had set out to preach repentance and the imitation of Christ. Soon many followed him into a life of apostolic poverty. In arranging for that unique Christmas Eve mass of 1223, Francis wrote to his patron, the mayor of Greccio: "I would like to represent the birth of the Child just as it took place at Bethlehem, so that men should see with their own eyes the hardships He suffered as an infant, how He was laid on hay in a manger with the ox and the ass standing by."

Franciscan street theater brought the mystical theology of the monks to the common people. It connected the crib to the sacrifice of the Mass and made the baby the one who suffers. This was the Franciscan approach: As God, who is love, loved and redeemed us in his dying, we, too, must learn to love, but we are blinded by sin. Devotees will aspire to a more human love if they are drawn to this little helpless infant. Here at this manger and in the Eucharist that follows it, love is reborn in the human heart. God, in this baby, is depending on us. The exalted theology of the Incarnation becomes comprehensible to everyone. As God descended into the human vernacular at Bethlehem, now Christian art and piety take the majesty of Incarnation theology to the eye-level of peasants on their knees at the crib. God has become a baby. Christ is re-humanized. Christ, in that child, is God's special gift to the poor. Christmas is the amazing day when God first sucked on a human breast, and Francis called it the celebration of celebrations. God makes himself a vulnerable baby who requires the affection, care, and protection of human beings. The next centuries saw a flood of religious literature that emphasized the human nature of Christ, his feelings and his physical pain. God had become approachable and sympathetic again in the face of doctrinal efforts to lift him high. God is a baby we are admonished to rock or to pick up.

The Franciscan crib traditions would make Christmas democratic and expand incarnational piety to encompass all sorts of people. Everyone was invited in, not just the ancient shepherds and wise men or contemporary churchmen. Still today, every Christmas Eve the people of Greccio relive the moment when Francis set up his crib among them. A costumed procession makes its way by torchlight from the town square to a Franciscan sanctuary with a hallowed grotto. On a mountainside, because the grotto is too small to accommodate everyone, there is a pageant with actors and living ox and ass. The sets are made at Cincitta, Italy's film production center in Rome, and many hundreds come to see.

In the fourteenth century, Margaretha Ebner, a Dominican nun, received a cradle with a baby-like doll as she was making her religious vows. The gift made a huge impression on her and inspired dreams; in one she is awakened by the child playing in his cradle, picks him up, kisses him, and suckles him at her breast. Small wooden cradles, a few still in existence from the fifteenth century, focused a particular kind of devotion. In the Netherlands noblewomen entering convents were commonly presented with a cradle that could hold a figure of a child, but more often they were elaborately carved and gilded miniatures. (If cradle-rocking focused on Christ's humanity, a splendidly ornate cradle might emphasize his divinity.) A devotional handbook of the period has meditation and prayer, personified, tucking the baby into bed and plumping his pillow: "One now gathers up the sweet little Child Jesus and lifts Him from His crib. As Jesus himself said, one must lift up the Son of Man so that all those who believe in Him do not perish, but may have eternal life." Nuns would sew clothes for baby Jesus dolls and rock the cradle at Christmas. But in Florence, the ever vigilant Savonarola accused nuns of treating their infant dolls like idols.

Carols provided musical accompaniment. In German lands worshipers would rock the baby's cradle and sing lullabies, a practice adopted from nunneries. In churches, the cradle would stand before the altar, with a brightly colored Christ-child visible within, and the priest—and eventually enthusiastic parisioners—would rock the cradle in time with the music of a cradle song:

Come, angels, come from heaven, appear!
Eia, eia, susani, susani, susani (hush; sleep, child)
Come sing, come pipe, come trumpet here!
Alleluia, alleluia, et in excelsis Gloria.

With softest touch let lutes reply
To soothe the Child with lullaby.

Some churches had two cradles, one for the priest to rock and another in the midst of the congregation, hung about with bells, for the children to rock. Carol-singers also carried cradles through the streets, props for their songs. In Provencal, Christmas celebrations included making model villages, complete with crib and vividly characterized villagers, and worshipers brought torches to light the way, as in the carol:

Bring a torch, Jeanette, Isabella.
Bring a torch to his manger bed.
This is Jesus, good hope of the village,
Christ is born, hear Mary's warning
Hush, hush, softly sleeps the child.

The manger scene did not disappear with the coming of Protestantism. For his children, Luther wrote "From heaven above to earth I come." As they gathered at home, they sang these verses:

These are the things which you will see
To let you know that it is he:
In manger-bed, in swaddling clothes
The child who all the earth upholds.

Look, look, dear friends, look over there!
What lies within that manger bare?
Who is that lovely little one?
The baby Jesus, God's dear Son.

O Lord, you have created all!
How did you come to be so small,
To sweetly sleep in manger-bed
Where lowing cattle lately fed?

Kneeling at the manger is meant to induce wonder at the juxtaposition of heaven and earth, power and vulnerability, grace and nature, God and a baby. An aria in Bach's *Christmas Oratorio* acknowledges how the little baby, surrounded by Herod's raging, could with a wave of his hand have called for heavenly reinforcements, but did not. Luther's hymn for Christmas Day proclaimed:

A manger choosing for a throne
While worlds on worlds are yours alone.

Francis had set in motion an artistic enterprise in which craftsmen would produce replicas of every village role, from butcher to housewife to playing children, and every village scene, and set them into the holy context of the original manger. In the enchanting Catholic imagination, all life was sacrilized. Common people were brought on stage. Like the more recent Dickens villages, manger scenes feature a colorful array of people from everyday life. These are pious, or casual, self-insertions into the orbit of God's presence. They are saying, presumably, "I too am in the picture."

The manger anchors, localizes, rivets, materializes the Incarnation. Every imaginable kind of manger scene, from the humblest to the most grand, has emerged in the material culture of

Christianity. The cities of Naples and Munich and the Metropolitan Museum in New York are contemporary repositories of this history. Bamberg, a city in Bavaria, stages each December the *Krippenweg*, along which lie more than thirty churches, museums, and public squares that display original crib scenes. The walk begins in the cathedral at the altar to Mary by the wood sculptor Veit Stoss. Pilgrims and tourists from there follow a route that winds through the city, where manger scenes range from life-sized figures to delicate miniatures. Set against local landscapes with half-timbered Franconian houses, the scenes are populated by people in vernacular costumes. The city sponsors a Krippenbauschule that passes on this four-hundred-year sculpting tradition to the next generation.

The Manger Scene as Home Altar

In nineteenth-century Mexico, drenched in political turmoil as reform governments struggled to limit the public power of the Catholic Church, some religious practices moved from church to household, where religious images and even home altars symbolized alternative religious space. Tin *retablo* art flourished for home devotional use throughout the country. While it resembles religious images placed in church altars and paintings on wood, copper, and canvas by European and Mexican artists from the fifteenth to the eighteenth centuries, it may also have pre-Columbian precedents in small household gods and clay votive figurines. This is the way Catholicism has produced an organic piety that plants Christian festivals in native soil. Domestic shrines and home altars reached their greatest importance during times of political turmoil. New legislation that sought to separate church and state reinforced the privatization of religion and paved the way for domestic devotions.

Arranged in highly personal ways, sacred objects facilitate human communication with God. These *sacramentals* are the Incarnation miniaturized in material culture. When sacred objects are displayed in place, a hallowed room becomes a church, a natural feature in the landscape a grotto, a bedroom chest a domestic altar. In fact, the first churches in Mexico were really constituted as enclosures around sacred objects brought by missionaries. The presence of God traffics back and forth between church and home or other sacred places. In the home different kinds of piety come to prevail, as one prays directly to Mary or the saints and expects a particular response not mediated by the clergy. Personal interactions are possible: one can dress sacred images, move them about, speak to them, change their appearance, and render them a homely part of daily life. This is a piety of seeing and touching, in which the sacred turns into a visual, tactile experience. It is a profound example of the indispensability of material culture in the rooting of Christianity in heart and mind, in the sacred spaces of public squares and private homes.

A sacred space within a Roman Catholic household may be compared with practices in Hinduism or Buddhism. A Hindu household shrine, tended daily by women, brings balance and welfare to the family and serves as a microcosm of Hinduism throughout the land. Home, family, clan, religion are all marked as a sacred cosmos, just as was also true in the Christian Middle Ages and sometimes today.

Protestants, too, became comfortable with manger scenes, even if few other religious images are displayed in their homes. Indeed, evangelical Protestantism took Christmas home to the family after it had proscribed Christmas as a churchly (and Catholic) festival. A later chapter displays the trees, decorations, cards, lights, and cooking that certainly fill every Protestant home with the material culture of Christmas. If not precisely the Catholic visual image of an invisible God, not quite an Orthodox icon, it is yet a staple of popular culture. What does the ubiquity of manger scenes imply? Do such objects of popular culture reflect the determined will of people to express themselves in folk art? Or is it mere mass market from a capitalism whose tentacles leave no marketing space unreached? It is not possible to tell, either for Catholics or Protestants, whether store-bought religious images and accoutrements are thoughtful extensions of an inner piety and symbols of a larger world of meanings—or relatively meaningless decorations created in Chinese factories.

Every child's first manger scene is likely to be under the Christmas tree at home. In the 1950s, many American homes had a cardboard manger scene with a perforated star at the top that allowed a bulb from the tree lights to reach down and shine on the baby's face. The finer the tree's ornamentation, however, and the more abundant the presents, the more likely the manger scene will be concealed, so a special display table might be arranged. Manger scenes are cardboard and papier-mâché and wood and resin and glass and ceramic and fabric. Usually their figures are movable, so individuals can place shepherds and wise men and animals and the baby in the feeding trough just right, with Mary and Joseph satisfactorily hovering. They are cheap enough to be replaced every year or dear enough to become heirlooms for the next generation.

Protestantism and Material Culture

But when the manger scene morphs into home altar or household shrine, or even holy image, the Protestant sensibility becomes jittery. Until recently, the descendents of the sixteenth-century reformers John Calvin and Ulrich Zwingli suspected that a deeply flawed human imagination would thwart the capacity of the image to reveal the divine to which it referred. They feared God would be reduced to something manipulable by humans and the divine essence confused with material form. For this theology, the original is in heaven, not on earth. But for Luther, heaven has emptied out onto earth. God is to be found in the manger, where Jesus is, not up in a heaven the soul tries foolishly to ascend by spiritual ladder. For Luther, and of course for Catholics, there is a visual and musical rhetoric of immediacy. The body, and embodiment, are not despised as organs of knowing. The image and the crib evoke an emotional relationship to God that can personalize belief and make a homely material culture central to the practice of devotion.

But for much of Protestantism, it is much harder to make the material body an instrument of grace. Instead, it is the unruly seat of the passions. For the early American Puritan Jonathan Edwards, authentic faith is signified by a selfless, disinterested contemplation of God's beauty. The visual imagination cannot get to that important place because it is bound to deceive by inverting the proper relation of humanity to its sovereign God. There is disagreement on how extensively conservative Protestant homes feature religious or devotional images, though the use of bumper stickers and T-shirts and other signs of a religious counterculture is not in doubt. It seems to be the case that evangelical Protestantism, even considering its penchant for Holy Land trips and its fascination with the materiality of the nation of Israel, prefers memory and time to sacred space, because the latter is too easily idolatrous—or Catholic. God is perceived to occupy not sacred space but individual hearts and minds. Yet, evangelical Christianity produces an embodied friendship with Jesus in the life of Christian communities, and contemporary Protestant mega-churches seem to have caught up to Catholicism in a relatively benign view of popular religiosity. Prayer, song, testimony, and Bible study carry the sacred, even if the only true sacred space is heaven.

It is an interesting question whether Protestant suspicion of material culture as a location for incarnational theology helped abandon a churchly Christmas to the secular world, where, its divinity discarded, it became, by turn, a site of harmless domesticity or rapacious capitalism. The ironical Protestant contribution to the celebration of Christmas was to help empty holiday of any residual holy day. Iconoclastic Protestants know how to make a manger in their hearts, but find it difficult to believe in the sanctity of a manger made with hands. But like all people, they have a hunger for material culture, because they live an embodied existence. Their homes are filled with reindeer, their lawns with snowmen. They have emptied material culture of its theology, in order to make it secular and safe. But a Protestant world from which divine Incarnation is subtracted is very different from the one centuries of Christianity thought Christmas had enchanted. The word for it is secular.

Sometimes secular production values far exceeded those of the church, as when store windows display breathtakingly beautiful tableaux. Of course, they charmed shoppers and made it easier for those with holy day consciences to enjoy holiday. Even factory goods from China, when religious meanings are attached, form the texture of everyday life. Images help secure the world of belief and establish the boundaries of a genuine physical world in which believers find their existence. A manger scene may fill the angle of everyday vision in a way that makes a constructed environment congruent with mind and heart. Material culture makes room for the meanings one wants to hold on to. It "takes space" for religion to "take place."

Since the Incarnation seems to challenge the religious imagination to widen a space for divine presence, material culture arises to fill that space and attract thoughtful attention or devotional reflection. The material culture of religion marks identity, just as national or ethnic or class symbols do. Any home altar, any prized manger scene, piles up material objects that bridge the divine and human worlds. Like family heirlooms, they stimulate the memory of things past and pass them on to new futures. Around them, a life of religious rituals and devotion can be constructed and maintained.

Encroaching on the Public Square

But when manger scenes today move into the public square, they provoke conflict, in the United States though not in Europe. While few protest carols in the mall or Christmas trees in public spaces, the manger scene, no matter how trite, is unavoidably a religious icon. As such, it has come to bear the weight of dissent in church-and-state arguments and in concerns about assertions of Christian hegemony in a pluralistic society. Does a manger scene on public property constitute an "establishment of religion," give evidence of national and historic traditions, or merely provide a pleasantly legitimating stimulus to consumerism? Several cases have been brought to the United States Supreme Court. A nativity scene on a public lawn in Pawtucket, Rhode Island, was narrowly approved, but a crèche in a courthouse was not. Based on one court decision, municipalities began to adopt the "plastic reindeer rule": the greater number of secular symbols surrounding the religious one, the more likely to pass court muster.

Toward the end of the twentieth century, the courts seemed to tilt away from weighing the First Amendment "establishment clause" against its "free exercise clause" in favor of moving towards the "free speech" clause. *Religious* speech cannot be singled out for prohibition. One solution was to allow private parties to erect a crèche on public land if the space functioned as a typical public forum in which any and all citizens could express their views. Government may not discriminate regarding the content of free speech. The presence of religious symbols is then accepted because the government is not presumed to endorse everything that occurs in a public forum, especially one more or less removed from the seat of government. But for many Christians, a public manger scene is a deliberate means of reclaiming Christmas as the birthday of Christ, "the reason for the season." Or does Lawrence Ferlinghetti get it right in his poem "Christ climbed down," in which Jesus tries to escape his burial under tinsel, ornaments, and gifts?

6

Re-Presenting Incarnation: The Role of Theology

In the beginning was the Word and the Word was God.
The Word became flesh and lived among us and we have seen his glory.

—John 1:1, 14

Without any doubt the mystery of our religion is great:
God was revealed in flesh, vindicated in spirit,
seen of angels, proclaimed among Gentiles,
believed in throughout the world, taken up in glory.

—1 Timothy 3:16

Strong Son of God, immortal Love,
Whom we, that have not seen thy face,
By faith, and faith alone, embrace,
Believing where we cannot prove . . .
Our little systems have their day;
They have their day and cease to be:
They are but broken lights of thee,
And thou, O Lord, art more than they.

—Alfred, Lord Tennyson, "In Memoriam"

After early Christianity had taken its first centuries to ponder the meanings of its experience of Jesus, it gave the world Christmas as the birth announcement of a turning point in human history. Christmas would be the jewel in the crown of an incarnational theology whose singular idea is that the ultimate self-disclosure of God is the one in which God appears in earthly form. The art of theology, one of many human gifts offered at Christmas, defined, expounded, interpreted, and extended the Incarnation. Theologians directed the festival play, prepared the audience, and advertised its message to the world. Incidentally, theology defended the material culture issuing from this holy day not as a fall from a spiritual golden age but the human shape of religion in the world, the perennial flowering of a divine word seeding the earth. Theology integrates incarnational meanings into an entire Christian worldview, both by rendering them rationally coherent and by magnifying their mystery. In a post-Christian world, theology also addresses the question whether divine incarnation transcends Bethlehem and whether Jesus transcends Christianity. Theologians must also worry whether Christmas can survive as a religious festival. Yet another risk of Incarnation is whether theologians can ever get it right.

Telling the Incarnation in Ever-New Vernaculars

The nineteenth-century Danish philosopher-theologian Søren Kierkegaard offered a fanciful story to account for Christmas, "The King and the Maiden." Long ago a king loved a humble maiden. Since he was all-powerful, his love could easily triumph in its claims. While his servants were certain that the maiden would be grateful at her elevation, the king wondered. Would she ever be able to forget the distance between them? He feared she might be happier to be loved by an equal. But even if she were quite willing to come to the king as nothing, this would not have satisfied the king either, because of the way he fully loved her. How then could the king truly love and make his love understood by the maiden? Perhaps the king could elevate the maiden, transfigure her, cause her to forget her former self.

This might have satisfied the maiden but not the king. Instead, he hit upon this plan: If a union cannot be brought about by an elevation, it must come through a descent. But it will not be sufficient for the king to take on a humble cloak in disguise. The king must take on a genuine clothing that will be his true form and figure, for the unfathomable nature of love is that it desires equality with the beloved. So the king determined to take on a servant-form, not as an outer garment but one in which he suffered all things, endured all things, experienced all things. Instead of changing the status of the maiden and perhaps concealing it from her, he changed his own position and became like her. Love alters not first of all the beloved but itself.

Incarnation implies indigenization, God swaddled in homegrown materials. To become human, God authorized divinity in the vernacular. And Incarnation seemed to require ever new vernaculars. Christmas was, in a way, a book with mostly blank pages, though with a provocative introductory chapter. Although Jesus is deeply rooted in first-century Judaism, the *Incarnation implies a dangerous freedom* with regard to all human cultures. God appears open to every human form. Being a first-century Jewish male, for example, is not definitive. In the ministry of Jesus and in the theology of Saint Paul, the New Testament authorizes inclusion rather than exclusion, opening divine residencies in every new place and ethnicity. Saint Paul staked his mission to the Gentiles on this insight, but it was nearly lost as the gospel gradually took the form of European Christendom. Though the Incarnation established *continuity* between God and all human life, *discontinuity* was established between Christianity and non-European cultures, and, much later following the Enlightenment, between Christianity and the high culture of the West. Theologians of Incarnation insist that the nucleus of the gospel is not European, that Christ seeks ever new conception. Even faith itself, the heart's grasp of God, comes clothed in culture and does not float above history.

Theologians may be thought of as dramaturges who advise on the evolution of Incarnation. They study the original play, fix on its meanings, consider changing audiences and circumstances, and propose new stagings. No doubt, they sometimes confuse holding on to the original story with insisting on a certain manner of telling it, but at their boldest they disclose more than contain, set free rather than control. The endowment of a Christian theater, to stay with that metaphor, is Christian faith set convincingly and coherently over time into a humanly constructed world of thought, social institutions, and material culture. The point is to portray Christianity and Christmas as attractive to and sufficient for human life in the world.

Not everyone applauds. For some moderns, calling oneself spiritual rather than religious is a way to escape the tiresome claims of theology, to get free from dreaded dogma, to escape ecclesiastical constriction and definition. No doubt many visitors to Christmas Eve services come with their fingers crossed. The piety of those who live and work in their heads is also sometimes in doubt. Even in a medieval "age of faith," Bonaventure was warning against elites who think "that it suffices to read without unction, speculate without devotion, investigate without wonder, examine without exultation, work without piety, know without love, understand without humility, be zealous without divine grace, see without wisdom divinely inspired."

How should the reader think about this chapter that tours the galleries of historic theologies? Surely an admiring traversal is appropriate, just as one appreciatively visits museums and churches where enduring works of art are displayed. That the Renaissance found renewal in the classical world and the Romantics mystery in the Middle Ages suggests that no age is in a position to discard gifts from other times, to turn away from the inexhaustible gene pool of the past.

Historic Theologies of Christmas

Beside the infancy narratives of Matthew and Luke considered earlier, New Testament theologies of the Incarnation issue from Paul's epistles and from the Gospel of John. For Paul, Christ is the second Adam. The first Adam had been created to manifest the image and likeness of God but failed, so Christ is the new creation who succeeds, by way of the tree of the cross, in becoming the image of the invisible God on earth and the demonstration of God's befriending of humanity.

John portrays a Christ of the abundant life, as when he turned water into a prodigious amount of wine at the wedding at Cana, a Gospel story read during Epiphany. But John's most important legacy was his "logos theology." The Greek word *logos* could mean word, mind, power, deed, reason, structure, purpose. John claims that the God whose word first brought creation into being now clothes that word in human form and registers it as the poetic source of human existence. The mystery of Christmas thereby illuminates the mystery of being human. An absurd universe (both celebrated and lamented in the modern world) would be one bereft of logos. The early church fathers made the audacious claim that God became what humans are so that humans might become what God is. Christmas re-enchants the world and makes of "man fully alive" the glory of God.

A Negro spiritual asks, "What you gonna name that pretty little baby?" Early theologians, struggling to express fully the community's experience of Jesus, moved beyond "rabbi" and "prophet" to ever sturdier titles like Logos, that could bear the heaviness of divinity and symbolize the mission of Christ. They required a language that would not collapse under the weight of what the church believed, as Jaroslav Pelikan says. First, the language of Trinity became necessary to account for the mystery of what had happened, and how, at Christmas. Then, the Christological controversies tried to resolve the question: What is the relation of God to God and God to you and me in the person of the earthly Jesus? The legacy of those days goes wrong when paradoxical and metaphorical language is changed, later on, into the literal language of modern science.

A fourth-century theologian, Athanasius, tells the Incarnation this way: "You know how it is when some great king enters a large city and dwells in one of its houses; because of his dwelling in that single house, the whole city is honored, and enemies and robbers cease to molest it. . . . You know what happens when a portrait painted on a panel becomes obliterated through external stains. The artist does not throw away the panel, but the subject of the portrait has to come and sit for it again, and then the likeness is redrawn on the same material. . . . Men had neglected to consider the heavens before, and now they were looking in the opposite direction. So God came from that direction. . . . He used his body as his instrument. Does not even Plato say that the Author of the universe, seeing it storm-tossed and in danger of sinking into the state of dissolution, takes his seat at the helm of the Life-force of the universe, and comes to the rescue and puts everything right? What then is there incredible in our saying that, mankind having gone astray, the Word descended upon it and was manifest as man, so that by his intrinsic goodness and his steersmanship he might save it from the storm?"

In the early fifth century, Augustine became the greatest intellectual in the Christian tradition and a preacher who rendered Christian life in the declining Roman Empire imaginable and practiceable for his hearers. His diagnosis of the human dilemma reasoned back to the divine prescription for its illness. If the Incarnation is the cure for a world gone bad, then what ails humanity must be a *loss of original goodness.* The meaning of Christmas, then, is the reestablishment of the ultimate Good as that which gives meaning and place to penultimate but distracting goods.

But Augustine knew the limitations of theology, and he did not make pious belief depend on the resolution of mystery. In a Christmas sermon he told his congregation: "Since we can as yet form no conception of his generation by the Father before the daystar, let us keep the festival of his birth of a virgin in the hours of the night. Since it is still beyond our understanding that his name endures forever and existed before the sun, let us at least recognize his dwelling that he has placed beneath the sun. We cannot yet behold him as the only Son, abiding forever in his Father, so let us recall his coming forth like a bridegroom from his chamber. We are not yet ready for the banquet of our Father, so let us contemplate the manger of Jesus Christ our Lord."

At the dawn of the Middle Ages, missionaries moving out from Rome and the British Isles gave central and northern Europe its first Christmas. "Pagan" Europe was encouraged to celebrate the glory and fame of a Christ who filled all of "middle earth" with the new light of his coming and his transformative power. Attendant miracles to Christmas began to be chronicled (seven days before

Christmas the sun began to shine at midnight), as an eclectic medieval Christianity connected itself to popular beliefs and existing religious and cultural traditions. Christianity embraced Anglo-Saxon vigor and heroism and made the great battles between gods and giants into the likeness of the conquering Christ.

In the thirteenth century, Thomas Aquinas envisioned a medieval synthesis of grace and nature in which God comes down not to negate human nature and culture but to complete them. As God and the world reconnect, transcendence enjoins particularity. As Augustine had seen, already on earth are many goods, but God now redirects them toward their proper end in the Good. The point of a theology of Christmas is the praise of life and its origin. Godfathering Aristotle into the Christian tradition, Thomas sanctified the senses as windows of the soul and opened Christianity to emerging science. It is said that when in doubt, Thomas believed in more reality rather than less. Although the Renaissance that followed is now viewed as the triumph of an early secularism, its elaborate celebration of the human can also be seen as a further advance of Christian incarnational theology.

A materialization of the medieval telling of Incarnation is the Corpus Christi festival that blossomed at this time. The doctrine of the transubstantiation of the bread of the Eucharist into the body of Christ was a bold assertion about material culture with profound implications for Christian ritual. In every Mass, many times a day, the Eucharist would become a new miracle on par with the virgin birth. Corpus Christi festivals paraded a material Christ in eucharistic bread through the streets, incidentally expanding a vernacular life beyond institutional walls.

Among the radical visionaries of the material were medieval nuns. Though a male power structure discounted their artful seeing, they persisted in fixing on a Christ who makes exercising the senses necessary, not superfluous. Women do the art of theology—with their bodies. Teresa of Avila said: “Christ has no body now on earth but ours; no hands but ours, no feet but ours; ours are the eyes through which his love looks out to the world; ours are the feet with which he goes about doing good; ours are the hands with which he blesses now.”

Martin Luther and the Protestant Christmas

Martin Luther is the patron of a Protestant Christmas, the festival that enchanted Luther's theology, his personal piety, his family life, and the music he made for the church. The immensely influential Luther Bible was an instance of cultural incarnationalism, through which God spoke and his followers sang in the vernacular. If Luther could make God speak German, he could also incarnate Christmas in the German forest and home. He inaugurated a period in which Germany would produce a unique culture of Christmas, much copied in North America.

As a preacher, Luther sounded like this: "I don't want to hear of any other God but Mary's baby. . . . Matthew counts four notorious women in Jesus' genealogy. Why? Jesus was determined to be born into a large family, one that included sinners, foreigners, and outcasts. . . . Jesus did not pass through Mary like sunshine through a glass, but brought her flesh and blood along with him. . . . The Incarnation happened so that reason could not apprehend it, but faith would be required. . . . The devil came close to ruin us, but he didn't take our nature; God came closer, to save us, and was willing to take our nature. . . . The angels envy us; God didn't take their form, but ours. . . . This ladder of Incarnation he placed on earth so that we might ascend to God on it—don't try any other way to get there."

For Luther, Christmas empties God out of heaven onto earth, and this divine emptying becomes, following Saint Paul, a theology of the cross. Jesus was God's demonstration that "the finite is capable of the infinite," that earth can fully embody the divine presence, that God does not hold back divinity in heaven. So Luther "horizontalized" his theology into a social ethic that insisted on finding Christ in the neighbor and redirected Christmas giving from the festival hall of the church to the poor. Everyday life, not the mystic journey, becomes the locus of spiritual transformation. The Lutheran Reformation was determined to turn wonder into personal good news: God as a baby overcomes our terror of a distant God. The new mantra was: "To know Christ is to know his benefits."

The other great Protestant reformer, Calvin, should not be passed over too quickly. Calvin's sacramental Christology is not, like Luther's, about God's presence in material things but Christ's actions among us by way of *our* actions with material things, a shrewd insight. It makes the Incarnation a warrant for a more radical Christian transformation of society and politics than Luther allowed himself to imagine.

Modern Incarnational Theologies

The theological meanings of Christmas have come under close examination, even assault, in the modern world. These are some of the questions raised in the last two centuries: How can the church continue to affirm mystery in a world where reason and science rule? Is a divine-human being not an unbelievable absurdity? Does the eighteenth-century Enlightenment (as Thomas Jefferson, for example, believed) supercede the Greek thought world in which early Christianity rendered its beliefs, making them no longer tenable? Is it believable that the immutable master of the universe would make a midcourse correction? Is the New Testament itself locked in the mythology of a three-story universe that no modern any longer accepts, and does this make a modern telling of God's movement from above to below impossible? Can intellectual honesty continue to live with ancient orthodoxies? If reason has triumphed over metaphor, disenchantment over enchantment, how can Christmas be taken seriously except by children? In the face of new appreciations of all the world religions, how can Christianity continue to claim one unique Incarnation of God in Christ? Has an aesthetic worldview (or pop culture) replaced the theological as the only avenue left to Christmas? Is it really possible any longer, as Christianity has claimed in the past, to construct an entire system of meaning, intellectually astute and culturally rich, on the Incarnation celebrated at Christmas? Is Christmas, in fact, so bound in middle-class materialism, so compromised by modernity, that there is no way back to its original message?

Each of these questions has elicited some of the most penetrating theological responses in the history of Christianity. While many believers, Catholic and Protestant, are convinced that the church's mission in the modern world is simply to repeat, unchanged, the formulations of the past, many theologians are committed to the relentless pursuit of formulations adequate to changing cultural circumstances—lest the church make itself an unintelligible island that the world sails by in indifference or disdain. No doubt the questions and the answers are part of the course (and risk) of Incarnation in the world.

C. S. Lewis (1893–1963) launched a popular attempt to portray Christianity as the rediscovered missing page that clarifies an entire book. In his tellings, the human story is always about the use of power and the search for the good. So the surprise in the New Testament is a story about laying power aside (also a theme in Tolkien's *Lord of the Rings*). Fastening on this point, the New Testament depicts Satan shrewdly tempting the adult Jesus, at the beginning of his public ministry, to take his power back, to reclaim the prerogatives of divinity, to *reverse the Incarnation.* In Lewis's imagination, following Augustine, the point of Christianity is to redirect the human race to its ultimate Good, while recovering the worth of all the goods. Lewis lamented the Christian response to modernity that literalizes the Bible's best story and makes of the Bible itself an inelastic rule book whose key is a legalistic decoding. In Lewis's hands, poetry and metaphor and imaginative story save Christianity and Christmas from rationalism.

Still, the modern celebration of Christmas takes place in a world where Enlightenment rationalism prevails, where aesthetes reduce the meaning of Christmas to fine art, where people of good will congratulate themselves on their escape from ancient dogma that ruined Christmas. But, some Christian philosophers say, the confident assertion that a divine-human being is an absurdity assumes that humans know all there is to know about humanity and divinity. It is not inconceivable to them that an Infinite behind the universe entered creation in finite human form and expressed an ultimate nature and will in a finite human mode. What if human consciousness is the only possible expression of God's presence, the very means by which the universe comes to self-reflection? It is an interesting wager, they suggest, that a benevolent God might choose to cover the distance between divinity and humanity, between absolute transcendence and utter immanence. If difficult times for belief occasion despair, they can also provoke a deepening self-understanding. Cosmic night and homelessness in the universe are suggestive settings for the celebration of Christmas.

The nineteenth-century liberal Protestant option was to rethink the entire Christian tradition. Friedrich Schleiermacher (1768–1834) was active in the University of Berlin at a time when an age of reason had triumphed throughout Europe and a Romantic protest was setting in. But he found that his closest friends in the Romantic circle were "cultured despisers" of religion. How could he persuade them to join him in celebrating Christmas? He jettisoned supernaturalism and reversed the order of reflection on Christ. Instead of beginning with the eternal Word who condescended to human existence, he began with the human Jesus, as many thinkers still do today. He saw Jesus as the completion of the creation of man. Jesus finally demonstrated a complete "God-consciousness," a sense of absolute dependence that is the essence of religion. Those who followed this tack in the twentieth century emphasized Jesus as "the man for others," the one who shows how to be fully human and so embodies God's intention for everyone. The task of theology is to give an account of how the God-consciousness of Jesus and all human self-consciousness could unite.

Does Christmas imply a change in God's mind? That is the argument of Jack Miles's recent *Christ: A Crisis in the Life of God*. Because the Old Testament plot did not turn out as God had been hoping, a crisis was provoked in the life of God and a major mid-course correction was made. We call that the Incarnation, and Christmas is its festival. When God comes out of silence to reappear in Jesus, the deep changes are obvious. In the baby Jesus God expresses utter vulnerability and abandons the role of the warrior God. In the ministry and preaching of Jesus, God refuses to recognize distinctions between friend and foe. God's virtue, enacted in Jesus' life, is universal love. God disarms. From then on, everything that Jesus says, does, or suffers should be regarded as said, done, or suffered by God. Exemplifying the new divine nature, Jesus turns what seems like bad news into an ironic kind of good news. Jesus is God with a changed mind. This will be a grander promise, a more poignant and heart-stopping story. By a surprising fusion of identities, God-as-God solving a divine problem by becoming God-as-human, the crisis in the life of God is resolved. This change of heart and mind cost God the crucifixion. Through Incarnation and then death, Jesus infuses the experience of being abandoned by God with a new meaning that transcends rather than negates old meaning. So in Miles's literary analysis of the Gospel-writers, the divinity of Christ is embraced by the biblical authors as the only way to get the story right.

The German New Testament scholar Rudolf Bultmann (1884–1976) proposed to save the message of the Gospels by first demythologizing them and then reestablishing their point of connection with modern life. The three-story universe of antiquity, in which God comes down to earth and then returns to heaven, is no longer meaningful, Bultmann believed. So he looked for the "preunderstanding" that lay behind the New Testament gospel and found it to be the same existential crisis in which moderns find themselves: the insistent question how one can live authentically in the face of anxiety, finitude, guilt, and insecurity. Into this setting, ancient and modern, God comes to address humanity through the message of Jesus, calling for a radical decision about the meaning of life, and offering a new freedom to live authentically. But the Christmas message must be stripped of its format of mythological story in order to expose the authentic understanding of human existence that is its heart and to avoid needlessly alienating modern hearers. The point of Christmas is not its historicity but its existentialist claim that grips us with the offer of a new way of understanding human life in the world. This is good news that requires not irrational credulity but a decisive choice about what we will do with our life.

In total contrast to Bultmann's approach, the neoorthodox theologian Karl Barth (1886–1968) revived ancient orthodoxies in the belief that they still told essential truths about the human condition. He emphasized that humans do not know themselves, by themselves, but must be told the truth about themselves through the epiphany of Jesus Christ. The voice by which we learn who God is and who we are is the voice of Christ. So this is where theology must begin, not with the upward-striving religious quest through which some hoped to save God for the modern world. Everything depends on what comes down from above, and the community of believers who gather at Christmas must be vigilant to see that they expect everything from Christ. Christianity, and Christmas, is the predicate to the subject that is Jesus Christ. When others were describing early Christian doctrine as the distortion of primitive Christianity by Greek metaphysics, Barth insisted that its Christology was indispensable and irreplaceable for a proper understanding of the New Testament proclamation. Christmas is the free act of the faithfulness of God in which he takes up the lost cause of humans who have denied him as creator and in so doing ruined themselves as creatures, and makes it his own in Jesus Christ, carrying it through to its goal and in that way maintaining and manifesting his own glory in the world. In Christ, God stands before humanity, and humanity stands before God. In Christ, God's plan for humanity is disclosed, God's judgment on humanity fulfilled, God's redemption accomplished, God's gift fully present, God's claim and promise declared. As Kierkegaard had seen, God did not dishonor himself when he went into the far country and concealed his glory, for he is truly honored in his concealment. In his condescension is the image and reflection in which we see him as he is. His glory is the freedom of the love which he exercises and reveals in the Incarnation.

It is said that the age of reason and the modern bureaucratic way of the market have disenchanted the world and stripped culture of the metaphors that nuance and deepen human life in the world. Life is flat and mystery gone. In response, some Christian theologians want to *remythologize* the biblical message as the prescription for an age dying for lack of metaphor. Religion—and a true account of Christmas—requires a language that is concrete, poetic, imagistic and hence inevitably anthropomorphic, not one that is "enlightened," rationalistic, or abstract. The times call theologians to be poets, not rationalist philosophers.

But what of the world religions, that most college students learn about and every traveler encounters? Is it not preposterous and arrogant that Christianity claims the one and only Incarnation of

God, when all about one can detect other movements of the spirit? In response, theologians like Sallie McFague (1933–) appear to deemphasize the Incarnation in first-century Christianity, in favor of a God who appears concretely everywhere, all the time. They worry that typical celebrations of Christmas limit God and excuse humanity from anything more than asserting the historicity of one special miracle. The real miracle is *every* joint venture between God and humanity, in every time and in every place. The real miracle is God and material life coming together. Too many Christians are spiritualizing away the real meaning of Christmas, which is the transformation of nature and the re-enchantment of the world. God's hands are on everything, and no political economy is safely beyond divine reach. Jesus is paradigmatic of what can be and must be evident everywhere. All things, not just a single instance in the first century, become the sacrament of the presence of God; all creation reawakens to the divine image. If the Incarnation of God makes everything new and precious, then the gifts of Christmas must be justice for all and the care of the earth. Everyone gets to come to the festival, even the birds of the air and clean-flowing streams. The world is filled up with God, there is no place where God is not, and the glory of Christmas is every creature fully alive.

In some ways, Western theologians are catching up with Eastern Orthodoxy's long celebration of the material earth as a sacrament of God's presence. For such a view, the Incarnation is a prism that refracts an entire world and human culture. This trend has evoked a new theological aesthetic that correlates the beauty of the earth with the beauty of God. Doestoevsky said that beauty will save the world, and Aquinas had imagined beauty as one of the properties of being that opens humans to God. The beauty of the Incarnation and the beauty of the world are signs of the exchange of love between creator and creation, the blending of grace and nature at Bethlehem. As a way to see God, beauty offers an experience of transcendence even for those who do not believe.

Lovers of Christmas wish, as they believe once was true, that its meanings could mantle an entire year, its theology become an entire Christian worldview. This is the aspiration of the most influential Roman Catholic theologian of the twentieth century, Karl Rahner (1904–1984). His incarnational theology carries forward the historic Catholic insight into the intimate relation between grace and nature. In densely argued philosophical reflection, Rahner stipulates the characteristics of human consciousness that make it possible to inquire about the coming of Christ. Is there a built-in thirst that prepares the human heart for the Incarnation? What do human longings imply about the nature of reality? How is it possible for humans to grasp the coming of God as the ultimate answer to their questions? Rahner saw the Incarnation as the climax toward which the world's evolutionary development was heading, the point at which earth achieves the life of God. This process is grounded in God's free giving to the world, which began at creation. Christmas means that the transcending of material reality into ultimate Good exactly coincides with God's self-giving to the world. Christmas discloses the essence of God to be self-communicating love to a creation that exists because God wanted a partner. And it portrays humanity's highest dignity as a complete openness to God. It is neither a myth to be demythologized nor a miracle that negates base nature, but a mystery available as a human experience.

As a theologian who speaks to the world as well as the church, Rahner needs to claim that it is possible to think intellectually about Christmas because divine self-communication with the world is thinkable, and this is so because humans have a built-in availability for closeness to God. Ever since the first Christmas, the church has struggled to delineate humanity and divinity in the person of Christ. Rahner asserts that Christ's humanity is not diminished but increased by union with God—as is ours. The Christian proclamation about Christmas begins not in eternity but on the ground, with the actual historical Jesus. But the life of the incarnate Christ becomes so profound and radical that we see in it the lived experience of the absolute and definitive presence of God to the world. Together with Christ, we come to see God as the ultimate horizon of our existence and our destiny. In the mystery of Christmas we see that to be human is to enter into the limitless question regarding God. And the God-question is not one possible issue to pursue in human life but the constituting question.

This is so because the live edge of our humanity is openness to the divine.

This open-endedness points toward God, the sky above every human head. Christmas reopens what had been closed. In Christ the human question and the absolute answer are brought to fulfillment. Christmas redirects our capacity for self-transcendence toward God. So now, wherever God is present in time and space, wherever human self-transcendence opens to God—there is Incarnation. When the world and humanity reach ultimate divinization, it is Christmas in the universe. Like Aquinas long before him, the profound philosopher insists on being a simple believer, when all has been said. Rahner claims: "If God's incomprehensibility does not grip us in a wonder, if it does not draw us into his superluminous darkness, if it does not call us out of the little house of our homely, close-hugged truths, we have misunderstood Christianity."

Liberating Christmas

> Chains shall he break for the slave is our brother
> and in his name all oppression shall cease.
>
> —"O Holy Night"

Mounting a social and economic critique of contemporary Christianity and the economic values it has accommodated, liberation theology emerged in the last third of the twentieth century on the Catholic soil of Latin America, spread to Asian and African Christianity, and soon transfixed much of the Protestant world as well. It argues that Christmas, and Christianity itself, has been hijacked by North Atlantic middle-class culture and the consumer capitalism that engulfs it.

While it is common in the First World to decry how holiday is overshadowed by consumerism, priests and theologians who work in Third World countries claim that the Bible itself and Christian life in society have been domesticated by the middle classes of wealthy countries. In this view, even well-meaning American Christians bent on keeping Christ in Christmas ignore its original setting in the lives of the poor and their own complicity in making it a festival of consumption. To the liberationist eye, the Christmas celebrated in the First World looks like a rival to biblical religion with an alternative message of salvation. They claim to see clearly what no one since Herod has seen, that this baby's birth is an explicit challenge to the power of political-economic domination systems to define life on earth.

Theology's calling is to examine the lived practice of believers for its congruence with the original message of Christianity. This has led to the claim that the First World is unlikely to get Christmas right until it listens to the readings of the poor and the marginalized. The martyred Latin American bishop Oscar Romero wrote:

> No one can celebrate
> A genuine Christmas
> Without being truly poor.
> The self-sufficient, the proud
> Those who, because they have
> Everything, look down on others,
> Those who have no need
> Even of God—for them there
> Will be no Christmas.
> Only the poor, the hungry,
> Those who need someone
> To come on their behalf,
> Will have that someone.
> That something is God.
> Emmanuel, God-with-us.
> Without poverty of spirit
> There can be no abundance of God.

Just after the Civil War ended, American blacks dared to imagine that genuine land reform might come to the South. Would the Christmas of 1865 be the season of dramatic social and economic reversal, a time of jubilee, as blacks who knew their Old Testament hoped? An American general was dispatched from Washington with the news: "Nothing is going to happen at Christmas."

On Not Doing without Theology

Theology is a difficult art, surrounded by pitfalls, and not everyone wishes it well. To speak, confidently, of God is already to risk going wrong, since God does not appear to be reducible to any theological system nor any ecclesiastical pronouncement. And when theologians become prophets calling for change, they meet the fate of all prophets who are discounted, ignored, and abused. Celebrators of holiday are not tolerant of reformers of holy day.

Still, theologians tell themselves, this art too must be brought to complement the Incarnation. When Augustine began writing his *Confessions*, which turned out to be a biography of God as well as Augustine's autobiography, he mused: "What can anyone say about you, God? And yet, woe to him who says nothing."

If Christmas and Christianity are not to appear foolish, incoherent, or irrelevant to the educated, if Christmas is not to be swamped by powerful economic forces, if sacred texts are not to be tamed for safe consumption, theologians go on believing that fresh and convincing takes on the Incarnation are required. Fashioning a gift of one's own is not a drab, stern, unwelcome assignment. W. H. Auden said: "I know nothing, except what everyone knows—if there when Grace dances, I should dance." Theologians mean to dance. Many carolers do not notice that it is God who speaks in a famous carol, initiating the reciprocity of sacred play:

> Tomorrow shall be my dancing day
> I would my true love did so chance
> To see the legend of my play
> To call my true love to my dance.

7

Second Thoughts on Incarnation: Taking Christmas Back

To the modern eye, Christmas may be sinking under the weight of incarnational extravagance. Did God get it wrong? It is not hard to find historical figures to say, I told you so. It is too late to reverse course, to take Christmas back. Have we now reached the half-life of Incarnation, when holiday overcomes holy day? The core religious festival is now nearly buried under a landfill of material culture produced by market forces. But the history of lament connected to Christmas long precedes the current triumph of consumer capitalism. Given Christianity's inclination for paradox, it is no surprise that caution should balance celebration, that yes and no should live in the same family. If, when, how, and where to celebrate Jesus' birth are questions with a long history of negative answers. Early Christianity feared the impact of end-of-year wildness on the new way of life the church wanted to pioneer. Medieval thinkers worried about holiday orgies swamping the asceticism appropriate to holy day. Puritans doubted that even the church was a safe place and argued there was no New Testament warrant for any celebration of religious festival.

It is never a long distance from holy mountain to golden calf. The drama of Incarnation lies in the question whether Christianity would lead the divine affirmation of earthly good or helplessly witness God's precipitous descent into every matter. Naysayers arose to save Incarnation by erecting doctrinal barriers to its downward slide, and they foresaw the likelihood that the church itself would become part of the slippery slope. If festival is determined to encroach on religion, would not the pious heart be a safer locale than the streets? But no one long ago could have predicted how completely the church as the festival house of the Incarnation would be overwhelmed by a bad neighborhood growing up around it.

Learning to Say No to Christmas

When the early church first set Christmas amidst the Roman saturnalia, it wagered that a hearty new theology could Christianize heathen celebrations, but planting Christmas in the wild fields of December was nevertheless a risk. Pagan rootstock might prove too persistent for eradication, and every Christmas season would likely harvest wheat and chaff. A radical solution is to burn down the field and try again, or to plant the Christmas garden behind walls and far from contagions. By the fourth century, though, the church made a full-scale attempt to counter, if not supplant, the pagan celebrations flourishing around late December and New Year. Christmas was the Christian entry in a contest over the calendar and its meanings.

Of course, early Christians recognized similarities between the beginning of the return of natural light at the winter solstice and the new coming of God's light in the nativity of the Lord. The solstice itself, anyone could see, was a way to clothe seasonal passages with sacred meaning. To make the birth of Christ that meaning was a bold assertion and a risky compromise. For thousands of years, seasonal cycles had thickened the texture of peoples' lives. Already in ancient Mesopotamia twelve days of New Year were celebrated with fires, presents, mumming, songs, and religious processions. These moved west to the Roman saturnalia. All looked for the replenishment of order through a temporary descent into chaos. As it moved to northern Europe, Christianity discovered that the winter solstice was also a great Nordic festival, with sacrifices, feasting, dancing, and nocturnal assemblies.

At first, Christmas could only be a thin Christian veneer over ancient and perennial pagan rites, as it often still is in much of the world today. The strategy was to *appropriate rather than eradicate.* This was the advice Pope Gregory sent to the early missionary to England, Augustine of Canterbury: make peace with local customs, transform December with the Christian gospel and Christian celebration. Later, as a missionary church began moving through Europe, it found that it could not ignore or suppress agricultural festivals that had both religious and economic meaning. It came to terms with them and endowed them with Christian significance. The church also accommodated itself to the social recreation and material culture of holiday seasons. *Gradual and deliberate stagings of Christmas across the new Christian world produced a fully alloyed culture of Christmas.* Whoever would ultimately "win," whether Christmas would be more sacred or more secular, the Christmas of today—and then—is no simple winter festival, but one of considerable private and social consequence, briefly uniting a disparate people in rites, sacred and secular, that hold universal appeal. But a determined no would have to balance every yes.

The twelve days of Christmas, elaborated in medieval Europe, provided ample foods for all palates. A special favorite was the ritual of reversal—the poor became rich, boys became bishops, and fools wise. The church went along but not without regret. Unauthorized liturgies were performed by minor players, including incensing the altar with the smoke of bratwurst, dressing in bizarre vestments, and turning upstart clergy into "lords of misrule."

It was all meant in good fun, but in an eleventh-century tale, an exasperated priest could scarcely celebrate Christmas Mass, so distracted was his congregation by revelers outside. So he cursed them to keep dancing without stopping for twelve months straight, hoping they would fall dead from revelry. In twelfth-century Worcestershire, a priest angered by all night escapades and amorous songs began the Christmas morning Mass chanting "Sweet lover, have mercy" instead of *Dominus vobiscum.* Holy days, like pilgrimages, are tailed by commerce or debauchery. Monastic reformers sternly admonished monks to cultivate a piety of the heart within monastic enclosure, instead of journeying about on frivolous holiday pilgrimages. Fourteenth-century Lollards, anticipating the Puritans, protested images that turned to idolatry and pilgrimage that gave rise to souvenir hunting, profiteering, and sexual license. They urged instead that people stay home, lead godly lives, give alms to the poor, and avoid superstition. In the sixteenth century, Erasmus satirized populist religiosity, and Luther suggested that holiday enthusiasms distracted from genuine Christian discipleship.

The Puritans audaciously attempted to reverse a history of hundreds, or perhaps thousands, of years of seasonal cycles and the festive exuberance attached to them. First in England, and then in New England, they hoped to suppress an entire cultural world. Their new piety grated against old custom. They argued that December 25 was not biblical but heathen, that Jesus would have disapproved of his birthday celebrations, and that Christmas was always just an excuse for Catholic syncretism, gross behavior, social upheaval, and drunkenness, no doubt aided by the lull in agricultural life.

During the course of the English Civil War, Cromwell led a Protestant assault on the traditional Christian calendar. Town criers were sent around to call out loudly, "No Christmas, No Christmas," shops were kept open, work was forced to go on as usual, and no one was to light a candle or eat holiday cakes. A poem of the day called mince pie "idolatry in crust." When evergreen decorations appeared throughout London, the lord mayor and his marshal had to ride about setting fire to them. All solemnizations in church or home were forbidden. The Puritan Parliament conducted business as usual every Christmas day from 1644 to 1656. When well before the Puritan ascendancy, King James had tried in 1617 to establish a Christian liturgical year in Scotland, including Christmas, the Scottish Calvinists refused and denounced Christmas as the return of Roman saturnalia. A rigid Sabbatarianism was the only ordering of holy time tolerated, and the deliberate profanation of Catholic holy days was encouraged.

The prohibition of Christmas ultimately failed. One seventeenth-century wag observed: "O blessed Reformation! The church doors all shut, and the tavern doors all open." Under Charles II, the Restoration Period meant also the restoration of Christmas. The mood was not unlike the repeal of Prohibition in the United

States. Yuletide came out of hiding. Yet even in the 1940s, Christmas had not yet become a holiday in Scotland. A traveler from London to Edinburgh described how the Christmas lights went out as he crossed the border into Scotland, "vanishing in Calvinist darkness." The Calvinist reformer John Knox had put an end to Christmas in 1562, and it stayed that way until the middle of the twentieth century.

The Puritans in America made similar and long-lasting attempts. The United States congress was at least officially in session on Christmas day from 1789 to 1856. Historians speak of New England's war on Christmas. The day went uncelebrated and was suppressed for a considerable period in early American history. The prohibition of a sacred calendar and holy days, indeed of a culture of alternating labor and festivity, could be seen as the apotheosis of the Protestant desacrilization of the world. In its wake, a new vernacular of material culture had to be constructed in the world of Puritanism, but not on religious grounds. The calendar, at the start, would be spare. In Massachusetts, Christmas was actually illegal between 1659 and 1681, though already from 1608 it was being celebrated by Anglicans in Virginia. It was said that in New England, Calvinists had to become Episcopalians or Moravians for a day, if they wanted to experience Christmas.

As late as 1857, in *Father and Son*, Edmund Gosse is recalling his father's railing against Christmas as popish idolatry, in the episode of the plum pudding: "My father had given strictest charge that no difference whatever was to be made in our meals on that day; the dinner was to be neither more copious than usual nor less so. He was obeyed, but the servants, secretly rebellious, made a small plum-pudding for themselves. . . . Early in the afternoon, the maids kindly remarked that 'the poor dear child ought to have a bit, anyhow' and wheedled me into the kitchen, where I ate a slice of plum-pudding. Shortly I began to feel that pain inside which in my frail state was inevitable, and my conscience smote me violently. At length I could bear my spiritual anguish no longer, and bursting into the study I called out: 'Oh! Papa, Papa, I have eaten of flesh offered to idols!'" When he led his father to the accursed thing "he seized what remained of the pudding, and with the plate in one hand and me still tight in the other, ran till we reached the dust-heap, when he flung the idolatrous confectionary on to the middle of the ashes, and then raked it deep down into the mass."

(Amidst all the piling on, a few scholars are raising the question whether American historiography on the Puritans is overdone. It is suggested that such scholarship was never at home in the Catholic fusion of sacred and profane but in an alleged Protestant understanding of the world as an absolute opposition between sacred and profane, a bifurcation perhaps also inherited from Durkheim's unacknowledged Jewish milieu that possibly drew more from the Old Testament than from social science research. If this critique has merit, then scholars were determined to find what they already knew. Did not the Puritans in fact experience their lives as worlds of wonder? Models of reality and models of Christmas past are always, in part, historical constructs.)

The Christmas that entered the American cultural mainstream, between 1730 and 1800, was undoubtedly tempered with a compromise that allowed both mirth and moderation to prevail. This history can be traced through American almanacs that ranged from the complete deletion of Christmas to its restoration as a red-letter day. Congregational clergy gradually made their peace with Christmas. Before the end of the eighteenth century, Christmas was becoming a public ritual but not yet a domestic or commercial one. In the nineteenth century, Christmas moved back into the church, and business was suspended on Christmas day. Legal recognition came as late as 1850. It may be argued, however, that it was not religion that displaced the holiday as a house of ale, but the new cult of domesticity and the emerging practice of commercial gift-giving. Santa prevailed where Christian prohibition had failed.

Sometimes *religious denial unwittingly produces secular affirmation.* The Protestant suppression of street festivals may actually have made proletarian frivolities *more secular.* Disconnecting public gaiety from organic connections to community and culture may have rendered it *more* dangerous and threatening. Were the Puritans asking for it when they extracted holy day and holiday from the social order that Catholicism more or less succeeded in making sacred? Did a now completely secular festival of Christmas return by the back door? Everyone will have a material culture, and even conservative Protestants could not do without one. Perhaps, then, public and secular festivity at Christmas were providing a relatively austere, anti-liturgical evangelical Protestantism with the lush new corporeal forms they in fact longed for—but not on religious grounds. The ultimate irony is that evangelical Protestantism abolished the Christian calendar, with Christmas as its most splendid ornament, only to welcome back a safe—because secular and hence not idolatrous—material celebration. In a spectacular failure of theological imagination, these Protestants seemed to believe that idolatry lay only in the contamination of (Catholic) ritual and the material culture of religion but not in the economic and secular ways of the world. Snowmen, reindeer, and mountains of gifts pile up where religious ritual and image have been banned.

By the late nineteenth century, Christian piety was being fully integrated into the Christmas market. Department stores became cathedrals where many devout Protestants shopped for Christmas. The Puritan desacrilization of Christmas in the seventeenth and eighteenth centuries had set Christmas free to go its own way. Late-nineteenth-century Baptists explicitly welcomed Christmas back as a domestic holiday but not as a holy day. Conservative Protestantism was pleased to accept, now, a (secular) material culture it never knew or had long since abandoned to Catholicism. Consumer capitalism took over the festival grounds vacated by disapproving religion.

Not every no is spoken by theologians. Some attacks on the commercialization of Christmas are attacks on festivity itself, as an embarrassment and perversion of human virtue and value. This is the old contest between clear-eyed aesthetic and merely bacchanalian celebrations, between Appolonians and Dionysians. A version of this is elite culture expressing its distaste for popular culture, highbrow indictments of the low-brow predilections of the masses, kitsch patrols.

Toward the end of the twentieth century, a quite different prohibitionism emerged. A great fear swept intellectuals and secular guardians of national culture that religiosity was making, via Christmas, untoward inroads back onto public space. A cartoon satirized this with a manger scene in a department store window and the caption: "Isn't that just like the church, horning in on a good thing." So crèche squads took their responsibilities seriously. Wherever a manger scene encroached on what they insisted was secular space, they went to court, their yuletide work never done. While others frolic, the grinches are on patrol, censoring nativity scenes in public parks and working tirelessly to eradicate religious symbols. In response, conservative Protestants, at the beginning of the twenty-first century, launched public relations campaigns against "the war on Christmas." In the midst of this clash, some Jewish Americans were becoming nervous—not because they feared persecution but because of the potential disappearance of a secular civic culture that allowed Jews to feel like full citizens rather than a tolerated minority.

If secular watchdogs guarded against religious overreaching and moderationists against Christmas excess, still others were sorry to see how few of their ambitious hopes Christmas fulfilled. Christmas did not succeed in converting men and women to their finer selves. Human nature persisted in looking unredeemed, despite the promises of the season. In "Christmas: 1924," Thomas Hardy laments:

> "Peace upon earth!" was said. We sing it,
> And pay a million priests to bring it.
> After two thousand years of mass
> We've got as far as poison-gas.

Many wanted from Christmas a lasting peak experience. After recounting mounting excitement, children practicing for their roles in the Christmas pageant, and the decorations of the church, D. H. Lawrence laments: "It was bitter, though, that Christmas Day, as it drew on to evening and night, became a sort of bank holiday, flat and stale. The morning was so wonderful, but in the afternoon and evening the ecstasy perished like a nipped thing, like a bud in a false spring. Alas, that Christmas was only a domestic feast, a feast of sweet-meats and toys! Why did not the grown-ups also change their everyday hearts, and give way to ecstasy? Where was the ecstasy?" In his long poem "For the Time Being:

A Christmas Oratorio," W. H. Auden summarizes the day after Christmas: we overestimated our powers to love all our relatives; we saw the vision of Christmas but failed to make it real; we sent the child away who could not keep his word.

Guy de Maupassant took a hard and humorous look. In one ironical story, a Parisian bachelor with a special fondness for fat women goes out to find one to share his ample but lonely Christmas Eve dinner. After dining her and finally getting her to bed, she begins to groan and surprisingly delivers a child. The bachelor kindly allows them to stay until the child can be sent away. Now the young woman has fallen in love with him, but since she is no longer fat, he cannot reciprocate.

Balancing Yes and No

The social sciences offer a more nuanced understanding of human festival and gift-giving. It is naïve to imagine that a great religious celebration like Christmas is or must be either sacred or secular. Holy days and holidays are not opposites, but jostling siblings. Already in the Middle Ages liturgies were turning into street dramas, and ecclesiastical Latin was giving way to popular vernaculars.

In all cultures, ethnographers report, commerce and celebration, social relationships and gift exchange, come together. In medieval life there was the church's time and the merchants' time, and fairs grew from open cathedral spaces. *Feria* (abstinence from work for religious observance) always leads to festival. Festivity always involves overdoing; excess is one of the meanings and purposes of celebration, a time off from hard work, self-control, frugality, and simplicity. People assign social meanings to play and consumption and gift-exchange; they recreate their physical world through goods and gifts. Material culture has expressive significance and symbolic power. All this cannot simply be reduced to conspicuous consumption, status competition, or capitalist conquest. So there is a complex relationship between a spiritual and commercial Christmas, between Christianity and consumer culture, one that is both symbiotic and conflicted, complementary and contested.

Still, the lament over commercialization remains one of culture's fondest jeremiads, across times and cultures. Today secular critics who are actually advocates for holiday still warn against the diminution of older traditions of genuine play, spontaneity, fantasy, and misrule in a society of commercialized leisure. They worry that we lose control of the meaning of holidays as they are effaced by advertising and merchandizing. They insist on a crucial difference not between holy day and holiday, but between holidays of genuine cultural festivity and holidays that are merely market-driven. Indeed, most American holidays would become unrecognizable without the trappings of the market. If Christmas is the great peak of retailing, marketers are lately trying to raise the height of the many foothills, relentlessly attaching opportunities for commerce to every single holiday, from Presidents Day to Martin Luther King's birthday, inventing Mother's Day, Father's Day, Secretary's Day and a host of others, and of course Valentine's Day and Halloween. It is suggested that the good of human society is not well served if holy day always is reduced, without remainder, to holiday, if the cultural substance of public memorial or celebration always erodes to market values alone.

Drawing the Line on Capitalist Religion

A surprise of recent decades is that the most passionate critics speak not on behalf of the church but in the name of a leftist critique of the pervasiveness of the market. Global capitalism's hostile takeover of Christmas functions like a computer worm that travels across the World Wide Web, invading every memory bank, insinuating itself into every address book, commandeering every message, leaving behind cookies that turn even the wary or unwilling to its purposes. Toward the end of the twentieth century, a new line of inquiry arose: Is there something qualitatively different in the way that modern capitalism disturbs the balance between holy day and holiday? Is something new happening that is warping any role for religion in society?

The debate over the cultural setting of the modern Christmas began in the Christian world. Modern theologians recovered the belief that the Incarnation reaffirmed the Jewish and Christian understandings that the world and matter were originally and essentially good. All penultimate earthly goods have a built-in ultimate end that points to the ultimate Good. But they claimed a high-stakes difference between this view and that of the philosophy of materialism evident in Marxism and modern science. That view seemed to insist that there is no transcendent reality beyond earthly good. What you see is what you get. The spiritual discipline of "seeing beyond" is negated.

Given that trend, it was to be expected that Christmas in a materialist world would express itself as consumerism. Christmas would morph into the religious expression of capitalism. Or, perhaps, contemporary capitalism had become a kind of religion. The critics of religion would be pleased to see Christmas reduced to economic transactions, and celebrate the withdrawal from the public square of nagging religious symbols. But some, who carried no brief for or against Christmas, began to analyze the pervasive effects of capitalism on life and culture in the modern world. Were we really better off if capitalist triumphalism was displacing religious triumphalism?

Capitalism could be diagnosed as the worm in the Christmas apple, and this is how the analysis proceeded. When advertisers depict commercial consumption as the solution to a nostalgic longing for a Christmas of yore, or for some enchanted meaning, they lead us down a path of calculated deception. Holy day, they assure us, has always been like this. And the meaning of holiday has always added up to the accumulation of gifts. As the advertisers' story becomes so pervasive that one can no longer imagine an alternative Christmas, the deception becomes unquestioned. No one notices anymore. Converting Christmas into a festival of consumerism validates the religion that is the market, the only meaning that counts.

Christmas becomes not just a secular ritual, but a ritual of secularization. That is, unrelenting Christmas shopping implicates you in the idea that shopping is all there is. In a startling irony, practicing Christmas helps everyone become more secular. When Christmas is fully, and without remainder, ritualized as consumption, then human festival as holy day is no longer available to cultural memory. It is almost impossible to notice what has happened, and only leftist intellectuals seem interested in analyzing the transaction. The entire socioeconomic world in which holy day happens is mystified and disguised. Everyone knows how to look *at* religion, the way you look at a play or a sports event. Hardly anyone notices that secularity is what people look *through*. It's the only way one can see, consumer capitalism the glasses you cannot take off. Even theologians were rather late to notice that the Christmas once expressed as the divine re-enchantment of the world is now received as the expressive power of commodities, the mystification of commerce as the meaning of life. In a word, Christmas is the religious expression of capitalism. Religious culture's inbox has been colonized, and all sent messages are now in someone else's hands.

Many cultural historians now argue that the American Christmas of recent decades is something quite different from the perennial synergy between holiday and holiday, between festival and commerce. No doubt Christmas was already commercialized in the nineteenth century (and in the Middle Ages), but commerce since then has fundamentally changed. Now commodities are the essential carriers of meaning, which advertisements helpfully portray. Ads tell an all-encompassing story about the emptiness of human life that products can fill. Since none of the media could exist without the advertising revenue that is their indispensable source of funding, the market comes to control all domains of culture. All twelve months of the year are under its sway, not just the magical time between Thanksgiving and Christmas.

In a cancer-like invasion of an original nucleus, a Christian holy day is redirected to become the holiday of a rival system of meaning—global consumer capitalism. So powerful is the appropriation of Christmas as the expression of market capitalism that *it is much easier to opt out of religion than out of the American Christmas.* A kind of religious authority has been transferred to secular behavior. Shopping is invested with the meaning of life, and it is therefore obligatory. The capitalist penchant for turning culture and even religion into purchasable commodities seems nearly complete. Consumer capitalism is now the leading worldview, at least in Western societies and those most influenced by them. Its mantra is that the meaning of human existence is best expressed as the accumulation of material goods. The acids of modern capitalism disfigure the face of Christmas. Market forces dislocate the incarnational account of human life and relentlessly erode its cultural substance. The meaning of the Incarnation is thrown into reverse. *Human attention focuses on all the materials that claim to be good instead of on the Good that claims to be material.* A philosophy of materialism supplants a theology of Incarnation.

While theorists influenced by Marx or "critical theory" offer their accounts of this process, Saint Augustine offered the original theological diagnosis of the worm in the apple. He confessed to God: "You were within me, and I outside; and I sought you outside and in my unloveliness fell upon those lovely things that you have made. You were with me, and I was not with you. I was kept from you by those things, yet had they not been in you, they would not have been at all." He was expressing a theme taken up in the twentieth century by C. S. Lewis, that matter is good but it has lost its original Goodness, which must be recovered if matter is again to contribute to substantial joy and pleasure. Augustine's cure was the famous sentence from his autobiography: "You have made us for yourself; and our hearts are restless till they rest in you."

The Christian campaigns that began in the late twentieth century to "put Christ back into Christmas" or to make Jesus "the reason for the season" do not sufficiently penetrate the modern social and economic situation in which Christmas steadily loses its significance as a holy day. These sloganeers fail to notice their own deep investment in consumer capitalism as the meaning of life the rest of the year. As many recent works argue, at least in the United States, capitalism as an ideology mostly goes uncriticized. Religious conservatives offering jeremiads on nearly every modern excess give economic systems a pass.

In a provocative work, *Consuming Religion: Christian Faith and Practice in a Consumer Culture,* Vincent Miller takes on not the materiality of religious festival or even consumerism itself, but *the fate of religion in consumer culture.* Miller's thesis is not the obvious one that the market competes with religion in product offerings, but that the market effectively retrains believers to function as consumers *precisely when they are behaving religiously.* Believers well-trained in consumption bring the habits and dispositions of consumerism to sources of meaning and practice like religion. Consumer culture is an infrastructure capable of absorbing all other cultures as content waiting to be commodified, distributed, and consumed in highly individualistic acts. Consumerism trains believers to encounter and use Christian symbols as shorn of their connection to living traditions and communities, thus *preventing them from actually influencing or changing their lives in fundamental ways.* Incarnation is just another ornament. Religious symbols, beliefs, and practices abstracted from their original contexts and valued outside them simply become additional consumer products dispersed and de-centered in a network of libidinal attachments and emptied of ethical substance. They are religious merchandise selected as part of the urban outfit.

All this is set in motion by what has been called capitalism's "commodification of culture." This means that all of culture, for example, material things, religion, education, and art, are turned into stuff that you buy as decorations for your lifestyle, and that you interact with it as a commodity. Liquidating the traditions and communities and worldviews in which religion was once meaningfully embedded, such a culture renders them all as store-bought attractions selected for decorative uses. The religious practitioner shifts from being to having. A rich texture of religious symbols is no longer a means of spiritual or moral transformation, but an array on offer to window-shoppers. All the Christmas-celebrating individuals in a capitalist culture may be thought of as the terminals of media networks that seek ever-increasing bandwidth. Holy day is simply a splendid opportunity for hollow holiday outfitters.

A different, though congruent, analysis is that of Richard Horsley, who sees Christmas as the essential festival of consumer capitalism. Connecting the dots of religion and political (and economic) power, Horsley posits across cultural history a threefold schematic in which religion may be used to *transcend* the power of competing worldviews, to *resist* them, or, in fact, to help *constitute* them. He is convinced that the American Christmas serves the latter goal by helping to establish the political and economic power of global capitalism. It is natural for those in power to want to make an ultimate value of their power relationships because power is what counts most to them. So religion becomes, at Christmas, both the authorization of consumerism as the meaning of life and the constitution of capitalism as the mode of such religion. While aligning religion with its own interests, the pervasive power of the market simultaneously appears to be keeping religion sacrosanct and completely separate from economics. The market defends itself through the subterfuge of the separation of church and state, or by labeling all challenges to capitalist world domination "fundamentalist" or "socialist," or by fencing economic life off from religious critique.

Observers of religion unwittingly cooperate with these strategies when they postulate religion as purely a matter of personal belief and close their eyes to its connections with power. Because a consumer-capitalist Xmas is in fact the dominant *religious* festival, capitalism has become the chief manifestation of the American civil religion. A secular enterprise posing as the purveyor of ultimate meaning requires religious support and celebration, and, with an irony few notice, Christmas provides precisely that. But because Xmas looks simply like a secular shopping festival, its *religious function* as the legitimation of capitalism goes unnoticed. The true miracle of Christmas is this: *A once-religious festival that now is mostly secular provides a socially compulsory "religious establishment" of capitalism.* Neither the ostensibly religious nor the clearly secular can any longer opt out. Because the way of capitalism is to cannibalize every dimension of the public sector, turning all of culture into commodities, it should not surprise that religion, too, has been invaded and taken over.

Much more powerfully and effectively than the church, the mass media control the means of (symbol) production. They define what Xmas is, and they depict salvation as the acquisition of products. They preach a convincing story about shopping as the achievement of higher meanings and purposes. Religion lends its magic, its aura, and its mystery to consumption. Martin Luther and many others have said that a god is whatever you put your trust in, what you are loyal to. The god worshiped and served at Xmas is consumer capitalism. This analysis might lead one to expect that capitalism's most passionate secular critics would join forces with theologians attempting to renew Christmas as a genuine holy day. But such an alliance will only occur when theologians and religious leaders themselves practice an economic analysis of the world in which their holy day is celebrated.

"Yes, But"

The "alternative celebrations" movement provides an interesting "yes, but" in its response to Christmas. It has the advantage of registering affirmation instead of lament, disapproval, and ascetic recoiling. It is said that the better response to falsehood than censorship is more truth. The better response to the negation of Christmas as the civil religion of capitalism is the affirmation of Christmas through effective retrieval of its religious (and playfully festive) core, and its renewal as the most important alternative to a civilization of materialism.

During Advent, the time for the desperate and usually losing attempt to save Christmas from consumerism as its only meaning and expression, some Christians pray: "Father in heaven, the day draws near when the glory of your Son will make radiant the night of the waiting world. May the lure of greed not impede us from the joy which moves the hearts of those who seek him. May the darkness not blind us to the visions of wisdom which fill the minds of those who find him." As *alternative celebrations*, caroling and visitation, especially of the lonely, are revived. Commercial abundance is not foresworn, but redirected to those who actually need something. The idolatry of things is subverted by giving them away. A book titled *Unplug the Christmas Machine* urges its readers to take the Christmas Pledge:

> "Believing in the true spirit of Christmas, I commit myself to
> Remember those people who truly need my gifts;
> Express my love in more direct ways than gifts;
> Examine my holiday activities in the light of my deepest values;
> Be a peacemaker with my circle of family and friends;
> Rededicate myself to my spiritual growth."

To a rhythm of demand and supply created by advertising and the satiety that eventuates, simplicity and thoughtful alternatives are proposed as the most effective response.

To be sure, one alternative may be ascetic renunciation, an age-old way of seeking God and re-forming the self. But that can take a joyful form, as displayed in the earlier American Shaker Christmas, a true counterculture. Their most famous song was "Tis the gift to be simple, tis the gift to be free," and its wonderful melody was used by Aaron Copland in "Appalachian Spring." Mother Ann Lee commends a hallowed and hallowing Christmas celebration, devoted to cleaning the house of the spirit. Sins are confessed, grudges resolved, restitutions made, peace and union restored, and simple gifts—first of the spirit, then material—are shared. The chief gifts are gifts of song and remembrance and personal talents and ritualized expressions of love for the community. Many of these are ingeniously metaphorical, acted out in pantomime. Always the poor are remembered, and garments and goods for them are carried to the post office on Christmas Eve. Christmas Day begins at 4:30 a.m., when an elder proceeds through the communal halls singing:

> Lo the Savior has come with a bright shining band
> Bearing love and salvation in heart and in hand
> Crying rouse up my children be bright and alive
> And for gifts pure and holy let each of you strive.

Part Three

Incarnational Extravagance

All the World's a Stage

Now Christmas is come
Let us beat up the drum
And call all our neighbors together.
And when they appear,
Let us make them such cheer
As will keep out the wind
And the weather.

—Washington Irving

So now is come our joyful'st feast;
Let every man be jolly.
Each room with ivy-leaves is dressed,
And every post with holly.
Though some churls at our mirth repine
Round your foreheads garlands twine,
Drown sorrow in a cup of wine,
And let us all be merry.

—George Wither, "Let Us Sing Our Roundelays"

The Third Act

This book is a religious and cultural history of Incarnation, a kind of Bildungsroman, in which Incarnation grows up, develops, expands, changes, and is performed in the festival of Christmas. Scripted and plotted in the texts of the New Testament and staged in the festival house of the Christian church, Christmas soon enough exceeded sacred page and precinct. The argument here is that this evolution of a religious festival displays the risky course of Incarnation in the world. The third act of Christmas plays in the public square, the market, the home—all the world's the stage. Accepting roles they cannot resist, the players, whether pilgrims or scallywags, seem determined to display, complete, stretch, amplify, decorate, furnish, display, and unfold the Incarnation of God in human culture and festival. Propelled by incarnational extravagance, Christmas ends up everywhere. Who knows whether this grand tour comes to pass by divine design or profane imagination? Who can evaluate with certainty the risky course of divine Incarnation in the world? Whichever, the splendid, over-the-top popular culture of Christmas embeds itself in the memory of everyone who experiences it. In the trenches of 1914, English infantrymen later recalled, a brass band played carols and the German troops shouted across the abyss, "Merry Christmas, Tommy." Was God incarnate there?

It is customary to speak of great traditions of religion and little traditions, of sacraments and sacramentals, of high culture and popular culture. Contemporary studies of "lived religion" no longer privilege the first term of each of these pairs. If all the world's the stage of Christmas now, all manner of gifts are piled in the wings or stacked at the manger. They seem incongruous tokens of God's bounty now brought for consecration—or perhaps betraying no awareness that this is a sacred play. Factories in China and their outlets at Walmart are part of the process. Goods received and hallowed are diminutive instruments of grace in everyday life.

Consider the broad landscape of Christmas. As the collects of Advent call God to "*Stir up* thy power and come," generations of Anglican women turn to thoughts of baking. In Christmas afterglow, an Epiphany Gospel features Jesus turning 180 gallons of water into wine for a wedding. If Bethlehem skies sang with angels and oxen breathed on God, Germans answered that all of nature is "ensouled," and the evergreen stands in for the eternal in a deciduous world. Saint Nicholas's gold coins provoke a still unstoppable avalanche of gifts. Carols carry crowds across the threshold of the everyday to enchantment, and kitsch paints the way.

Is Everything Fit?

But is everything fit to be a prop in this play? Must popular religion say yes to everything that auditions? The following chapters chart a relentless course from Christmas as Christian holy day to an unrestrainable holiday on a post-Christian festival stage. The course of Incarnation as religious festival is uncertain, though the piously hopeful believe there is a beguiling path from seeing God to seeing religiously, from experiencing Incarnation to practicing inculturation, and finally a predisposition for noticing traces of divinity everywhere.

The front doors of the Abbey Church (now Basilica) of St. Denis near Paris are inscribed: *Mens hebes ad verum per materialia surgit* (the dull mind rises to true reality through the material). But there lingers a certain suspicion of material or popular culture, beginning already with Plato. The early desert monastics left the senses behind in striving for an intense spiritual discipline that escaped the body. Mystics deride the material as a lesser avenue to God. Bernard of Clairvaux and other Cistercian monastics mandated unadorned churches and simplified song. Some traditions of the Protestant Reformation were hostile to images and suspicious of music, permitting only a severe unaccompanied Psalm singing within white-washed walls cleared of art. Many Protestants took the golden calf story in the book of Exodus to represent the fallen human imagination gone wild into material culture, though Augustine noticed that the Egyptian gold from the melted-down calf was used later to adorn the sacred Ark of the Covenant.

Some believe that a religion purified of materiality will protect God from human manipulation. Because in this view the divine original remains in heaven, attempts to portray it in the popular arts are fraught with danger. The disciplined mind, not the body, is the safer organ of knowing. While the masses seem to require material culture—which, in this view, is itself suspicious—it would be better if they could transcend it. We have already seen elements of this viewpoint expressed in the second thoughts on Incarnation discussed in chapter 7, even attempts to reverse the Incarnation, talking God back into the box, as it were. Minimally, these concerns are expressed in resolute attempts to confine Christmas to the church's festal house and keep it away from the corruptions of the world stage—certainly a hopeless task.

But does this well-pedigreed prejudice overlook popular culture as a way to seek God or find religion? "Lived religion" is not confined to ideas or Platonic forms. Recent intellectual trends set faith into the landscape of the senses and take notice of efforts to see, hear, and touch God. Paying attention to the public stage where Christmas happens avoids the false dichotomy between sacred and profane, spirit and matter, piety and commerce, and discloses how religion actually settles into lived experience. What believers actually do is *scramble the categories of sacred and profane*.

When Emile Durkheim made these categories oppositional in the early years of European social science, he may have been playing out an (unacknowledged) Old Testament iconoclasm in which God remains always the disembodied voice interacting with embodied human beings. But the Incarnation's great reversal authorizes a material Christianity replete with theological meaning. The Christianity that went public after the conversion of Emperor Constantine moved quickly to foster its connections to the material world. Nevertheless, the old suspicion that when people lose their faith in God they turn to popular culture to construct graven images of the divine or to substitute for lost theistic meaning lingers in Christianity as well. There can be no doubt that forms of sensory delight significantly determine how Christmas is experienced. To make, merchandise, purchase, and give, to taste and smell and hear and see and handle all the artifacts of material culture is not only to be enjoying Christmas. It is to be involved in creating and maintaining an entire social and cultural world.

The Bells of Christmas

This book portrays a Christmas of spirit and matter, sacred and profane, holy day and holiday, the world as real and imagined. A revealing way to think about the interpenetration of religion and culture and resulting contests over social meaning over time is a recent study of the role that bells have played in the aural imagination of France. In the nineteenth century, Longfellow wrote:

> I heard the bells on Christmas day
> Their old familiar carols play . . .
> And thought how, as the day had come
> The belfries of all Christendom
> Had rolled along the unbroken song . . .
> Then pealed the bells more loud and deep:
> God is not dead; nor doth he sleep!

For much of French history, bell-ringing had marked both religious and secular time, calling citizens to pray or celebrate a religious festival, summoning angels, inviting assembly, warning of danger. To control the bells, the French Revolution saw, is to control the symbolic order, the rhythm, the loyalties of everyday life. Municipalizing church bells could bend them to the national interest. The revolutionaries melted down one hundred thousand bells from sixty thousand towers. To attack the bells was to disenchant the landscape, to free civic life from the sensual dominance of religion, to subvert ancient markers of the holy. But long after the revolution had run its course, the populace decided that they could not live without their bells.

To understand the bells is to decipher an aural culture that mixed the sacred and the profane together. Villages had competed to be thought of as a "ringing town," as neighbors today outdo one another in their decorations. Castings on site were great occasions, expert advisers were called in, drinking bouts followed, finally the bell was baptized, even with godparents. Mayor and priest competed to control the community's biorhythms, but the priest held the key to the tower. After the revolution, on every Bastille Day the mayor insisted the bells were his and if necessary seized the church tower and hung from it the national flag. Clerical insolence could be expressed by ringing a funeral peal in protest or perhaps a ding-dong to scoff. In the modern world the bells were thought to compensate for the dumbness of human voices that had lost the habit of prayer. The steeples spoke for the church in a secular landscape, still trying to shape and crown and consecrate, to offer a dominating verticality amidst a prevailing horizontality. But the modern urban milieu found the bells an interference with sleep and the right to silence, even a torture from which a secular relief was demanded.

Like the bells of France, the material culture of Christmas carries national significance. The American colonists, with their spare calendar, needed a national holiday, and Christmas would be it, easily outdistancing the Fourth of July in its eventual cultural impact. During the nineteenth century, the American Christmas was fashioned in part as a nationalistic sentiment that could draw all people together in a kind of civil religion. Conveniently, its benefits were commerce and even excess, divinely sanctioned. Only grocery and liquor stores profit from Thanksgiving, but Christmas invites a multitude of conveyors. Congress made Christmas a federal holiday in 1870, after many states had already done so. Christmas would inaugurate an annual, temporary state of national prosperity.

But if this was to become a modern American festival, what of Jews and Muslims and agnostics who did not share the Christian tradition? The Christian particularities of Christmas would be reduced—and later eliminated in the public schools—to be replaced by the civil religion of consumerism or winter celebration, a perfected American religion that could unite everyone. A manger scene could not be the defining prop, but secular carols, kitsch, and Santa easily could. The material culture began to shift to other stages. "Keeping Xmas" as a sign of being American was the contribution of the twentieth century. The Jewish Irving Berlin created a national anthem sung by the Catholic Bing Crosby, "White Christmas." The continuing popularity of Dickens's *Christmas Carol* was a modest mitigation of seasonal excess and an invitation to recover benevolence as the true spirit of Christmas, close to or far from religious precincts. Some persistent corrections were necessary. Every year, newspapers reprinted Frank Church's 1897 essay "Yes, Virginia," to remind a post-religious Santa of his deeper meaning. Christmas television specials about Charlie Brown and the Grinch would admonish Americans that Christmas cannot be bought in a store and that children, perhaps, can save it.

The Panoply of Incarnation

The popular culture of Christmas mostly makes people happy. It is not clear whether this should be read as Christianity's success in sacramentalizing every earthly matter or as a puzzlingly enthusiastic venture in burying the lead. Whether as a total immersion in divinity or in consumerism, *God gets carried away at Christmas.* The prevailing sentiment is to love Christmas for its feasting, toys, wrapping, and lights (chapter 8).

Much of Christmas has a good-bad-good quality to it. Saint Nicholas was once a symbol of holiness and generosity, a patron of our best impulses. Then Santa seemed to become a cynical advertisers' shill. But if magic and mystery deteriorate in the modern age, that process leaves reminders. There are bread crumbs on the path, beckoning us to find our way home to enchantment (chapter 9).

The visual trajectory of Christmas runs from the settings of Christian worship to a Christian artistic culture mostly embedded now in museums to the modern construction of a festive landscape for the eye that runs from market to home and often plays as kitsch. The ability to "see religiously" may be an uncertain vestige of Incarnation in a post-Christian age (chapter 10).

Carols carry the delight of meaning on both sides of the divide between Christmas past and present and between holy day and holiday. They are popular emblems of a rich Christian musical culture that runs to Bach and Handel and to many before and after them. They invite us to reflect on the power of music to move us to hear religiously (chapter 11).

GALLERY

Part I. Origins of Christmas

The original Christmas story is embedded in the texts of the New Testament. The narratives of Matthew and Luke retain their incantatory power when read aloud, carrying modern hearers back to the beginning even while authorizing incarnational trajectories far beyond Bethlehem.

Fig. 1

Saint Luke at his writing desk: The Incarnation extended to every written vernacular and to the culture of the book. *Photo courtesy of the Yorck Project (http://commons.wikimedia.org/wiki/File: Byzantinischer_Maler_des_10._Jahrhunderts_001.jpg).*

Saint Matthew at his writing desk: The original Christmas story is embedded in the sacred texts of the Christian New Testament. *Werner Forman / Art Resource, NY.*

Fig. 2

Fig. 3

The Dream of Saint Joseph: Guided by an angel, Joseph is the hero of Matthew's infancy narrative. *© National Gallery, London / Art Resource, NY.*

Part II. Christian Images of Incarnation

Christianity comes to understand itself as a theater of Incarnation with the church as its festival house. As the living body of Christ, the church is called to annual performances of Christmas amid the ever-changing conditions of lived Christianity. Centuries of festal days have laid down rich accumulations of Christian culture.

Fig. 4

The Annunciation: Every age created its own image of the "Annunciation," this one from the nineteenth century. *Photo courtesy of Wikimedia Commons.*

Fifteenth-century nativity scene: Instrumentalists at the nativity play music as the artistic accompaniment to Incarnation. *Photo courtesy of the Yorck Project (http://commons.wikimedia.org/wiki/File:Piero_della_Francesca_041.jpg).*

Fig. 5

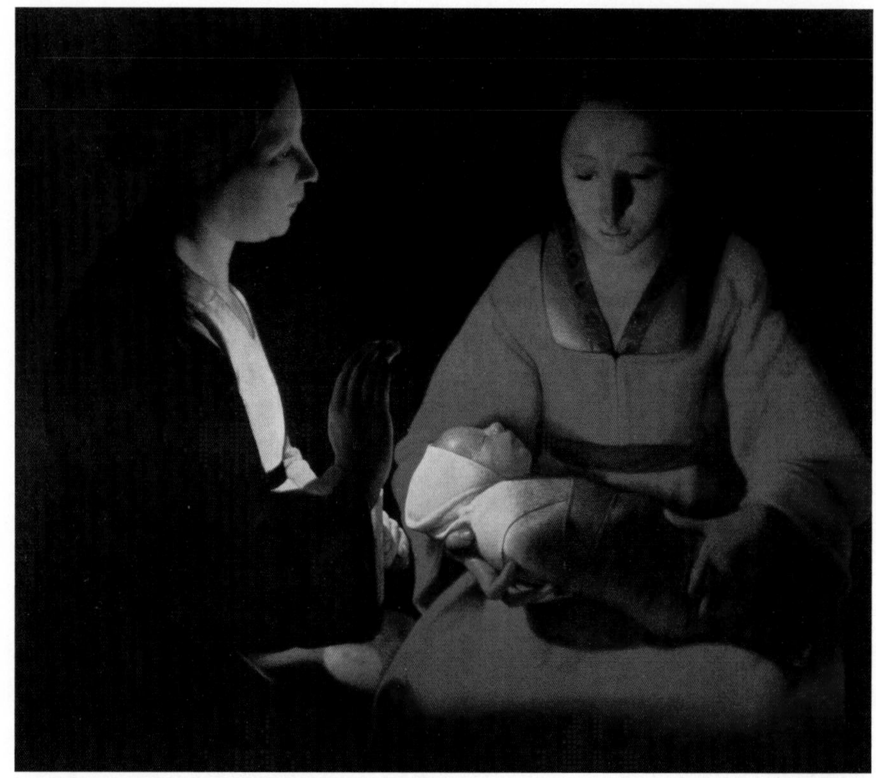

Fig. 6

Seventeenth-century Mary and Jesus: Christian themes appear in the vernacular of each century so that believers can find themselves in the art of their day. *Photo courtesy of the Yorck Project (http://commons.wikimedia.org/wiki/File:Georges_de_La_Tour_020.jpg).*

Fig. 7

Sixteenth-century devotional reliquary: Homely cradles suggested Jesus' humanity, while stylized cradles like this one suggested his divinity. Many were rocked during Christmas worship. *Réunion des Musées Nationaux / Art Resource, NY.*

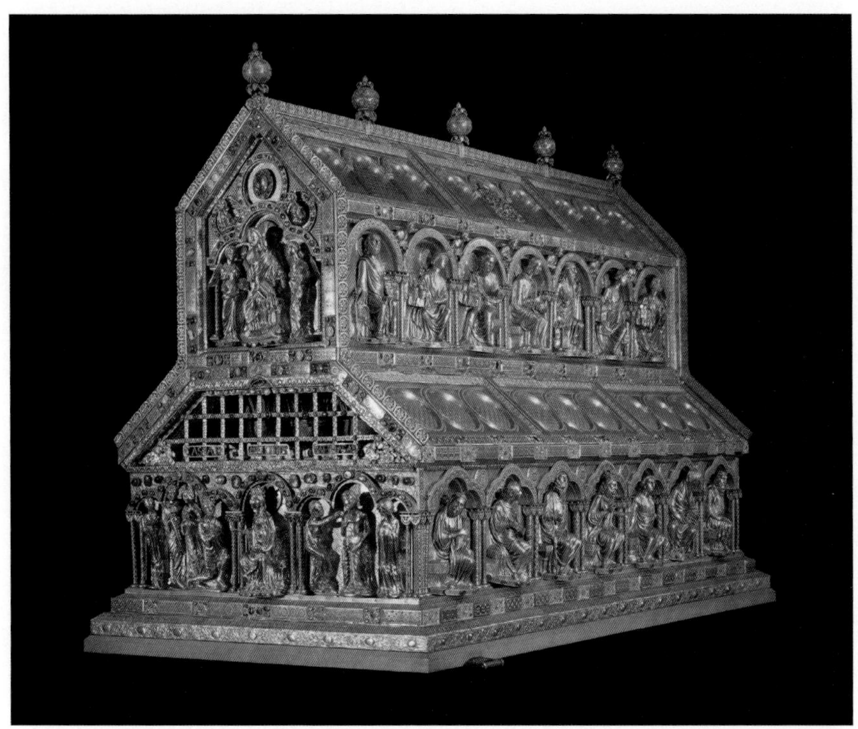

Fig. 8

Medieval reliquary: After migrating across Europe, the relics of the magi came to rest at the cathedral in Cologne, Germany, in this splendid shrine. *Erich Lessing / Art Resource, NY.*

Tenth-century Adoration of the Magi: The magi are ever shifting shapes in the Christian imagination, here painted into a sacred manuscript. *Scala / Art Resource, NY.*

Fig. 9

Fig. 10

Adoration of the Magi: It is a surprise that a Christmas scene can be imaged in the fashion of twentieth-century cubism. *The Newark Museum / Art Resource, NY.*

Book of Hours—The Adoration of the Magi: Illuminated devotional books occasioned one of the highest art forms of the Middle Ages. *Erich Lessing / Art Resource, NY.*

Fig. 11

Fig. 12

Stained glass representation of the Magi: This beloved art form that reached its zenith in the Gothic cathedral still interested artists in the twentieth century. *Photo courtesy of Wikimedia Loves Art Project.*

Fig. 13

Nativity scene of the Holy Family: The twentieth century saw whimsical and naïve portrayals of the nativity scene. *Banque d'Images, ADAGP / Art Resource, NY. Copyright © 2010 Artists Rights Society (ARS), New York / ADAGP. Paris.*

South American crèche: The nativity scene takes on myriad forms in religious art, as this straw crèche from Ecuador shows. *Alfredo Dagli Orti / Art Resource, NY.*

Fig. 14

Fig. 15

Music from a church organ: Much Christian music, like that of Bach, originates in the church's liturgies.

Snark / Art Resource, NY.

Fig. 16

Religious procession: The earliest and lasting celebration of Christmas is staged in its festal house, the church.

Nimatallah / Art Resource, NY. Copyright © 2010 Artists Rights Society (ARS), New York / ADAGP. Paris.

Part III. The World as a Stage for Incarnation

Spilling far beyond sacred scripts and churchly precincts, the "cultural performance" of Christmas makes all the world its stage. Holy day and holiday jostle together, God is spun into every matter, all of life is decorated with festive celebration. Christmas plays as incarnational extravagance.

Fig. 17

Angelic madrigal singers: Throughout Christian art, angels make music a central dimension of Christian festival.
Cameraphoto Arte, Venice / Art Resource, NY.

FIG. 18

NINETEENTH-CENTURY AMERICAN CHRISTMAS CELEBRATION: For many, Christian or secular, Christmas celebration happens in the home.

Bildarchiv Preussischer Kulturbesitz / Art Resource, NY.

Fig. 19

The Metropolitan Museum's Christmas Tree: Elaborate manger scenes, or crèches, sometimes in the presence of a tree, expand the investment of the Incarnation to every regional vernacular.

Christmas Tree with Neapolitan Crèche; "Angel Tree." Eighteenth to nineteenth century. As installed in Medieval Sculpture Hall; facing east. Gift of Loretta Hines Howard, 1964 . Location: The Metropolitan Museum of Art, New York, NY, U.S.A.

Image copyright © The Metropolitan Museum of Art / Art Resource, NY.

Fig. 20

Byzantine icon of Saint Nicholas: Nicholas as bishop and saint was a holy day figure long before he morphed into a holiday fixture. *Photo courtesy of Wikimedia Commons.*

Saint Nicholas as gift-giver: When Saint Nicholas threw gold over the transom to provide a dowry for three poor girls, he forever connected gift-giving to his image. *Erich Lessing / Art Resource, NY.*

Fig. 21

Early nineteenth-century image of Santa Claus: On his long evolution into the American Santa, Saint Nicholas first becomes Father Christmas. *Victoria & Albert Museum, London / Art Resource, NY.*

Fig. 22

Christmas celebration (the Twelfth Night of Christmas): The riotous exuberance of holiday is also a dimension of Christmas. *VEGAP / Art Resource, NY. Copyright © 2010 Artists Rights Society (ARS), New York / VEGAP. Madrid.*

Fig. 23

Fig. 24

Christmas commercialized: This storefront of Macy's in San Francisco, California, announces the secular advent of Christmas in a most powerful and arresting way. *© Tinou Bao. Used under the Creative Commons Attribution 2.0 Generic License.*

8

Ornamenting the Incarnation: The Popular Culture of Christmas

Follow me in merry measure.

When we hear the fife and drum
Christmas should be frolicsome.
When we hear the fife and drum
Dance and make the village hum.

Deck the halls with boughs of holly
'Tis the season to be jolly
Don we now our gay apparel
Troll the ancient yuletide carol.

—Nineteenth-Century Carol

Though not without second thoughts over its historical course, Christianity sacramentalized nearly every human artifact, not holding back divinity from every earthly imaging. Of all the Christian holy days, Christmas most conspicuously clothes itself in the material world, becoming a celebration of material culture. Hopeful medieval mystics said that God is in all things and all things are in God. For those able to believe this (often in spite of much evidence to the contrary), Christmas is the ideal festival.

To those who love the world and every material piece of it, Christmas is the consummate occasion. How is it that Christmas has so attached itself to earthly life? In one view, the Incarnation sacramentalizes material culture with a total-immersion baptism, leaving no matter untouched by divinity. A flood of grace lifts all boats. In another view, market forces (compounded with human longings) surround and engulf every spark of divinity, rendering it as a purchasable commodity. In either view, God gets carried away at Christmas.

To venture into the mall in the middle of October, two weeks before Halloween, six weeks before the beginning of Advent, and two months before Christmas, is to enter a candy-land of Christmas display. A determined wince soon gives way to enthrallment. One cannot look away. Men have visions of ever larger pre-lit faux wreaths hung on their chimneys, six-feet long trains moving along the ridge of the roof, insouciant reindeer, heads moving mechanically up and down, grazing on their winter lawns, angels with electronically fluttering wings blowing their horns in the trees. Christmas overdone is magical, and expected. The holiday imagination wants to leave no square foot untouched by gewgaw or flashing light. Even aficionados of high art and highfalutin scorners of kitsch find themselves racing to the lowest common denominator of incarnational extravagance. It is the least they can do for holy day. In the rhythm of life, this is the one month for every fling with bright, shiny material, for gilding all things visible with Christmas spirit. Mothers dream their own dreams, unpacking with care a lifetime of ornaments, staging domestic fantasies, getting in the holiday spirit. Like God at creation, they name everything anew and pronounce it all good.

Of course, the Christmas spirit is not Christianity's entire message. There is the stern "No!" of Good Friday and the complex "Nevertheless!" of Easter. But at Christmas, no matter is too low to disclose divinity. Let reservations about the world and worry about human overreaching calendar themselves elsewhere. Each season, each mood, gets its due, when its themes are played for all their worth. On one's twenty-first birthday one does not spend time meditating on mortality. Strolling in spring gardens as nature comes alive is not the season to ponder the dying of the light. Only very tightly-pinched prohibitionists ruin Thanksgiving by insisting on baloney sandwiches in honor of the hungry. Let Christmas sparkle—is the dominant view. Let huge evergreens stand in transplanted magnificence. Wrap the world in delight. Decorate every sentiment.

Feasting

> Now thrice welcome Christmas, which brings us good cheer,
> Minced pies and plum porridge, good ale and strong beer;
> With pig, goose, and capon, the best that can be,
> So well doth the weather and our stomachs agree.
>
> —Poor Robin's Almanack

> Wassail, wassail all over the town
> Our toast it is white and our ale it is brown
> Our bowl it is made of the white maple tree
> With the wassailing bowl we'll drink to thee.
>
> —Traditional English Carol

In *A Christmas Carol,* Dickens describes the extravagant Christmas Eve street scene the sour Scrooge cannot avoid witnessing: "The poulterers' shops were still half open, and the fruiters' were radiant in their glory. There were great, round, pot-bellied baskets of chestnuts, shaped like the waistcoats of jolly old gentlemen, lolling at the doors, and tumbling out into the street in their apoplectic opulence. There were ruddy, brown-faced broad-girthed Spanish Onions, shining in the fatness of their growth like Spanish Friars; and winking from their shelves in wanton slyness at the girls as they went by, and glanced demurely at the hung-up mistletoe. There were pears and apples, clustered high in blooming pyramids; there were bunches of grapes, made, in the shopkeepers benevolence, to dangle from conspicuous hooks, that people's mouths might water gratis as they passed; there were piles of filberts, mossy and brown, recalling, in their fragrance, ancient walks among the woods, and pleasant shufflings ankle deep through withered leaves; there were Norfolk Biffins, squab, and swarthy, setting off the yellow of the oranges and lemons, and, in the great compactness of their juicy persons, urgently entreating and beseeching to be carried home in paper bags and eaten after diner."

Eating and drinking together is a constant of human festivity, in Christianity both a sacrament and a lesser sacramental, so mythologies about abundant food and treasured recipes are common. While many Christians are content with the culture of candlelight and candy canes on Christmas Eve, others believe that the Midnight Mass must feature a eucharistic meal. To those with amplified imagination, the Eucharist is the visible extension of the Incarnation, an icon of the day when all the world gets a seat at God's table. As gifts are brought to the altar, the liturgy sings:

> Let the vineyards be fruitful, Lord, and fill to the brim our cup of blessing.
> Gather a harvest from the seeds that were sown, that we may be fed with the bread of life.
> Gather the hopes and the dreams of all; unite them with the prayers we offer now.
> Grace our table with your presence, and give us *a foretaste of the feast to come.*

From the Middle Ages, Christmas has been constituted, celebrated, and evaluated, in part, by its feasting. The groaning board of the old English manor was a means of conspicuous consumption that also allowed the poor a taste of its riches. Occasionally, royalty had to remind the nobility to do their duty: get out of London at Christmas, return to their estates, and set a table whose bounties trickled down to everyone. The Christmas Dinner, as also religious ceremony, centered Christmas. *Poor Robin's Almanack* of 1700 admonished:

> Now that the time has come wherein
> Our Saviour Christ was born
> The larder's full of beef and pork
> The granary's full of corn.

As God hath plenty to thee sent
Take comfort of thy labors
And let it never thee repent
To feast thy needy neighbors.

The Cratchits' simple but uplifting meal is the heart of Dickens's *Carol*. The family comes together in want and sickness, but finds reasons to rejoice and even to toast Scrooge. The goose was small and so was the pudding, but Tim's blessing and mother's worrying and the family's gratitude made it the perfect Victorian dinner scene. The Dickens dinner would birth public charity meals in England and the United States.

Not everyone gets it. Isak Dinesen's short story and later film, *Babette's Feast*, describes what is surely meant to be a consummate sacramental meal. A refugee who had been a famous chef in Paris but now does humble housekeeping for two spinster sisters in Scandinavia, devotees of a severe Christian sect, has won the French lottery. With every exotic ingredient shipped in from Paris, she spends her entire winnings on the most fabulous meal imaginable, which she convinces the sisters to accept in honor of their sainted father. The little congregation invited to the meal, together with the sisters, conspire ahead of time to say No to divine delight, by not allowing themselves actually to savor any taste, lest it overwhelm the palette of their sanctimonious piety. So they manage to miss the presence of God in the incarnation of a Paris chef dressed as a humble servant and giving all she has.

But mostly people rejoice at Christmas feasting. Peacocks were once the prized chief dish at Christmas, brought to the table with great ceremony. The skin was stripped off with feathers still attached, the bird roasted, then sewn up again in feathered skin, and the beak—sometimes the entire bird—gilded with gold leaf. Stuffed with spices and herbs and with a cotton-wick saturated in spirits placed in its beak, it was brought, flaming, to the table. The Christmas goose is feted in carols, as are puddings and cakes. Carol-singers went wassailing (*waes hael* means "to your health"), singing for their supper of drinks. Germans prized gingerbread and used it in elaborate culinary constructions. Candy canes are said to have been created by a baker in Indiana who wanted to use his product as a witness for his faith. White candy symbolized the virgin birth, the shape was a J for Jesus (or perhaps a shepherd's staff), and red stripes represent Christ's passion. Or were they sweets to decorate German Christmas trees and first handed out at Cologne Cathedral in 1670 to keep the children quiet? One need not reconcile culinary etymologies, just savor them. The earliest ornaments of Christmas were edible, fruits and nuts, eventually cakes, candy, cookies, to be offered to visitors and taken to friends—and sometimes attached to the Christmas tree.

Besides many-coursed madrigal dinners the local college sponsors, and the splendid or excruciating family dinners that occupy the afternoons and evenings of Christmas Day, Christmas means many lesser occasions for feasting, as well. Even households that do not normally bake schedule cookie extravaganzas in which the family gathers to pour dough into favorite cookie cutters and consume considerable raw dough on the side. The tremendous variety of Christmas cookies reveals the propensity of Christmas to sugar the world. Families who have lost old-world languages can still pass down, generation after generation, old-world tastes and smells. Excuses are found to load confections with spirits, and many a cake is served heavy with bourbon or rum. An entire literature has grown up around the infamous fruit cake, which would fracture a toe if dropped and which is passed down year after year, uneaten but reverenced or ridiculed. The light and warmth December requires is added through flaming puddings and hot toddies. Never more so than at Christmas is eating an expressive act that bastes the holidays in joyful excess and draws family and friends together in festive community.

Gifts and Toys

This is Miss Manners on gift-giving and receiving: "Presents are never given because they are felt to be obligatory but because people enjoy expressing their affection and appreciation in tangible form. You choose a present when something catches your eye and suggests itself as a source of delight for a particular person. When you receive a present, your pleasure in it and in the feeling it symbolizes obliterates any awareness of its material worth. Do you believe this? Miss Manners is trying to. People keep interrupting her by asking if they have to give something to this person or that, how little they can get away with spending, how they can get others to give them something they really want rather than something of that person's choosing, and what do they do about people who give cheap presents or none at all. What a nasty, troublesome business it all seems to have become. Miss Manners is beginning to think that nobody deserves to get anything until we all manage to get greed under control."

Christians believe that God makes himself a gift to the world, and so, in imitation, the magi naturally bring treasures to Bethlehem and Saint Nicholas throws gold coins to girls in need of a dowry. Christmas is saturated with gift-giving and receiving. In fact, every culture weights gift exchange with social meaning. When Christians—and now nearly everyone—give gifts at Christmas, they are humbly mimicking a self-giving God, or gilding the Incarnation with their own efforts, or following perennial custom, as evidenced already in the Roman saturnalia, or succumbing to modern merchandising, or avoiding the guilt of stinginess, or relishing the feeling of generosity, or practicing reciprocity, or keeping up with the Joneses—or all of the above. Holy day stimulates holiday, and holiday envelops holy day. Unable to banish New Year's gift-giving, early Christianity baptized it by way of the magi. Even the Romans were not always satisfied with gift-giving. Although the upper classes gave gifts to the emperor to assure him of their loyalty, gifts soon enough degenerated into "useless little terra-cotta lamps, clay tablets with pictures of fruits, garlands or cornucopias with such inscriptions as 'Happiness in the New Year.'"

Except for the Christmas charity that lords of the manor owed to their serfs and the seasonal revelry with which the upper classes indulged the lower classes, gift-giving as we know it today was not a feature of the medieval Christmas and did not for a very long time come to pervade the European Christmas. Christmas in the good old days was delightfully organic, and its simplicity derived from an agricultural economy that produced most gifts. The English began to grow a culture of gift-giving in the sixteenth and seventeenth centuries, but until the nineteenth century adult exchange did not go beyond foodstuffs, perhaps a Stilton cheese or a barrel of oysters. The German *Christkindlmarkt* began to evolve in fourteenth-century Munich and came into its own in seventeenth-century Nuremberg. The emergence of the toy industry in nearby regions was not coincidental.

Following Puritan caution about Christmas, the early American colonists were very cautious about gift-exchange, except for food and drink. In 1745, American Moravians were following German customs when they gave gifts of scarves, handkerchiefs, hats, neckerchiefs, and apples. As Christmas Day 1805 fell on the great Lewis and Clark expedition, Lewis gave Clark a shirt and socks. From their men they received a pair of moccasins and a small Indian basket, and from the Indians two dozen weasel tails. For a long time, most gift-giving went one way, from upper to lower, a token of status obligations. Eventually this yielded to reciprocal gifts among family, friends, and neighbors.

The nineteenth century saw the growing of the American Christmas into a festival of gift-giving and consumer exchange, stimulated by the transition from a rural economy to a full urban and industrial order that could produce manufactured gifts in abundance and that would lead to the demise of handmade gifts. To the masses concentrated in cities, store-bought items became available, and, in any case, industrial laborers did not, like farmers, have free time before a winter holiday. When holiday was brought inside and centered in the family, gifts of food and drink no longer made sense, and the Christmas present as we know it was born.

The first advertisement for Christmas presents may have appeared in Salem, Massachusetts, in 1806, placed by a local bookseller. Boston and New York ads in 1808 featured shops with 450 kinds of Christmas presents and New Year's gifts, especially toys, children's books, paints, pencils, and penknives. Besides books, the first commercial presents were manufactured for children. An 1865 Harper's engraving portrayed as Christmas gifts: pocket watch, teething ring, china doll, doll carriage, picture books, wooly lamb on wheels, easel and boxed paint set, tool chest, drum, sword. For adults there were pipes, perfume, and books. No doubt Ralph Waldo Emerson could see where all this was going when he insisted that gifts must bear the identity of the giver. "The only gift is a portion of thyself. The poet brings his poem, the shepherd his lamb, the farmer his corn, the painter his picture. It is right and pleasing when one's biography is conveyed in a gift."

In *Little Women*, set during the Civil War when the father of the house is away in battle, the four girls assemble with chastened hopes on Christmas morning. Each gets only one little present and before they can sit down to an almost luxurious Christmas breakfast, they dutifully decide to give most of the fixings to a poor family nearby, from whom the youngest March girl subsequently contracts smallpox. Already in 1850, Harriet Beecher Stowe wrote a Christmas story in which she remembered that when she was a little girl, children were perfectly delighted with a single piece of candy, but now as an adult she saw presents flying everywhere: "Christmas is coming in a fortnight, and I have got to think up presents for everybody! Dear me, it's so tedious. Everybody has got everything that can be thought of. Every shop and store is glittering with all manner of splendors." The most interesting gift during the Civil War period may have been General Sherman's. He telegraphed President Lincoln on Christmas Day 1864: "I beg to present to you as a Christmas gift the city of Savannah."

A century before liberation theology and probably innocent of Marxist influence, J. H. Ingraham, a contemporary of Dickens, exploded the niceties of a Victorian Christmas in a short story where the poor live a desperate existence and the rich enjoy lives of hard-hearted self-congratulation. Upon the snow-covered Boston Common lands a radical Santa. He sends his helpers to inspect every house to see who has abundance and who not and to right things by taking from the rich and giving to the poor. Santa as the great distributor is a fond American myth; Santa as a redistributor is a rarity in American life, and probably a communist.

After Victorian patricians transformed Christmas from lower class excess to genteel family celebration, merchants transformed it again from evidences of homemade kindness to commercial exchange. There seems to be "a natural history of gifts," from homemade to retail, from food and drink offered to neighbors and the poor to special items chosen for each member of the family, from baking and whittling to store-bought. But the more gift-giving became an engine of commerce, the less of a role did the poor play as recipients. Gift-giving and charity came apart. Dickens's *Carol* tried to right that wrong, but no social gospel could dent for long the individualistic currents of American religion. American Christians, taking a cue from the Puritan search for evidence of their divine election, were prepared to see gifts and the ability to lavish them as evidence of divine reward. "Godliness is in league with riches," preachers assured.

From the middle of the nineteenth century, advertising released giving behaviors, just as alcohol releases other sorts of behavior. In the early nineteenth century, few would have thought that consumer capitalism and civic virtue went together. Relentless advertising and capitalist success changed that. Christmas would become a powerful market stimulus, the time when people who cannot afford it splurge. Just as medieval holiday produced rituals of reversal, the modern holiday would upend the normal rules of economic behavior. Women tended to take control of gift-giving, perhaps because they are the appointed custodians of relationships and the guardians of kinship ties. As capitalist success grew, a new consciousness would have to be shaped. Santa was employed to market Christmas toys to one's own girls and boys, but as a non-commercial commercial transaction. Store-bought gifts would be dressed in sincerity, magic, and, of course, religion. Retailers, of course, did not invent gift-giving, but rushed to seize new opportunities. Christmas and consumerism are reciprocal, each marking up the other.

The Christmas market Americans invented in the nineteenth century, with the *Saturday Evening Post* the chief purveyor of holiday iconography, would be perfected by Macy's in the twentieth. The Macy's parade first delighted the crowd and then brought them straight to Macy's windows to gaze on dioramas of a perfect world of gifts. Advertising reminded consumers of the reasons for the season. Early retailers were capable of generosity and ruthlessness. At the turn of the twentieth century, Woolworths invented the Christmas bonus, but also insisted on cheap help in order to offer cheap goods. When women clerks demanded better pay, managers were instructed to wait until after the holidays and then fire the agitators. Late in the twentieth century, many thought the gift chase had become a cancer on Christmas, a single-dimensioned material culture gone malignant. Indeed, gift-exchange was showing a much greater capacity for consecration than the ancient Roman New Year celebrations. Wags said that Santa and Rudolph turned folklore into folk-lure.

Some confess that the best gifts are for oneself, because who else knows so well what would please me? Collectibles are an example. Miniature villages, added to each year to the extent one can afford, emerged in the late 1970s. It is said that one-third of Americans collect something. Christmas is the perfect time of year for it, and a village of one's own brings utter perfection within reach. The faultlessness that is missing in life comes to brief display in one's own living room. Ersatz scenes, gently arranged and softly lit, retrieve childhood mythologies and provide an idealized setting for Christmas sentiments. When produced in limited, signed editions, the perfect village promises to be a good investment as well.

A certain irony should be mixed with Christmas giving, if we are to get some distance on our toys. O. Henry's "Gift of the Magi" tells of a young husband who pawns his finest inheritance, a gold watch, in order to get the money to buy his wife an exquisite comb for her beautiful hair, while, meanwhile, the wife sells her hair to get money for a gold chain for her husband's watch. It is commonly remarked that little children appreciate the boxes more than the expensive toys that came in them, which break anyway in one week and are dogged by dead batteries. But parents and grandparents keep building mountains of toys because they cannot help themselves. Each year there are brief bouts of insanity when they cannot locate on store shelves the year's most pumped-up presents and must do business with scalpers on eBay. To complicate things further, self-appointed toy critics scornfully analyze whether toys stimulate childhood imagination and the spirit of play, or overexcite with an easy novelty that quickly bores children because of lack of intrinsic stimulation.

Those who watch with cynicism or amusement the annual outrageous extravagances offered in the Nieman-Marcus catalog cannot utterly condemn it all because they secretly long for such purchasing power and status-confirming gifts. Christmas resolutions take the form of shopping only in catalogs this year, spending more but saving time for more important things—we forget what. Newspaper stories gently ridicule corporate gift procurers who do the work to impress someone or other (even the busy CEO's own children) with just the right gift. Just as rules of thumb stipulate a diamond engagement ring must cost two months' salary, gift-givers suffer considerable anxiety determining the meaning of their gifts and how much should be spent on them. We see on television the wife or lover who leads her man, blindfolded on Christmas morning, to the red Porsche parked in front of the house, sporting a huge red ribbon, and wish we had such a wife or lover.

It turns out that adult gifts are freighted with anxiety. They display social roles, of course, by marking men or women or children, lovers or friends, employers and employees, rich and poor, with what is au currant and what is "so last year." More worrisome is the implication that the gift will inevitably convey "what someone really thinks of you." Gifts become accurate markers of relationships, or not. So great is the stress that hinting about what one wants becomes permissible and then required. Genteel adults see that gifts of money would be a serious problem of symbolism, so the gift certificate is born; teenagers, however, have no qualms about stipulating and accepting cash. One function of advertising is to offer reassurance that the gift you are considering would be both proper and highly desirable. Those who make a present of something that was needed anyway, like underwear or socks, mistakenly believe they are going to achieve "gift credit." In fact, luxury gifts, meaning high monetary value and low utility value, are the most desirable. Men, always beset with phallic uncertainties, are susceptible to advertisers who insinuate, "Will your gift measure up?" If it is any comfort, retailers are all suffering along with consumers. Their preoccupations are whether they will have ordered too much or too little of a good thing and when they must begin to discount.

We pause to remember fathers who sat contented on Christmas morning and said they really wanted nothing more than all the children home and healthy, and we wonder if those times are gone. We think about the "alternative celebrations" movement, which coaches our desires: homemade presents, family adventures in holiday baking, playing together, homemade cards and meals, the gift of time or service, creating candles and their rituals, admirable charities that will not squander our gift. We are, momentarily, cleansed.

Wrappings and Cards

Material culture has its rules. All gifts must be wrapped, and gift-dressing is best done by women, since men are notoriously inept. Along with eye-appealing bling and the demonstration of exquisite choice, wrapping conveys the mysteries of containment and concealment. A classy wrap disguises the gift's origin as a mass-produced commodity, mediates the relationship between commerce and giving, and adds a layer of authenticity and personal feeling that would be missing from a straight marketplace transaction carried in a plastic bag.

Elaborate wrappings soon followed the culture of gifts, often making them seem more expensive than they were. Nowadays stores understand that their wrapping services purify merchandise just plucked from the retail floor and make it suitable for ritual use in the home. How to respond to the elegant sentiments of wrapping? Children, of course, tear through the wrapping paper with abandon, as do some adults, especially men. But the more genteel and well-mannered see that this is about ritual and so they unwrap slowly as everyone hushes and all eyes are on the person unwrapping and on the person who is giving the gift, just announced from the attached card. Some people even carefully remove the bows and untie the ribbon just so and are careful not to tear the paper and fold it reverently and neatly, not just for recycling but because this is the proper response to complete the wrapping/unwrapping ritual. Wrapping, but also unwrapping, should be nuanced and aesthetic, for each is an expressive act. Think how many possible methods there are to loop a ribbon around a box, and note which one was selected for this particular present: so much meaning on display.

The wrapping paper industry was born in 1917, when it was called "gift dressing," and Christmas is now unimaginable without it. Like every great invented tradition, it is now impossible to conceive a time when society went without it, even though through much of the nineteenth century wrapping Christmas presents was unknown and gifts were placed in stockings, hung on the tree if small, placed in very simple boxes, wrapped in very simple paper and string, or left open and undisguised. A new fashion returns to those days, as presents, with simple elegance taught by Martha Stewart, are wrapped in brown paper now stippled with metallic paint from homemade patterns.

Christmas cards have become a ubiquitous emblem of the season. They must be selected for image and message, addressed from a personal list that is added to and subtracted from each year according to rules of reciprocity, stamped with a secular or religious stamp, possibly dressed with Christmas seals, and mailed on time. (Or, this can all be done now through a custom service, or on one's computer.) They range from spectacular and expensive examples of classical art or the latest in graphic design to the cheapest and most trivial images. They foster friendships or business acquaintances. They provide a not very wide range of sentiments selected as one's own. They indicate whether the sender or receiver is religious or secular or nicely positioned on the fence between. They are a possible substitute for small gifts. Unfortunately, they replace an older custom of writing letters or making personal visits, but they allow some contact during an age of increased geographic distance.

Christmas cards were first created in 1843 by John Calcott Horsley, and they consisted of a postcard with three panels, the central one an English family enjoying the holiday and the others picturing acts of charity. They were inscribed: Merry Christmas and a Happy New Year to You. They spread among Victorians as a popular holiday custom. They were affordable to send because in 1840 a penny post had become available, and the British postal service even delivered on Christmas Day. New Year's cards had been in use well before this, but the Christmas card coincides with the Victorian revival of Christmas customs. Many still decorated their own visiting cards at Christmas time, or made their own cards. Commercial production accelerated after the 1860s. The invention of the steam press made mass production possible, and the German-born American printer Louis

Prang built Christmas cards into a mass market. His first design was in 1875, a color lithograph in eight colors featuring nativity scenes, nature scenes, family scenes, and eventually Santa. He enticed public interest by staging contests all over the country and offering prizes for the best designs. Today Christmas cards come in every possible shape and dressing, and the emblems of the season featured are a good indication of the range of material culture. They may feature obviously religious symbols, but also evergreens and holly, reindeer and squirrels and cardinal and robin, snowmen and puddings and bicycles, and, of course, eye-catching female figures.

In some cases cards are bought in boxes and selected for their images, with hardly a notice of the sentiment expressed, which narrowly ranges from the possibly religious Merry Christmas and Happy New Year to the carefully neutral Happy Holidays. But when cards are sent selectively rather than in mass mailings, people can be observed standing in stationary stories carefully reading card after card, until they find the one that precisely connects the sender and the receiver. The more educated or aesthetically refined may select cards much more for their artistic beauty and the elaboration of their design, high-end triptychs being in great favor. "Alternative celebration" enthusiasts may let it be known that they are instead giving to charity what they would have spent on large mailings, and in some Christian churches members place their good wishes on a simple card on a tree in the narthex, with the expenditure saved going to the needy. Charities flood households with Christmas card-like solicitations, that may also offer address labels with holiday images to encourage reciprocity.

The envelope holding an impressive card deserves a special seal. Christmas seals were invented in Denmark in 1903 to benefit tuberculosis sufferers. From Scandinavia they spread to the United States, where in 1919 the double-barred cross of Lorraine became the signature for the American Lung Association. Christmas stamps, lending holiday spirit to the mails, were invented in Canada in 1898 and came to the United States in 1962. A renaissance painting, Adoration of the Shepherds, by Giorgione, was the most popular stamp in American history, until the Elvis stamp.

Lights

As in the Holy Christ Child's name
This blessed wax shall feed the flame—
So let my heart its fires begin
And light the Heavenly Pilgrim in.
—Anna Hempstead Branch

A festival near the winter solstice must certainly light December night. The sympathetic magic of saturnalia lights was intended to coax the sun to shine again. European peoples worried the light in December and controlled the sun through the exertions of ritual. Light and darkness are powerful symbols in all religions. Among the Greeks light had intellectual and ethical connotations as well.

In the Old Testament, creation begins with the emergence of light, followed specifically by sun, moon, and stars. The psalmists sing of the light: "The Lord is my light and my salvation" (27:1) and "In your light we see light" (36:9). The prophets, too: "The Lord will be your everlasting light" (Isaiah 60:19) and "The sun of righteousness shall rise" (Malachi 4:2). Light is the irresistible icon of Christ, who called himself the light of the world (John 9:5). The Gospel of John (1:4-5) proclaims: "In him was life, and the life was the light of all people. The light shines in the darkness, and the darkness did not overcome it." Since the fourth century, Christians have confessed of Christ, in the words of the Nicene Creed, "God from God, Light from Light." Since the days of the early church, Easter vigil rituals have included a paschal candle carried into a dark church to a threefold acclamation, "Light of Christ." In light of the resurrection, every requiem mass invokes: "Let perpetual light shine upon them." The early Christians were called children of the light. In Christian art, light surrounds the heads of a saint as halo. Throughout Christianity, light became a root metaphor for Christ and, thus, for Christmas. Christmas music, too, is full of light. Luther's hymn for Christmas day sings:

Your coming in the darkest night
Makes us children of the light

Enabling us in realms divine
Like all your angels bright to shine! Hallelujah!

Consider all the carols that sing the light:

Yet in thy dark streets shineth, the everlasting light . . .
The highest, most holy, Light of light eternal . . .
And to the earth it gave great light And so it continued both day and night . . .
Light of life to all he brings, Ris'n with healing in his wings . . .
Silent night, holy night! Son of God, love's pure light . . .
Behold throughout the heavens There shone a holy light . . .

The festival of Epiphany, twelve days after Christmas, celebrates the showing forth of Christ's light to the world. The wise men are the Epiphany heroes who follow the light of a special star: "Westward leading, still proceeding, Guide us to thy perfect light."

In the Middle Ages, Thomas Aquinas wrote a hymn to the light:

Lord of lights, all gloom dispelling
Thou didst come to make thy dwelling
Here within our world of sight,
Lord, in pity and in power
Thou didst in our darkest hour
Rend the clouds and show thy light.

Monastic communities greet every morning with the fourth-century words of Saint Ambrose:

O splendor of the Father's light That makes our daylight lucid, bright;
O Light of light and sun of day, Now shine on us your brightest ray.

Candles, in particular, carry the light in Christian worship, but soon migrated to every home, suggesting romance and mystery. Their original religious function was to provide light in the catacombs. But they were much more important symbolically, standing in for life, immortality, and divine presence. Then they honored the martyrs and images of saints, which they somehow made present, sharing with the congregation divine life and light.

At first they were tallow, then wax when it became affordable. As a product of virgin bees, wax became an emblem of Mary's purity. Or, wax represented Christ's body, the wick his soul, and the flame his divine nature. Votive candles, as one sees in massive flickering display in Catholic churches, are meant to prolong prayer, to keep the sentiments just expressed by the believer going to God. The constant sacred use of candles requires ritual preparation, for those who attend to such things. So on February 2, the festival of the Purification of Mary and the Presentation of Jesus in the temple, also called Candlemas, candles for the whole year are dedicated through prayers, sprinkling of holy water, and incensing. They are made holy for liturgical use and for the health of human body and soul. Candles are regularly carried in procession, and they are used at momentous occasions like birth and death. In ages of hospitality and pilgrimage, candles were placed in windows to guide the Christ Child or weary travelers to shelter. Scandinavians believed that candle light itself bestows blessing, so they spread out food and clothing and silver and pewter that candlelight might shine in benediction on them. Today Christmas Eve worship seems to require a candlelight ceremony, including among Protestants whose worship life is not normally filled with sacramentals. An "eternal light," usually a candle in a red vase of some kind, symbolizes the constant presence of God in a church.

Candles inevitably made their way onto Christmas trees, especially in Europe, but there were problems. Magical illuminations that began with a candle or two soon became as many candles as the tree could hold, as many as four hundred on a twelve-foot tree. Lurid annual newspaper stories reported on rooms and entire houses burning down and many family deaths. Enthusiasts who were not to be daunted learned to stand ready with buckets of water or blankets to smother, as someone lit the candles, and they burned just long enough to cause the desired sensation. Inventors, of course, were determined to devise the perfect holder that would keep the candle upright and not weigh down the branches of the tree. The breakthrough in 1879 was the spring-clip holder. Still, insurance companies began to call candle-lit trees a "knowing risk" and refused to compensate for the many fires.

Ultimately, electricity solved the problem, and candles on trees went out of fashion by the 1920s. (In some twenty-first-century European churches, one finds banks of electric lights, switched on when one inserts a coin, to save altar and art from the depredations of candle smoke.) In 1880, electric lights first began to replace lighted candles on the Christmas tree. General Electric began mass-producing them in 1901. In the last hundred years, they have evolved from large energy-intensive bulbs, to the bubble lights of the 1950s, to tiny inexpensive lights now produced exclusively in China, to programmable strings that can make the light go forward or backward, on and off, and vary the colors. Most recently, LED bulbs with endless possibility and minimal power demands are making their way through the market.

When Christmas tree lights went outside, a battle of the bulbs ensued, each house on the block, each neighborhood, each town, competing with the next to see who could produce the most clever or extravagant display. Now electricity lights up every urban mall, every landscape, every city center—calling shoppers and admirers to the glory of December nights illuminated with human ingenuity. So pervasive is the material culture of Christmas that all lights on a string, no matter what time of year and on what occasion, are likely to be called Christmas lights.

In an eastern German village several years ago, I witnessed children and their parents celebrating the festival of Saint Martin of Tours, on November 10. This is one of the many smaller festivals that have sprung up in the suburbs of Christmas. After a party at church, where the pastor appeared dressed as Saint Martin, families were moving through the streets carrying colored lanterns on their way home. I saw a grandma holding tight a little child's hand and singing a favorite German ditty, "*Laterne, laterne, Sonne, Mond, und Stern*" (Lantern, lantern, son, moon, and stars). In a creaky voice the old woman sang to the light. From this little light to the great lights of the heavens, from this village to an enchanted world, from her granddaughter's life to her own as a little girl long ago, grandma sang of connections to each other and to the past and to God and the universe. She had been born during the Third Reich, she had lived through the purgations of East German communism, and she had survived to hold tightly the hand of the future and sing gently of the light.

Christmas Trees

The Christmas tree has become a national symbol. The first White House tree was set up in 1856 by President Franklin Pierce, to remind him of his native New Hampshire. In 1891, Benjamin Harrison's White House festivities included an "old-fashioned tree" for his grandchildren. Grover Cleveland ordered electric lights for the 1895 tree. Calvin Coolidge gave the country its first "National Christmas Tree," in 1923. Eventually, the 3,500-year-old General Grant sequoia in California was declared America's living Christmas tree. As a public display, the Christmas tree became a civic offering to the entire community, rich as well as poor, from small-town squares to the nation's capital.

Americans become aware each early December of an important rivalry between New York and Washington, D.C. Will the President's National Christmas Tree or the Rockefeller Center tree be lit first? When state secrets are leaked, New York is able to beat Washington by one day. There's more: inside the Beltway, the White House tree competes with Congress's tree for stature and first illumination. Once a new tree, from a different state, was cut and erected in Washington each year; now there is a permanent live tree on site. The Capitol tree, established by Congress in the 1960s, comes from a different national forest each year. The congressional tree must be placed by landscapers precisely halfway between the House and the Senate sides. There is an ongoing contest to determine whether these trees would be designated Christmas trees or holiday trees. In recent years and under a politically incorrect administration, Christmas won.

Evergreens are a miracle, trees that do not wither or die even during the dark days of winter, the presence of the eternal in a deciduous world. Their religious and cultural significance long predates Christianity, especially as a fertility symbol. Evergreens have always shared December with other greens—mistletoe, holly, and ivy. Mistletoe was prized by the Druids in Roman days, and priests would collect it from great oak trees, where it grew as a parasite, with a ceremonial golden sickle. When Saint Boniface brought Christianity to the Germans, he cut down a mighty pagan oak and planted a fir in its place.

The Christian Middle Ages called December 24 Adam and Eve day, and legend had them leaving Eden with a slip from the Tree of Life. In medieval iconography the scion of the Tree of Paradise is growing from Adam's grave. Christ, who is crucified on the tree of the cross, is depicted plucking the fruit of redemption from it. The connection between the tree of celebration and the tree of Christ's cross was made visible. On the stage of medieval mystery plays there was often a paradise tree, decorated with the apples that tempted Adam and Eve. From northern Europe come countless evocations of the magical power of the evergreen. It was said that when Christ was born, all the trees bore miraculous fruit, but the fir had little to offer, so God came down and lit its branches. Spruces, pines, cedars, and firs enliven the short daylight of winter with many shades of green. In December, Germans, at least, believe that all the trees of the wood sing for joy. Those paying attention can hear it.

One Christmas Eve, it is said, Martin Luther was out walking in the forest. Overcome with the beauty of creation, he brought a tree home and set it up indoors to lend his household the fresh smells of the forest and the cheer of green. He decked it with candles to represent the stars of heaven. By the beginning of the seventeenth century many German homes were setting up fir trees and, eventually, decorating them with roses cut out of many-colored paper, apples, wafers, gold-foil, and sweets. It may be that among some German Protestants the Christmas tree became an alternative to the Catholic crèche. Soon, Germans would be singing to their trees, and they have taught the world to do the same:

> O Christmas tree, O Christmas tree, With faithful leaves unchanging
> Not only green in summer's heat But in the winter's snow and sleet

> O Christmas tree, O Christmas tree, With faithful leaves unchanging.
>
> O Christmas tree, O Christmas tree, Of all the trees most lovely
> Each year you bring renewed delight Agleaming in the Christmas night
> O Christmas tree, O Christmas tree, Of all the trees most lovely.
>
> O Christmas tree, O Christmas tree, Your leaves will surely teach me
> That hope and love and faithfulness Are precious things I can possess
> O Christmas tree, O Christmas tree, Your leaves will surely teach me.

German customs spread to England when Prince Albert and Queen Victoria in 1840 set up their first Christmas tree at their Balmoral country home. This ignited popular enthusiasm throughout the English-speaking world. The British nation followed in creating the Victorian Christmas. The American epitome was a Christmas tree tied to a horse-drawn sleigh going through the snow from woods to home. The German Christmas came to America, via immigrants and through travelers who had visited Germany. The Christmas tree is a good example of American middle-class interest in the rituals of Christmas in Germany, which was thought to celebrate a purer Christmas and one less encumbered by commerce.

When Americans of the nineteenth century went in search of a Christmas culture that would not teach children to be selfish or ruin their character, they looked to Germany. The tree was at the center of a German culture that was thought to include seasonal surprise, folk authenticity, and apparently unselfish children under parental control. The word spread through literary channels, as much as through direct contact with German-Americans. One of many is Harriet Martineau's 1835 story about "Little Charley's Christmas Tree" that arises from her visit to the Charles Follen household, he a Harvard professor and German immigrant. Pennsylvania Germans began setting up trees in the early nineteenth century. In 1846, an enterprising pastor, William Muhlenberg, set up a tree in his Sunday school, and Christmas trees gradually became an incentive to attract neighborhood children to enroll. When in 1851 Pastor Henry Schwan put up a Christmas tree in the church itself, he nearly lost his pulpit over it, even though Christmas trees were already becoming common in homes.

From the mid-nineteenth century, New York entrepreneurs were advertising Christmas trees for sale. Not everyone rushed to buy, however, so some selling became necessary. A story in the 1887 edition of *Saint Nicholas Magazine* depicted a Puritan household from Plymouth, Massachusetts, in 1635. A crippled little boy lies ill in a desolate house, while his widowed mother tells him stories of a "great green bough that was lighted with tapers and hung with gifts for the good children" in olden days, "before mamma was a Puritan." Eventually, as the child is close to death, mother brings an evergreen bough to his bedside. By the end of the story, the boy is on the mend, even the lost father has reappeared, and the stern village elders have been won over. In a Harper's Young People magazine of 1894, a Puritan mother, under the benign influence of forbidden holly and mistletoe wreaths, finds herself making her little daughter a doll for Christmas.

Women supervised the tree's transformation from pagan fertility talisman to domestic moral decoration. Homemade confections and decorations and candles were already common, and glass ornaments were added in 1860. Today one sees the Christmas tree turned into a new fashion statement each year. But long before interior designers took over, the tree was being dressed in the vernacular. Just as in Naples, and then in many other places, people were populating manger scenes with contemporary villagers, craftspeople, merchants, and children, so, too, did the Christmas tree begin to acquire the accoutrements of local culture. The tree had become a member of the family, the Germans seemed to think it had a soul of sorts, and so people wanted it to look like themselves, to share in their indigenous cultures. Already in the seventeenth century, Scandinavians were draping their trees with fishnets.

By the mid-nineteenth century, illustrated magazines were telling Americans how to decorate their trees with "tiny tapers, strings of beads, tiny flags of gay ribbons, stars and shields of gilt paper, lace bags filled with colored candies, knots of bright ribbons" all made by hand, and, of course, with nuts, popcorn, seeds, and cookies as well. Eventually the tree attracted small gifts tied to its branches, and when these began to overwhelm the tree they were piled up beneath it. The tree became a display center for the material culture of Christmas.

Beside displaying the latest fashions or dressing in the local culture, trees had another symbolic role to play. Most nineteenth-century ads and stories depict the purveyors of trees on urban streets as destitute children or country innocents. In the face of the silk-hatted wealthy, the trees and those who bring them to the city stand for something sweet, unaccustomed, fresh, and natural. Greenery is alien to the city, a reminder of olden times and values of the past. That they should suddenly appear in the city every December was magical in itself, a retrieval of an agricultural golden age. City-dwellers did not live by agricultural seasons, so they depended on input from rural life to remind them of the rhythms of nature. Like Santa, the tree may have become popular through the avenue of commercial culture, but it was in the name of a pre-commercial folk culture.

Inevitably, the organic symbolism of an evergreen brought in from the forest gave way to refashioning as a central icon of Christmas culture. Losing its roots in nature, the tree of ungilded eloquence morphed into a new role as displayer of mass-produced ornaments, presents, and wealth. That too is a symbolic role. By 1991, fake trees began to outsell real ones, and the balance had already begun to tip in the 1950s. Artificial trees less and less make allusion to real ones, as they become pink or purple, are made of shredded aluminum or spun glass fibers, are flocked or dipped in many colors, and are so overcome by fashion statements that they are unrecognizable as a tree. Americans give as their reasons for choosing fake trees that they are fire-retardant and safe, a one-time expense, reflective of an ecological consciousness, and not messy. And, they achieve a perfection unknown to real trees.

Trees, at Christmas and other times, are always powerful symbols. They are icons of human longings and projection. When he was a young boy, Truman Capote and his eccentric aunt went to find the perfect tree. Dragging it home in an old baby buggy, they were offered fifty cents for it by a wealthy lady leaning out of her car. There's only one like this, they said, and declined her offer. The Grinch plunders the Christmas tree as the ultimate symbol of the season, without which Christmas is simply impossible, but in a triumph of childhood faith, the tree finally comes back to Whoville on the contrite Grinch's sleigh.

In his poem "The Cultivation of Christmas Trees," T. S. Eliot makes children the only caretakers who can be trusted with Christmas and the Christmas tree. While adults ruin Christmas with their unfitting attitudes, children actually believe that "the gilded angel/ spreading its wings at the summit of the tree/ Is not only a decoration, but an angel." Eliot sent this poem to friends and family as a Christmas card. It is the child who is able to see with clarity, brilliance, and absence of ego that the world pulses with divine presence. The Christmas tree is heavy with symbolic weight.

Dickens's *A Christmas Carol*

So pervasive even today is Charles Dickens's *A Christmas Carol* that it is easy to claim that it once saved Christmas. Some say that in 1843, when his famous work appeared, Dickens single-handedly revived Christmas in England and gave it no small boost in North America as well. It is easily the most prominent and repeated "secular" Christmas tale on both continents, actually achieving its greatest popularity in the second half of the twentieth century. So remarkable did Dickens's work seem to many Victorians, including his resurrection of charity as a key dimension of holiday observance, that they considered it too hallowed for the stage. Its sacred components certainly include its overnight status as a defining myth of the season, the rituals it portrays and induces, its capacity for modern hierophany and mystery, and its ability to produce unique bonds of community.

Dickens dramatizes opposing worldviews, contrasting the ethos of Ebenezer Scrooge and that of the Bob Cratchit family. It is a story of Scrooge's transformation, one that gives hope to those who wish for more from Christmas than they see. In a seasonal miracle, Dickens makes Scrooge more like the Cratchits, as he gets the true spirit of Christmas. Dickens offers a Christmas that actually changes things: from privilege by wealth to virtue in poverty, from seasonal numbness to joy and empathy, from being riveted to the industrial grind to home and family, from miserliness to generosity, from selfishness to brotherhood, from love of money to love of people. It has been noted that Christmas seems to draw to itself several of Christianity's seven deadly sins, like avarice, gluttony, lust, and envy. Dickens bequeaths a Christmas that turns us to virtue, as everyone at least hopes.

Customs around the World

Although "syncretism" is sometimes a dirty word in Christian theology, meaning a too-easy acclimation to "pagan customs" that betrays the integrity of the Christian tradition, it can also suggest the remarkable ability of the Incarnation to acculturate itself to every imaginable setting, as in the poet Hopkins's notion that Christ plays in a thousand faces. Folklorists, beside theologians, are perhaps the most enthusiastic chroniclers of Christmas. While it remains a question today, and not only regarding Christmas, whether American popular culture and films and television have led to a worldwide homogenization that produces "network standard" celebrations, many students of holiday remark on how Christmas still combines both global reach and local significance. There are many good books on "Christmas customs around the world." One can pick nearly any time and any place, in the history of the West and now worldwide, and discover how Christmas has drawn to itself or infused an amazing array of local rites and colorful customs, all wonderfully concrete and specific.

Good Family Times

It is common to hear theologians decry the "domestication" of Christmas as a family festival, its de-centering from the life of the church and religious traditions. They mean that the stage of divine action and human celebration has been reduced to the size of the nuclear family, that the radical proclamation of the Christmas gospel loses its capacity to address an economic, political, social world, or that a historic celebration has been trivialized and infantilized. They worry that a family-centered Christmas, which is to say a religious festival individualized in the home, will not successfully withstand the array of market forces intent on commodifying Christmas.

In December 2005, a major controversy broke out among American Christians when it became known that many of the most influential and trend-setting evangelical "megachurches," in the midst of seasonal culture wars over Christmas, were in fact canceling their services on Christmas Day, which happened to fall on a Sunday. Their leaders claimed that this decision was in keeping with their "family-friendly" approach, that their members were encouraged to watch a Christmas video in their own home or follow a streaming video on their computers, that they could read Scripture and sing a song before opening their presents and not have to run off to church. While the pastors of these churches emphasized that this was another example of their innovative approach, scholars noted that megachurches do not attach to holy days on the calendar or symbols and traditions, but to creative marketing.

But there is more to say about the role of the family at Christmas. It is a fact that the original Christmas occurs in a "holy family" setting, even if Matthew and Luke are also envisioning a world stage. The family is an idiom, and perhaps the first idiom, of a wider social world in which Christmas clearly occurs. It may be precisely a new Christian contribution to December festivities to identify them, as was not true of Roman life, with the nuclear family. The Christian Christmas, precisely, focuses on a mother, a father, and a child, and thereby alters the relationship between festival and family, making it more akin to Italian family-centeredness than Roman civic life. The early Franciscans, Italians to be sure, connected the Christ child, humility and innocence, and family life. Some scholars connect the public emergence of Christianity in the fourth century with precisely the development of new norms and practices of family life. Much closer to today, the English Christmas concentrates on rituals that incorporate the immediate family, but in a way that connects the divine family, the royal family, and every family. Only on Christmas afternoon can it be said that nearly every household in the United Kingdom is doing the same thing at the same time, beginning with a feast and culminating in more or less rapt attention to the Queen's Christmas address.

But it is commonly said by social critics that the modern family is in decline. Is Christmas, then, the great exception? Does family ritual create a sacred time that reverses everyday rules and reality? Not merely nostalgic, Christmas seems to evoke or reconstruct an alternative reality of a world in which the family momentarily regains its central presence and in which family values almost flourish. Is Christmas an embodiment of family values, the one conspicuous instance when kinship is celebrated and the family as a whole is deliberately valued?

While it is commonly argued that the family succumbs to the market, it is also possible to suggest that the family somehow manages to transform commercial exchange back into the deep structures of the social meaning of gift exchange. It may be that Christmas constitutes a ritual of reversal, in which one returns to earlier meanings of family, or one of reestablishment, in which new ground is won for the family in a world where it otherwise suffers conspicuous assaults. I spent Christmas 2009 in Germany and was surprised to see that all stores closed very, very early on Christmas Eve and were all locked tight on Christmas Day. Shortly after, a German high court decreed that large cities like Berlin were transgressing Sunday-closing laws and were told that even during Advent stores could only open on two of its Sundays. The reason given was the integrity of family life.

The family at Christmas is a microcosm, its individual meanings mirroring and mimicking larger meanings (as in "all politics is local"). The family at Christmas, at least ideally, stimulates the social imagination to the larger community—unless it precisely reduces the moral imagination and religious generosity to one's own kin. The more people believe that family Christmas celebration imitates a global action repeated by people everywhere, the more Christmas across the world seems to be the family writ large, an entire culture constructed from family celebrations. Or is this wishful thinking?

The Carrying Capacity of Material

Christmas brings an extraordinary panoply of material culture, and this chapter celebrates not high art but the pervasive culture that touches everyday lives. Christmas loves the material world, perhaps much more than capitalism does, whose marketing theologies load down materials with dubious meanings in order, precisely, to transcend material life. Consumerism traffics in symbolic meanings.

Meanwhile, the illustrious parade of food and drink, gifts and toys, bright wrappings and cards, lights and greenery, good family times—passes by the eye and through the memory. Material culture saturates both holy day and holiday with what we have come to call the Christmas spirit. It is a universal memory of the season, a spirit triggered in everyone by expectations and hopes associated with material culture. How much of Christmas is a sensory experience? What would Christmas be without the senses?

It may be that the question to ask of material culture is not whether it is high art or kitsch, but what is its carrying capacity for deeper meanings. Does it evoke and display or subvert and mislead? Religious studies scholars ask of symbols, old ones passing and new ones aborning, whether they are transparent or opaque, whether they imply narrow exclusion or widening inclusion, whether they produce self-transcendence or self-congratulation.

9

Saint Nicholas and the Enchantment of the World

The Divine Patronage of Saints

Ancient Christianity believed that the birth of Jesus re-enchanted the world. In such a paradise saints could emerge, new blossoms of Incarnation. The stories of these saints were like security deposits to assure that God has not left earth and to promise extraordinary human beings as continuing signs of divine presence, as when Gerard Manley Hopkins writes:

> . . . for Christ plays in ten thousand places,
> Lovely in limbs, and lovely in eyes not his
> To the Father through the features of men's faces.

During the fourth century, a story arose about a young Christian named Nicholas, who would become the patron of school boys, sailors, girls looking for husbands—and of all who do good by stealth. When he happened to be the first person through the church door by the name of Nicholas, answering a dream of the church elders, he was appointed bishop while still almost a boy. When he threw little sacks of gold through the window of a house where three young women were in danger of entering lives of sin for lack of a dowry, he sanctified a gift-giving that would attach itself to Christmas. So pure was Nicholas seen to be, retrospectively, that even at his mother's breast he observed the Wednesday and Friday fast days of early Christianity.

When Russia was being Christianized in the ninth century, and Kiev was becoming a Christian city, the cathedral there was named after Saint Nicholas. From then on, miracles proliferated in his name, and he became the most important personal saint in the Russian Orthodox tradition, reaching all the way to the reindeer people of Siberia. Eager for his cachet, Norseman in the eleventh century raided Nicholas's burial site at Myra (in modern Turkey) and took his remains to Italy, where, in 1087, a shrine and tomb were erected in his honor at a Norman basilica. Statues of Nicholas were soon paraded through towns on festival days. The Normans carried Nicholas and his new symbolic accoutrements throughout Europe, where he became the patron saint of towns and guilds. Since the twelfth century, gifts were given in his name on the eve of his feast day, December 6, eventually placed in shoes which perceptive children carefully placed for reward. After a Russian princess was married to Otto II, Germany embraced Nicholas. Hamburg, Trier, and Cologne became centers of his cult. In Holland he became, via Spain, Sinter Klaas, who appeared in late November dressed in bishop's vestments to spend two weeks checking up on children. Finally, he was prized throughout Christendom and became the patron saint of Christmas. Such are the vagrancies of the saints—and Incarnation—in the life of the church.

Special devotions would emerge around new saints, spreading their dispensations among the common people. These chips off the block of Incarnation would lend magic to everyday life. When monks in an eleventh-century French abbey requested permission to try out the new liturgies of Saint Nicholas, their abbot opposed mixing modern inventions with ancient traditions. But as the abbot tried to sleep that night, Nicholas appeared in fearful demeanor and upbraided him for his obstinacy. With many fierce blows Nicholas taught the abbot to sing the new liturgy of Saint Nicholas. The next day the abbot apologized to the community for his hardness of heart and took the lead in chanting Nicholas's new liturgy.

Nicholas kept evolving to fit new settings. As he moved north, his dark beard turned white. He began to look a little like the pagan god Odin or Wotan, who played at winter solstice. When the disciplining of children became attached to Christmas festivities, this was too undignified a task for the gentle Nicholas, so he acquired darker companions like Hansruhpart, Rumpaus, Krampas, or Knecht Ruppert. While Columbus christened his landing place in the West Indies Saint Nicholas Harbor, having come ashore on the saint's feast day, December 6, 1492, it was the Dutch who staked Nicholas's claim to the new world. In 1626, the ship *Goede Vrowe* (good housewife), with Nicholas on its prow, landed at Nieuw Amsterdam, to become a Dutch village at the southern tip of Manhattan. When the British took control of New York after 1664, they allowed the Dutch to continue their customs, even though the Puritan style of the time was to outlaw Christmas. The New York Historical Society was the first to celebrate Saint Nicholas Day in America, December 6, 1810. In the early nineteenth century, New Yorkers of English extraction were looking for a patron saint to counteract the British Saint George. The traditions of their Dutch antecedents inspired them to re-create Saint Nicholas as Santa Claus, who soon became a cultural fixture in New York, assisted by the stories of Washington Irving and, above all, by Clement Moore's poem. Among German immigrants in Pennsylvania, *Christkindl*, the Christ Child of Protestant devotion, migrated into Kris Kringle, who paralleled and then was united with the Santa Claus figure. Today, only the hanging of stockings is a remnant of Nicholas traditions, though in most homes that custom no longer occurs on the eve of his feast day, December 6.

The Transformation of Patronage

> The stockings were hung by the chimney with care,
> In hopes that Saint Nicholas soon would be there . . .
>
> — Clement Moore, "A Visit from Saint Nicholas"

Clement Moore's "A Visit from Saint Nicholas" has become the sacred text for the American Christmas, with the power to make every home a place of magic and everyone who hears the poem an eyewitness to a primal scene. Probably more people can recite "Twas the night before Christmas when all through the house" than know "Now it came to pass in those days that there went out a decree from Ceasar Augustus that all the world should be taxed." But now historians of the American Christmas claim that Clement Moore wrote these hallowed words in order to commercialize Christmas for the merchants and make its festival comfortable for the middle class. Is nothing sacred?

This is how they say it came to pass. The setting is Moore's ten-square-block estate in Chelsea, lower Manhattan. There, high-church Episcopalian, seminary professor, and patrician, he lived the ideal of a politically conservative family man. He fenced his homelife with a Knickerbocker antiquarianism that Washington Irving had invented from early Dutch and English traditions. But outside his estate lay a very different world. Rapid population growth and a careless industrial revolution were unloading in the middle of the city poverty, vagrancy, homelessness, and public violence. The noblesse oblige that drove Old World nobility to share a little wealth during the holiday season was a scarcer commodity in the new world, where seasonal unemployment and rowdy street demonstrations that looked like genuine social protest were beginning to frighten the middle and upper classes. The Protestant suppression of street festivals and public gayety had disconnected such proletarian frivolities from an organic Christian society and made them more secular, dangerous, and threatening.

Upon this urban landscape fell Moore's re-enchanting poem. (Today it is heard in Cajun, firehouse, redneck, and many other dialects.) Moore was reimagining Christmas traditions within the trappings of a new consumer culture. He brought Christmas indoors, wresting it from a menacing urban proletariat, and refocused it on women, the home, and children. In a wonderfully guilt-relieving way for those whose cultural memories still recalled the obligations of the old world, one's own children stood in for the poor as objects of benevolence. By the twentieth century, children would come to be the very saviors of Christmas, like the wise little girl in the film *Miracle on 34th Street,* the crippled boy in the opera *Amahl and the Night Visitors*, and the exuberant youngsters in *How the Grinch Stole Christmas.*

Against the dangerous currents of the early nineteenth century, Moore helped invent an American Santa Claus who was not so much continuous with earlier traditions as a useful pseudo-Dutch confection for new times and purposes. Santa was an Old New York response to new immigrants. The new Santa would win out over the bringer of ales and whiskeys and the patron of merrymaking on the streets. Santa's visit coincided with larger domestic changes and reforms. When gift exchange was brought inside, no longer a matter of community food-and-drink hospitality, it became a commercial, store-bought, mass-produced enterprise. From about 1820 on, patricians, fearful for their authority, threw their weight behind these domestic reforms of Christmas. They were reinforced by merchants who needed streets clear of drunks and rowdies, by shoppers who required secure public spaces, and by newspapers interested in advertising. Early consumer capitalism and civic virtue were brought together. Moore's poem was just the beginning of the process through which Americans were creating and constructing the Christmas they needed. *As participant in change, indicator of change, and instrument of change, Christmas had become serious cultural business.*

Like Christmas itself, the American Santa continued to evolve, becoming central to gift-giving and to the magic of Christmas Eve and morning. He progressed from Clement Moore's whimsy to the chief mediator of spiritual and material worlds. Towards the end of the nineteenth century, every December *Harper's Weekly* had Thomas Nast illustrating Santa's iconic course. In 1881, Nast produced his first official portrait: a round-cheeked, white-haired and bearded old fellow in furry red coat, with pipe. But the national anthem of Christmas, "Santa Claus is comin' to town," was not written until 1934. From a tall, austere Bishop Nicholas, Santa nicely softened to a fatter and mellower jovial visage good to all. His punishing duties to bad children and his mischievous trickster associations fell away.

But if Santa was a kind of opium for the masses of children (as Marx thought of religion), he soon escaped parental control and took on a life of his own. The "Yes, Virginia" editorial that newspapers utterly dependent on holiday advertising trot out each year is, in part, an attempt at image control, if also a paean to magic and wonder. In each year's wide reprint of this famous essay the public is reminded who Santa is supposed to be—a kind of secular saint loaded with religious feeling. Consider the similarities between Christ and Santa. Each works miracles, each responds to the prayers of children, each has uncanny knowledge about what humans need. As Christ had apostles, Santa has elves; as manger animals accompany baby Jesus, reindeer surround Santa; each accepts the token offerings of humans; as Christ came to have carols, Santa stars in songs of his own; each emanates from a heavenly place of whiteness and purity.

Then, in the middle of the twentieth century, Santa was employed to sell Coke. His red and white colors nicely matching those of Coca-Cola, he became an ideal corporate logo for marketing a cold beverage in the middle of winter. In images newly conceived every year between 1931 and 1964 by Haddon Sundblom, Santa became the colonizer of Christmas for Coke. The Coca-Cola archives, like a Vatican museum, preserves all the Haddon Sundblom paintings. In the Darwinian competition of images, advertising evolved the fastest.

So pervasive is Santa's patronage, so calculated are the uses of his image, that second thoughts were inevitable. Was his American transformation such a good idea? Some say Santa corrupts parents and children, that his existence requires parents to lie, and that he encourages children to think only about presents. Theologians wince that the good news to all the people proclaimed at Bethlehem has morphed into a prize for getting your behavior checked twice. Churches are concerned that children will mix up Santa and Jesus and be disillusioned of both.

In 1951, Father Christmas was burnt in effigy by Sunday school children in the precincts of Dijon Cathedral, which caused an uproar throughout France, with Catholics weighing in on behalf of the deed and secularists denouncing it. This occasioned a famous analysis of the meaning of Father Christmas by the preeminent anthropologist Claude Levi-Strauss: Not exactly a hoax, Santa represents a deeper conflict between life and death. Each year parents beseech their children to believe in Father Christmas so that the parents can keep believing in their own lives.

More persuasive is the critique of Santa as the icon of consumer capitalism and its aggregation of all holiday meanings. In this view, Santa comes to disguise the fact that store-bought presents are mass-produced commerce. He softens the gift exchange that happens in all cultures and protects it from coming off as pure capitalist excess. In the arms of Santa, abundant gifts seem to partake of an ancient custom. Mystifying mass production and personalizing distribution, Santa is a perfect noncommercial commercial marketer. He solves the problem of the modern Christmas: he persuades everyone to buy commodities, but he allows them to forget this is a commercial exchange. With Santa as its patron saint, a flourishing consumer capitalism fast becomes the civil religion of America. If Santa is the symbol parents use to shape their children's attitude toward the world, merchants use him to make sales transactions quasi-religious. In the powerful myth of Santa, Americans embrace both wealth and the search for spiritual meaning—or wealth *as* the search for meaning. If the Nicholas tradition was replete with miracles, the American Santa's is the greatest miracle of all. In a very impressive performance he romanticizes American capitalism. As its official icon, he reigns over a vast empire, a true captain of industry, everyone whispering his name in awe. Somehow, each year he sheds all his wealth in a massive distribution system. Adults relentlessly hope that he images the idealistic world they want to create for small children, but the critics are quite certain that something far different is going on.

The Uses of Enchantment

> How I long to pull away
> to a world where a parade of dwarfs
> marches across the snow.
>
> —C. S. Lewis

This is what it was like in my childhood in Dubuque, and perhaps still is today for the few. After we children starred in the Christmas Eve Sunday school pageant, father drove us through the town, all loaded down with excitement, to look at the Christmas lights on the streets where rich people lived. My father was convinced the wealthy owed us this enchantment, as our family could only afford in-house magic. After the tour of the lights, we drove down to McGrew's Oil to see a real live manger scene, which never failed to astonish us—oxen breathing on God and all that. As soon as the family got home, we pestered mother to let each of us open one present. Eventually, each year, she relented, in a kind of encore to the service at church. Then, off to bed. All four of us are tucked in, say our prayers trying not to think of presents, allow the lights to be turned off, and mother and father leave to commence unknown business. I myself would get up once or twice, patter to the bedroom windows, run my fingers over Jack Frost's etchings (our bedrooms were very cold), and peer out for signs of Santa Claus.

Ultimately, every child returns to bed, pulls the covers over, and giggles with delight. Surely this is the most wonderful night of the year, but how can one ever fall asleep with a stomach full of unbearable giddiness? Somehow I slept while Santa came. On Christmas morning, my father woke each of us, and we all padded down the stairs in our flannel pajamas. We were made to wait on the bottom steps, with the door to the dining room firmly closed. My father would take forever to start a record of the Mormon Tabernacle Choir singing carols, turn the tree lights on, take one last look at the array, open the door, join my mother in saying "Merry Christmas," and invite us into the wonderland our living room had overnight become. I cannot forget those days, and I can summon my bodily delight better than my palate can remember last month's tastes at the finest restaurant.

Is there something more, then, to Santa? Doesn't he stand for parents' fondest wish for their children, and somewhat credulously for themselves—a return to wonder. C. S. Lewis, who could not forget the enchantment of childhood, wrote to awaken the imagination of a lost world. To discover it, Lewis first prepares his readers for new ways of seeing and makes them receptive to unexpected meanings. Though he had become a devout convert to Christianity, he knew that he would have to "steal past the watchful dragons" of Christian literalism. Ultimately, he intended to awaken longings which the reader can not readily identify or satisfy.

The millions who know Tolkien's landscape by heart are also searching. As are the countless children and parents who stand in line for Harry Potter episodes. Wiccans dance in midnight woods, and goddesses puncture hard masculine calculations. In the nineteenth century, the poets of Romanticism turned to nature to find the transcendence missing from their lives. Taking no solace from the coming triumphs of science, William Blake worried about a nature "sheathed in dismal steel" and wanted to be wakened from "Newton's sleep." In "Tintern Abbey" Wordsworth evoked the aching sense of longing for something beyond, and looked to a re-enchanted nature for melancholy, wonder, and yearning. "In Lamia," Keats lamented the scientific explanation of rainbow:

> Do not all charms fly
> At the mere touch of cold philosophy?
> There was an awful rainbow once in heaven:
> We know her woof, her texture; she is given
> In the dull catalogue of common things.
> Philosophy will clip an Angel's wings.

Myths and fairy tales are much older than these current yearnings. Ways of seeing the unseen beyond, myths save us from the overstimulation of facts on the ground. They set the human journeys on a larger stage. Like Christmas or Santa Claus, myths do not argue, they simply present. Students of myth find in them the sustenance necessary for genuine human existence.

Myth was on the mind of the editor of the *New York Sun* when he wrote his "Yes, Virginia" editorial in 1897 to caution that our minds are small and the world is large. Santa "exists as certainly as love and generosity and devotion exist. . . . How dreary would be the world if there were no Santa Claus. . . . There would be no childlike faith then, no poetry, no romance to make tolerable this existence." True wonders are unseen, and Santa "will continue to make glad the heart of childhood."

For Christianity, Bethlehem was the beginning of enchantment, but once would not be enough. The church held on to saints to demonstrate that God continues to work miracle and magic. However commercial Nicholas's present metamorphosis into Santa, the point is the thirst for enchantment. People look to Christmas, or to Santa, to freshen the wells of fascination and delight.

Can Santa save us? Saint Nicholas is an example of the so-called "invention of traditions." This is the way societies use culture to "mythologize the present" or to re-enchant the world. Invented traditions more recent than Santa Claus are the Olympics, Kwanza, and the twentieth-century British monarchy. For reasons of sport or ethnicity or nationalism or economics, societies do the work of culture when they invest new meanings in public life. Societies invent or rediscover ways to a usable past, in order to hallow an uncertain present or legitimize social change, or gird new aspirations. The invention of traditions is not simply about creating something new and pretending it is old; it is also about retrieving something old, at least as it was imagined to be, and still valuable.

Was the American Santa a Faustian bargain, a modern trade for lost magic whose price was too high, a prime example of the law of unintended results? Has childhood under Santa become more magical? What is it that parents catch from their children? Some say that the modern Santa arose when Protestantism abandoned Catholic mystery and accidentally achieved the disenchantment of the world. In this view, the magical world of medieval Catholicism, in which holy day and holiday, earth and sky, paganism and Christianity were all organically one, is lost, perhaps forever. Could Clement Moore have guessed what forces would take control of his Santa symbol? Had Moore himself pulled Santa, roots all dangling, from the rich loam of European Christianity and thrust him into the sterile soil of a market culture? Has the jovial figure Moore invented for his children's eyes been commandeered to do a wicked witch's bidding?

The evolution of Saint Nicholas shows how a suggestive symbol can acquire a life of its own, especially when its home community loses control of it. *When spiritual symbols come loose from religion and are no longer uniquely identified with or even used by the church, they become attractive and available to popular culture for fashion or for retailing.* Sometimes the change produces a complete inversion of the original meaning. In the music video "Like a Prayer," an icon of popular music who calls herself Madonna "turns on" a religious statue, rather than vice versa. Religion is aroused by commerce.

The social sciences have charted the move from rationalism to voracious capitalism, diagnosed the Protestant disenchantment of the world, watched the natural world get stripped of its magical properties and its capacity for meaning. But they also saw that humans are suspended in webs of significance they themselves have spun. Culture could be sublime, and anthropologists could be merchants of astonishment. "Thick description" of human life could carry the observer beyond too-easy rational explanation. In fact, society is a grand theater in which people tell stories to interpret themselves to themselves and play out their meanings in public symbols.

But while social science is read by the few, literature and film are available to multitudes. They evidence myth as a remnant from another world, where reason has not completed the eradication of mystery. When cultures are fully awake, divinities make their appearance. George Eliot wrote in *Middlemarch*: "If we had a keen vision and feeling of all ordinary human life, it would be like hearing the grass grow and the squirrel's heart beat, and we should die of that roar which lies on the other side of silence."

So what is now called *magical realism* infiltrated the world of reading and filmmaking. Parents have experienced how storytelling, including stories of Santa, can open their children's eyes wide and make their worlds magical. The equivalent occurs for adult readers when authors become shamans who join the world of daily life and that of the spirits. Magical realism creates space for diversity and disrupts the way things are said to be. Maybe there *are* elves in the woods and Santa on the roof. If magic is real, then reality is magical. Macy's is real, but so is a Santa who escapes Macy's windows. Readers are promised what every parent who tells bedtime stories hopes for: to transgress, blur, or pull together the polarities of myth and fact, enchantment and realism, moving us beyond the present exhaustion of our lives. Christmas means to surround ephemeral life with a fabulous aura, to grace our nature, to resist the assimilation of a besetting world. The repertoire of human possibilities is expanded.

No doubt symbols like Saint Nicholas will continue to migrate across times and cultures. Santa sits astride two worlds. On one hand, there is the apotheosis of Santa as a manikin of commerce, a market shill. On the other hand, in the name of Incarnation or romantic re-enchantment, Santa is an authentic descendant of

Saint Nicholas. The church may even be aroused to tend its symbols with greater care, re-embedding them in a rich ritual life and insuring they do not come unmoored from their organic connections to religious traditions. In "The Oxen," Thomas Hardy, no easy optimist, wrote:

> If someone said, on Christmas Eve,
> Come; see the oxen kneel . . .
> I should go with him in the gloom,
> Hoping it might be so.

The parent or child who falls asleep on Christmas Eve hoping it might be so is not alone but part of a much larger movement in the culture of the West.

10

Seeing Christmas: Visual Incarnations

Then let me see you everywhere I go.
If merely mortal beauty makes me burn,
How much more strongly I shall shine and glow
When to your fiery love at last I turn.

—Michelangelo, Sonnet LXXII

The Evolution of a Visual Culture of Christmas

The German carol "In dulci jubilo" has the refrain "Oh, that we were there," evoking the ecstasy of the eyewitness. What did the original Christmas, or Christ himself, look like? As Jesus was faltering on the way to the cross, a woman later tradition names Veronica came out of the crowd to offer a cloth to wipe his face. She later discovered that Jesus' features were miraculously imprinted on it. Veronica's image of Christ became the most famous in Christendom and was kept as a precious relic at Saint Peter's in Rome. The name Veronica might stand for *vera icon*, true image.

In the Jubilee Year of 1300, as pilgrims flocked to Rome, Dante was among them, saw Veronica's cloth, and wrote about it in the *Paradiso*. But, in fact, very few artists want to work from Veronica's cloth. They offer instead their own visions.

Even mystics who long for disembodied epiphanies admit to being stimulated by visual depiction. In the sixteenth century, Saint Teresa of Avila wrote that during a mass Jesus Christ deigned to appear before her "complete in his very holy human incarnation, indescribably beautiful and majestic as he is depicted in paintings of him resurrected. . . . I never saw this vision with the eyes of my body or any other, only with the eyes of my soul. . . . Sometimes I thought that what I could see was nothing more than a painting; but on many occasions it was obviously Jesus Christ himself, as he clearly wanted to reveal himself to me." As for Teresa visual culture is a way to God, Christmas itself can be experienced as a gallery of images more than an incarnational idea. The history of Christmas runs from Incarnation to inculturation, from the original presence of Christ met in the Bible to the diverse visual forms the Incarnation seems to have authorized in Christian and world culture.

Christmas as a public and visual religious festival begins in the fourth century as the church goes public. No one in the first century of Christianity would have predicted that the acclamation *Kyrios Kaisar* would turn into *Kyrios Xristos* (from "Caesar is lord" to "Christ is Lord") on the lips of the emperor himself. The conversion of Emperor Constantine to Christianity at the beginning of the fourth century, and the subsequent victory of Jesus Christ over the gods of Greece and Rome, had enormous implications for the culture of late antiquity. As Christianity became the official religion of the realm, a whole repertoire of images from pagan mythology were overtaken by the new visual world that Christianity was imagining and creating.

In the second section of this book, an Incarnation born into sacred texts comes to annual performance in the life of the church as its Festival House. To that end, there emerged over the next fifteen centuries an outpouring of creativity that is without parallel in the history of art. More than a patron, Christianity became the originator and authorizer and then the reservoir of the arts, from music and drama to visual symbols. But today these classics of the visual arts live mostly in museums, where some people now go to encounter the splendor of Christmas.

The staging of Christmas inspired a seasonal downpour of architecture, mosaic, painting, sculpture, woodcarving, illuminated manuscript, and stained glass that is utterly remarkable. It would not have been expected that the human response to God would change so quickly from the Jewish proscription of all material representation of the divine to its eventual full embrace by Christianity. It appears that the church's understanding and appropriation of the Incarnation became the inspiration and then the principal justification for an entire Christian visual culture.

Early Christian celebrations of Easter and then Christmas first flowered as architecture when great edifices arose to site the new Christian worldview. Christianity was able to move beyond the secrecy of times of persecution and open its worship and community life to public space. Christian architecture's first requirement was to provide a space sufficient to hold the congregation and to celebrate the peoples' liturgies. The original basilicas, with their nave and chancel and aisles modeled on Roman civic buildings, began as empty sanctuaries that soon enough filled up with material culture. They were stages awaiting liturgical drama, invitations to every art. Incarnational florescence suffused ecclesiastical space. Artistic forms followed churchly function. As images came to illuminate the texts and ritual of worship, the congregation could *see what it was believing*. Christian art parallels the creedal and doctrinal development of the fourth and fifth centuries, as a fast-indigenizing Christianity would confess and depict a religious development beyond its original texts. The Incarnation would acculturate in every artistic form.

But just this incarnational triumphalism, Christian iconography splashed everywhere, produced second thoughts on visual art, just as we saw in chapter 7 that Christmas and all its attendant materiality produced second thoughts on Incarnation itself. Those great reconsiderations of visual images of God became the *iconoclastic controversy*. The first attempt at a Christian aesthetic, grounded in the Incarnation, arose in the face of new attempts to destroy the culture of images—attempts born amidst the rise of image-rejecting Islam and efforts by Byzantine political authorities to control public expression. (The same thing occurred in the "left wing" of the Protestant Reformation, in which—outside Lutheranism—a virulent iconoclasm flourished.) The burning question was, what would be a fitting image of God in visual culture? Could any work of art be "one in being" with Christ himself? Only the eucharistic presence of Christ at the altar seemed to be a proper image, and the iconoclasts insisted the Eucharist precluded all other images.

But the defenders of icons argued that a Christian icon is not an idol, but an image of the Image. This became *the case for Christian art, and for the entire material culture of Christianity*. God was the first and original image-maker of the universe. Initially, images or paradigms for the world existed only in the mind of God, as Plato also thought. The gulf between the original, metaphysical images and concrete, historical images was bridged when the Logos became flesh, when God became man, when divine creativity materialized. In the view of some theologians, God had chosen to let godhood be seen. That initiative took the form of Christ, a visible self-portrait of divinity. Icons depicted an indissoluble union between the timeless nature of God and the corporeal nature of Jesus—and even the human race and a re-enchanted world. A new Christian aesthetic found room for beauty, as well as goodness and truth, and Jesus was seen as the fairest of the sons of men, as a later hymn sings it.

In short course, early Christian visual art was inspired by the Logos incarnate, then challenged by iconoclasm, and ultimately reauthorized by new theologies of Incarnation. Much later, Romanticism would argue that aesthetic experience is the *most* appropriate vehicle for appropriating religion, that a poetic and artistic understanding would supersede the dogmatic, moral, and historical understanding increasingly ravaged by rationalistic skepticism. You can't argue with art. The visual art of Christmas could survive a post-Christian age. (A great surprise at the beginning of the twenty-first century is that thousands of holy icons are being brought out of hiding in Russia, and the nearly lost skill of creating or refurbishing icons is born again.)

With the justification for a Christian visual world established, the Incarnation drove art in every imaginable direction. The greatest deposit of Christian visual art portraying the Incarnation lies today in museums and in the churches and monasteries of Europe. Because of the unique and compelling divine-human exchange involved in the coming of God into human form, what is everywhere called "the Annunciation" of the angel Gabriel to the Virgin Mary is the most depicted event in Western Christian art, all attempting to capture the exquisite moment when Gabriel appears to surprise Mary with God's plan, and Mary, quavering, offers her consent. After that are innumerable Madonna and Child scenes, no doubt related to the vast escalation of the role of Mary beyond the New Testament texts, to the idealization of Mary, and the celebration of female innocence and virginity. Because the magi, or wise men, proved far more captivating (and usable) than the shepherds to the European imagination, the worship of the magi, together with their exotic entourage at the manger scene, was also portrayed in widely dramatic ways. There are also diverse portrayals of the shepherds, the Holy Family, an ever more populated manger scene, and the attendant angels.

As earlier piety had deemed visual art necessary for the illiterate, the late medieval *devotio moderna* sought to forge a personal identification between the contemporary believer and biblical characters. The point was to connect directly with Mary or Joseph or the Baby through intense meditation on their lives and internalization of their experiences, aided by the stimulus of visual art. The "distance" between image and viewer enjoined on modern museum visitors is precisely the opposite of, for example, images of Mary that subvert that distance between a New Testament figure and a pious believer. *Seeing is a religious activity*, and what Germans call *Andachtsbilder* (devotional images) enhanced liturgical worship and personal spirituality.

It is a mistake, however, to reduce religious art, then or now, to utilitarian purpose, a mere didactic aid to the uneducated pious. The visual art of Christmas is iconic, a full mediation of its subject. It does not *point to* the sacred; it *is* sacred. It is a sacred "text" in its own right, worth its own consideration. The visible image is equivalent to, while different from, the verbal image. Religious art aspires to direct communion with God, an especially valuable aid to those suspicious of dogmatism or ecclesiastical authority. Many contemporary Christian worship services would profit from less word and more material, less self-satisfied preaching and more art, music, and ritual movement, more for the eye and somewhat less for the ear.

The visual art of Christmas represents the course of Incarnation into inculturation, as Christ and Christian belief embedded in ever new Christian cultures. Any art is disclosive of its times, and in Christmas art over time can be observed the itinerary of divinity into every human form. Just as biblical texts did not drop down from heaven but emerged in particular contexts, even while also proclaiming truth larger than their settings, the art of Christmas emerges in the forms and colors of its environment. By observing the portrayals of Incarnation, for example, one can follow cultural and theological change, as when Christ takes on an imperial visage during Byzantine times or becomes the baby in need of human care in Franciscan piety.

What does it mean for the modern course of Incarnation when the Christmas art we see now only in museums is so distant from the "audience practices" of earlier public or private devotional settings, large spaces in which great liturgies were performed or small shrines dedicated to a local saint? Sometimes devout or religiously curious collectors have assembled collections long since removed from their origins in order to reconstruct a vision of how things once were or should be. Abstracted from liturgical settings, the art of Christmas takes on new (and perhaps quite different) meanings for the contemporary viewer. As the context in which art is seen changes, so does the resonance of the work. In an exhibit of medieval Christmas art, for example, the intellectual, cultural, and physical contexts in which the art was first experienced have shifted so drastically that we are *seeing something new, and losing something old*. Now the art is no longer touched and kissed, or gazed on amidst ritual sounds and postures and the smell of incense, but viewed unencumbered—by its past and, perhaps, by the viewer's vacant religiosity.

When the context of the signifiers changes completely, what is signified is also altered. In the Middle Ages, the church was the repository for the material expression of a community's collected memory, but now other institutions fill that role, and the art of Christmas may be abstracted from, even disengaged from, lived

Christianity. Fragments of a once religiously embedded art now float free in museums and books and on the art market—and in modern advertising. Napoleon took the treasures from the Basilica of St. Denis, jigsaw pieces of a once all-encompassing religious life, and displayed them as trophies of military victory; modern advertising does something similar. In contemporary museums, Christian art acquires new meanings as objects of aesthetic devotion or of meditations on changing styles or the history of human achievement. The Romantics and a Roman Catholicism in search of lost splendor similarly looked to the Middle Ages to valorize an ideal time by which the present could be judged and renewed. In effect, they were saying to Protestants, Do you really want to give all this up? Self-satisfied Protestants who scorned anything with a Catholic association, often said yes, gladly.

Enthusiastic aesthetes transform art once defined by a devotional code into independent objects of beauty. Museums and collectors become another stage in the evolution of the Christian culture of Christmas. Viewers wonder what a lost age of faith was like. But what rituals is art a part of today? What beliefs and values surround the contemporary viewing of the art of Christmas? Once a processional art moved from church to town to countryside, consecrating everything along the way. The sacred in a public stable had gone indoors to the great edifices of Christianity, but was eventually carried back to the wider spaces of its original enchantment. Is this the modern course of Incarnation, or the end of the road?

Once Christian art transfigured physical setting into sacred space, shaping belief, and guiding the faithful toward a fuller comprehension of the incarnational word. Signs in holy places today admonish possibly indifferent visitors not to imagine these great spaces as "museums for the curious." Then and today, they are pilgrimage destinations; New York's Metropolitan Museum of Art displays annually its crèche collection that counts even for secular visitors as destination art in December. The altar in the pilgrimage church at Creglingen, Germany, by Tilman Riemenschneider, may be the greatest woodcarving in the world. The guidebook invites visitors not simply to marvel over a wonderful sight but to immerse themselves in the piety of the past that produced it.

But the course of Incarnation moves on. Even if, assisted by docents who coach us on *relearning the past and unlearning the present,* we momentarily recover the "audience practices" of the past, is it really possible (or desirable) to approach the great visual art of Christmas as original viewers did? If not, is its essence then missed, or a different one conveyed?

But did the seminal power of the Incarnation on fine art come to an end in the seventeenth or nineteenth century, as the visual arts moved in new directions and art and Christianity mostly lost their intimate connection? Was this due to the exhaustion of incarnational influence, or the church's seemingly careless inability to maintain a vital connection to the visual arts? Of course, powerful economic forces were also driving new patronage of the arts, including rich merchants rather than churches and monasteries, and new patrons and new prevailing worldviews moved to different subject matter. The Protestant Reformation no doubt also played a decisive role, and there was no longer a single unified vision of Christian presence. Indeed, Protestant art moved in quite different directions from the increasingly splashy baroque art of the Catholic Counter-Reformation.

Unless one wants to protect the Incarnation from baser portrayals and implicitly claim that God only inspires highbrow artists, one has to notice the ever accumulating Christmas art of the twentieth century—which is often called kitsch, a word I will try to redeem. But beyond that? After considering the unstoppable production of Christmas kitsch, I close this chapter inquiring whether the Incarnation lingers in the sensitivity that art teaches us to see in new ways, to "see religiously," suggesting new places to look, so changed religious content does not mean the end of incarnational art.

Kitsch as Vernacular Performance

People determined to delight the eye with the visual splendor of Christmas do not await coaching from theologians about what is proper subject matter or from art historians about what is refined. Rather, they *graze* in an image-rich landscape. They go about assembling and maintaining a material culture that portrays an entire social and cultural world, certainly including the individually constructed world of family life. Every devotee of Christmas has heavy investments in material culture. Of course, Christmas goods may display power and social status or bad taste, but they may also secure the continuity of family over time. They remember things past, and mark who we are, what we believe, how we feel. If the Incarnation is present to these self-assemblages, it is not in the direction of avante garde ways of seeing but toward popular religion and culture.

We live in a densely visual culture. What catches peoples' eyes in their everyday lives? What does it mean to them? Where does one look for Christmas? How one sees and what one sees is a matter of culture (and economics), not optics. Do contemporary images of Christmas occur under religious auspices or aesthetic or commercial? Does the market control the production and placement of images? Flashy material culture provides beguiling cover illustrations to get a viewer to look inside the book, but the book may be not a sacred but a commercial text. *The act of looking and what is seen are culturally performative*; together they constitute one of the rituals of Christmas.

Is Christmas kitsch to be celebrated as indispensable to the décor of festival? It is lately fashionable to reimagine the term kitsch, including redefining "taste" as a bought accoutrement of education or social class, cultural capital spent to display and impress oneself. So every social class, perhaps also every brand of Christianity, finds its way to visual expression with its own logic. In every assembly of artifacts, including kitsch, entire social worlds present themselves, chosen identities are created. That these universes of meaning are not constructed independent of economic forces is at least as true for Nieman Marcus as for Walmart shoppers.

Aesthetic guardians of the visual landscape decry kitsch as imitative, an inferior copy of something else, cheap and mass-produced, lacking creativity, style, imagination, and nuance. Guardians of high culture believe that kitsch is anti-art in the same way that much popular culture is anti-intellectual. Christmas bathos is "shallow emotion deeply felt." Theologians say that Christmas deserves better than sentimentalizing the infinite, and that the church has a nearly inexhaustible storehouse of ideas and images waiting new presentations.

But the boundaries are muddied today when "real art" and kitsch combine in surrealism, camp, pop art, and the current market conditions among art buyers in lower Manhattan. Some artists turn "fine art" on its ear, packaging it in irony or disdain. If kitsch challenges the pretensions of cultural shrines, assails the elitism of the wealthy, aspires to decorate hovels, perhaps it offers a morally shrewd and theologically relevant gift to Christmas.

Might kitsch lovers have Incarnation on their side? What if contempt for kitsch hides a refusal to value feelings of sweetness, tenderness, and sentimental longing (Christmas collectibles)? What if kitsch speaks to devout needs in a voice that is not imposing or authoritative but dressed down to the level of everyday life? Are critics who sneer that kitsch reduces God to human scale forgetting the point of the Incarnation? Is highbrow art conceptually difficult, abstract, disinterested, noninstrumental? Is kitsch and pop art useful, interested, reassuring, confirming, purposive, available, illustrative, and functional (think Norman Rockwell)? Whatever is treasured and enjoyed probably fits the user's image of the beautiful or the spiritual. What should the nativity look like?

Many who appreciate the material culture of Christmas are looking for a *religious* (or perhaps sentimental) experience, not an aesthetic one. Much religious behavior, and much of the material culture of Christmas, would have to be ignored if only the criteria of connoisseurs of high art are accepted. Outside the ken of many critics, there is an entire piety of looking and seeing. In it, what is thought to be holy, or perhaps only "special," becomes available to everyday life. As believers have done with saints and icons and relics since the Middle Ages, one handles the holy, one dresses a statue. *Is no gift piled up at the manger to be disparaged?* Is this, in fact, a meaning of Christmas?

Christmas Invites Seeing Religiously

There is an unbridgeable chasm between the present and the age when Christian art grew organically out of a world of Christendom, when political rulers and great patrons and the church shared a common view into which an entire Christian culture was sedimented. That age also brought an audience practice that is no longer recoverable. Even for a time after the Protestant Reformation there still flourished a common Christian heritage for those who wanted to claim it. But then came the Enlightenment, the rise of modern science, a historicism that relativized Christian claims and certainties, and political movements intent on getting free from religious authority. Even though one can enter that world through museums and pilgrimages to great European Christian sites, there is no longer traffic back and forth—except perhaps in the imaginations of the devout or the determined.

Since religious art can still be found, it might be said that it has migrated from *view to viewpoint*, from obvious portrayals of Christ and the characters of the Christmas story to indefinite or suggestive evidences of spiritual seeking or tracings of the divine. This art that could be called religious often offers nothing literal or even representational. There is no easy availability of nor desire for traditional personages and themes that so dominated the Christian artistic vision of the past. Still, some contemporary artists say they are on a spiritual quest, or that they are pioneering alternative ways of seeing. But Christianity and artists have come uncoupled, the church having lost its imagination for patronage and its need for vital connections between theology and the arts, while modern artists display little desire for the tutelage of the church.

Still, some artists and their work evoke the common ground of spiritual vision. Can one see intimations of Incarnation—ambiguous, unpredictable—certainly well beyond ecclesiastical control or even commission? To represent the divine in the human (incarnation) is an aesthetic (not to mention theological) challenge in any age, and certainly today. To paint the infant Christ is to take a view of his nature, and of human nature. The artists of Christendom accepted the aesthetic problem involved when turning religious themes into archetypes of human experiences. That respectable and historic project, when identified and embraced, could open up modern artists and viewers to reconsiderations of creating and "seeing" religious art.

Perhaps Christmas itself is awaiting modern reimaginings, bolder incarnational wagers, recovery from loss of nerve. The lamentable but insufficiently recognized decoupling of Christianity and the arts over the last several centuries involved not only the slipping away of churchly patronage, but also the more serious erosion of deep connections between theology, liturgy, lived Christianity, and the presence of artists and arts. Much of Christianity seems actively disinterested in the arts, and cannot notice that that may have contributed to headlong detours from bold new inculturations toward ever more stultifying and confining literalisms. Could secular artists help train the church to see again?

Early American Protestantism privileged preaching and Bible study as the means to revitalize Christianity in a new world. Hoping to imitate literally the early Christianity of Bible times, it did not look to the arts, which seemed a dubious preoccupation of the upper classes that was far from the heart of simple religion. The medieval populism inherent in some forms of the new Protestantism saw in the visual imagination a major source of the corruption and abuses of the time. The moralization of Christianity intended to strip it of mystery and image and to substitute clear language in its place. English Protestants were a hearing culture, in which the eyes were told what to see.

When Protestants in the new world finally began to produce religious art in the nineteenth century, it was not typically commissioned or encouraged by churches but by individual patrons for private or civic spaces. The dominance in America of one Protestant viewpoint meant that religious art would, on principle and for some considerable time, be mostly absent from the American churches. This would mean a *disappearance of Christian substance from visual culture.* We saw in chapter seven how much of Protestant Christianity deliberately—and with considerable self-congratulation—abandoned visual culture to the world. So "the world" came to dominate the contemporary visual landscape of Christmas. Contemporary Catholicism knew better than to abandon a sanctifying and sanctified material culture but readily allowed and fostered its reduction to kitsch.

In 1964, the Second Vatican Council offered a special mass for artists and called for a revival of the bond between artists and the church. A decade later the American Catholic bishops issued an encyclical on the artistic environment in which Catholic worship should be occurring. In Europe and the United States there were bold attempts to invite leading nonreligious, even nonbelieving artists to offer new contributions to lived Christianity. Aesthetically sophisticated theologians kept reminding the church that great religious art had first to be great art. It was an incarnational wager, for example, to make of a powerful earth mother a compelling Madonna. Art, like religion, will be the child of its time. Easy theological or artistic efforts that aspire simply to repristinate the past produce stillborn children in the present. The cozy sentimentalism of most commercial religious art seems to be an embarrassment both to artists and to theologians.

The question has to be asked whether the Incarnation has run out of steam, whether what a confident early church called the *logos spermatikos* has ceased to impregnate every or any creative impulse. Are religion and art even on speaking terms? Or, do religion and art, like religion and science, perhaps speak different languages, in different spheres? Are they dialects grown apart and no longer understood by each other? Sociologists like Robert Wuthnow have uncovered hundreds of artists who see themselves on a religious quest, even while they keep their distance from institutional Christianity. Some Web sites devoted to contemporary Christian art offer spirituality "without a religious aftertaste."

Of course art does not readily reduce to the categories of religion, and cannot usually be relied on to do its bidding. Artistic images can incite a religious devotion that is not controllable and conformable to the self-image of the church. Art connoisseurs and theologians are equally distressed to visit a cathedral where a monumental work of art is on display, only to discover that all the traffic is flowing to a cheap statue steps away that has a light bulb inside, or bleeds. Ancient optical theory saw a religious image as the object of a quasi-physical ray that streams from the eye of the viewer to the object. The form of the object then moves back along the visual ray to imprint itself on the memory of the viewer. This old theory emphasizes the viewer's initiative and active engagement, not so different from postmodern theories, but in the present it seems to be visual advertising that takes up most of the bandwidth of the viewers' perception.

Could the religiously inclined hope that material culture would be transparent, a window on the transcendent? Could new attempts to "see Christmas," or to see incarnationally, bring everyone together again? To the eye of a theologian, at least, beauty holds eschatological significance, like the transfiguration of Christ that reveals his essence and anticipates the kingdom of God. Theologians wish that artists would transform the world as it is into the world as it should be. They say things like, "Beauty is matter in anticipation." But who is listening? Who is volunteering for such belief-ful seeing? Any modern poet can admire the lines of the Catholic Gerard Manley Hopkins:

> The world is charged with the grandeur of God
> It will flame out, like shining from shook foil.

And even the devout nonbeliever can look at Byzantine art, for example, and settle for awe, for bedazzlement by aesthetic pleasure. The believer thinks that the icon not only shines on divine reality but actually contains it. The believer wants the great art of Christmas to hold the presence of Christ in reserve (like the sacrament), waiting to be activated by the fervor of the faithful who still come to see religiously.

Art (like religion) creates frames of perception through which humans interpret experiences, and order and ornament their lives. Seeing religiously alters the way we see in general. It values, and then transforms, material culture. Both art and religion aspire to the situation in which the eye turns away from a religious or aesthetic experience to see a changed world. Great artists impose on the world by altering the way we see. College students are taught that they should not expect good art to relax them into reality, but to disturb them with wonder and consternation. Van Gogh said that art is troubled man added to nature. To fellow artists, Georgia O'Keeffe says, "Art is not what you see, but what you make others see." John Dewey made of art a pregnant woman with child, not a truck transporting goods. Leonardo's painting is not *about* the Last Supper, it *is* the supper, performed daily for the monks in Milan in whose refectory it was hung.

Art is independent expression, its own meaning. "If I could have said it in words, I would not have had to dance it" is a well-understood line from one called to be a ballerina, not a philosopher.

The images of Christmas are ends in themselves, not just means to a text. Of course art can be decorative, illustrative, or didactic, but it can also be symbolic and iconic, a direct access to the holy. Great architecture, for example, *is* worship, not just a house for worship. Speaking its own language, it catches the congregation up in the dynamic of faith in stone.

Art historians and anthropologists pay attention to many things as they study visual culture: the visual images themselves; the relation between the medium chosen and the apparent message; the identity and motivation of the artist; what explanatory or unspoken cues may be present in the immediate milieu; the social, economic, and cultural context of the art; who sees it and responds; and the way society, politics, and culture cross in front of the image. Seeing religiously, if it happens at all, occurs in this thick context.

Then and now, art frames human perception, including the ability or the propensity to see religiously. Rembrandt's visual Calvinism created a single space of light framed by overwhelming darkness, while baroque Catholicism's triumphalism splashed the true faith across every canvas. Each approach constituted a religious seeing, a training of eye and mind in how to see and where to look. The modern celebration of Christmas is also an exercise in seeing. Studies of visual culture notice what people are looking at and who is providing the images and to what ends. Once historic Christianity schooled its adherents in a spiritual discipline of seeing; today the market is a leading purveyor of what to see and where to look.

Granting the significance of the dilemmas and opportunities just detailed, one should not deny oneself the obvious joy of great Christmas art still created by fine artists and experienced by enthusiastic worshipers. For example, every year compelling Advent-Christmas art is created by artists and destined for liturgical settings as a vital part of the festival of Christmas. How does this happen? Extravagant visual art is commissioned, especially by great Episcopal and Catholic cathedrals but also by many a humble parish, and becomes available for all, evoking an audience practice of a different age. Often, this art does not arise from church members but from the best local artists one can identify, who for various reasons are eager to accept a connection to Christian architecture and liturgy. Such new art requires artistic ambition that sets high standards and attracts talented local artists and also adequate funding to commission them. The glimmerings of Incarnation grace the festival once again.

One can go looking for such art, and why not? Pilgrimage to art is still a way for moderns. This book has made pilgrimage an ideal metaphor for the perfect response to the festival of Christmas. I have seen it as an attitude of the heart and of the mind. But in closing I suggest a literal pilgrimage that many readers could readily take if they find Christmas in Germany a promising site for the performance of Christmas.

In northeast Bavaria, not far west from Nuremberg, lies the beautiful, artistically rich, and ancient cathedral town of Bamberg. I have twice walked the path of Bamberg's *Krippenweg*, which is a fairly well-marked walk through the entire city, beginning at the cathedral, to witness an astonishing array of manger scenes or crèches, some outside in the cold of winter and many inside. They range from tiny miniatures to expansive landscapes, outdoing one another in vernacularizing the Incarnation in Franconia. There is a long tradition for this, and so the manger scenes have steadily multiplied. A craft school for creating such art has also grown up in the area. There are two enchanting museums devoted to this crib art, one next to the cathedral and one in the city's historical museum.

The impression they leave is of overwhelming incarnational extravagance, and not a network standard art but a regional art in which all the figures of daily life proudly show themselves and invite reverent inspection. Of course, this is not a display of classic fine art, whose residue is everywhere in museums and the great churches of Europe, but simple, beguiling folk art. If the pilgrim's task is not completed until return to one's own locale, liberally sharing and sprinkling about the enchantment recently encountered on the way, then the return trip of many pilgrims may evoke, across the land, new celebrations and anticipations of incarnational extravagance beckoning the modern eye to see religiously again.

11

Hearing Christmas: Musical Incarnations

Let men their songs employ.

My heart for very joy now leaps
My voice no longer silence keeps
I too must join the angel-throng
To sing with joy his cradle song.

—Martin Luther

Since I am coming to that holy room,
Where, with thy choir of saints for evermore,
I shall be made thy music; as I come
I tune the instrument here at the door,
And what I must do then, think here before.

—John Donne, "Hymn to God my God, in My Sickness"

Some to church repair
Not for the doctrine, but the music there.

—Alexander Pope

This book locates the festival of Christmas in the pages of the New Testament, in the performance life of the church, and on every imaginable stage to which incarnational exuberance has carried it. Christmas is a much richer festival than contemporary commercial samplings, or even many church services, might suggest, and this is true of its musical incarnations as well. There are already great evocations of music in the texts and circumstances of the New Testament, still available to every reader and hearer who take time to ponder them. These have given rise to the long and dense development of liturgical music in the worship life of Christianity. Early Gregorian chant, without ever losing its core, was also carried forward by an incarnational flourishing to the likes of Bach and beyond to the secular world of "classical music," though Bach himself mostly erases the differences between art song and liturgical music by giving it all to God. While art music, even that of Bach, mostly exists today outside the church—at least in America—the great carol tradition seems equally at home in holy day and holiday, and so carols are loved and treasured, if not always understood, by all.

If the great deposit of Christmas visual art is mostly found today in museums, or in European churches, the best-loved art of Christmas, music, still carries meanings on both sides of the divide between past and present, believers and onlookers. Like the festival of Christmas itself, Christmas music thrives on the far side of the threshold one crosses into sacred ritual, but sounds equally alive when one returns to daily life. And if more difficult choral music can no longer be performed in the churches, no student in a high school or college choir, nor any modern concertgoer, escapes the fact that the overwhelming preponderance of the great choral music of the West is Christian. But even as the Christian culture of Christmas grows more mystifying or problematic or irrelevant (to commerce) in the modern world, Christmas music still seems transparent and approachable—to the believer, the aesthete, and the only mildly interested. Why is this so?

The Power of Music

What is happening when music moves you so, transports us to times long ago, evokes some mystery we cannot pronounce? The ancient world imagined that music arose as heavenly spheres moved in their harmonies. They found a material connection between the music we hear and the nature of the universe. Medieval learning made a required *quadrivium* of the subjects that went together, arithmetic, geometry, astronomy, and music. Moderns have not entirely lost this sense of musical interconnections. In case there are other beings able to tune in, astrophysicists have broadcast a Bach fugue to interstellar space. At least to physicists, sound could be the bridge between spirit and matter, which is now seen as the vibration of particles dancing. The tiniest bones in the body, hammer, anvil, and stirrup, resonate to every sound. Mystics are pleased to imagine that God actually *chanted* the "Let there be" that brought the universe into being. All kinds of music, certainly not only religious music, transcend the sayable and carry us far beyond the analyzable. Of all sensuous experiences, music affects the soul the most. The Roman poet Ovid was sure that Orpheus's music could tame the savage mind.

In Hinduism, Shiva, the Lord of the Dance, accomplishes creation through music, and the cosmic order is his dance. In one of the hands at the end of his multiple arms, he holds a tiny drum that he beats with his finger; with this rhythmic sound he brings the world into being. A second-century apocryphal gospel has Jesus dancing at the Last Supper. The Orthodox tradition subsumes the Word in a total work of art in which liturgical performance integrates all the senses through architecture, icons, candles, light, incense, gesture, chant, harmony, and—of course—utter mystery.

Music stores up in the body and soul the reveries and emotions of childhood, of memories born of pregnant occasions, of beloved traditions repeated like a child's best-loved stories. Lived Christianity embodies the power of hymns sung long in common, both reverent and familiar, and this works as well for the unsophisticated and those who have no other contact with religious poetry. In ways beyond understanding, rhyme and meter satisfy deep instincts, just as folk songs and verse are incantatory. In the memories of many who sing them, tunes and texts are inseparable and also inseparably part of their religious experiences.

Philosophers of music wonder what must be the nature of reality for the phenomenon of music to occur. Wise "primitives" believed that musical instruments were animated, that magical power came from the spirits housed in them. They reverenced the materials from which they were made because they believed in a physical-metaphysical continuum. While all the senses happen in real time, music especially is the aesthetic performance and perfection of time, full of delayed gratifications when unresolved tensions are prolonged into exquisite resolutions. In his "Song for Saint Cecilia's Day," she the patron saint of all who sing, John Dryden makes of music nearly everything:

As from the power of sacred lays
The spheres began to move,
And sung the great Creator's praise
To all the blessed above;
So when the last and dreadful hour
This crumbling pageant shall devour;
The trumpet shall be heard on high,
The dead shall live, the living die,
And music shall untune the sky.

The Evolution of the Musical Culture of Christmas

How did this elemental power evolve into the rich musical culture of Christmas? Following the presentation of this book, it began in the sacred texts of the New Testament, flourished extraordinarily in the festival house of the church, and soon enough played on every possible stage. Everyone knows that angels sang a *Gloria in excelsis* over Bethlehem. The New Testament set Christ's birth to music. Christ *was* music: the early church called him God's song. Borrowing from ancient Israel's musical traditions, early Christianity carried forth at first in the praise songs of Easter. "Who sings, prays twice," the church believed.

The New Testament songs of Christmas have laid down a rich deposit in the worship life of Western Christianity. Mary's praise song is a form of musical outburst rooted in the Old Testament where response to divine surprise calls forth "musical shout." Since the fifth century the *Magnificat* has been the chief song at vespers, sung by every generation of monks and by many other Christians who gather for evening worship. It has inspired innumerable musical settings, culminating in works like that of Monteverdi, whose operatic treatment was meant to impress the listener with the power and majesty of Christ and the church, and Bach, who made it a jewel of liturgical worship.

At the naming ceremony for John the Baptist, his father Zechariah's tongue is untied to sing of John's mission as the forerunner of Jesus in God's plans and purposes. This *Benedictus* ("Blessed be God") has for centuries been sung at morning prayer in monastic communities and by many other Christians. At the presentation of Jesus in the temple and the purification of Mary, the old prophet Simeon, representing expectant Israel, acclaims Jesus to be God's agent of salvation and registers the passing of the old order into the new. This third song in Luke's nativity narrative is called the *Nunc dimittis* ("Let me now depart"), and since the fourth century it has been sung by all monks at Compline or evensong, and eventually at Candelmas, February 2, the Festival of the Purification of Mary. Bach dramatically set it into Cantata 82 for that festival, and by then it was often associated with the Christian's ability to face death calmly because of redemption in Christ. These songs of Christmas entered the liturgy long before carols, and their ever more elaborate artful settings became a permanent musical legacy of the West.

Around 105 C.E., Pliny the Younger, spying on the Christians, reported to Emperor Trajan that they were accustomed to meet early in the morning and sing hymns. The New Testament alludes to Christian hymn-singing (Mark 14:26; 1 Corinthians 14:26; Acts 16:25; Ephesians 5:19; Colossians 3:16), and Christian poetry set to music flourished in the early centuries of Christianity. Hymns as a verse form within the liturgy sung to specific tunes began to proliferate in fourth-century public worship, so that Christmas and Easter began to acquire rich and lasting musical accompaniment.

In the fourth century the church father most associated with the emergence of the Christian hymn, Ambrose of Milan, wrote "Veni, Redemptor gencium," which eventually became an Advent hymn sung in monastic liturgies. Martin Luther translated it into German, adapted its plainchant melody, and gave it to the Protestant tradition as one of its most substantial, musically as well as doctrinally, Advent-Christmas hymns:

> Savior of the nations come, Show the glory of the Son.
> Every people, stand in awe, Praise the perfect Son of God.
>
> Not of human seed or worth, But from God's own mystic breath,
> Fruit in Mary's womb begun When God breathed the Word, his Son.
>
> Wondrous birth, Oh, wondrous child Of the virgin undefiled.
> Mighty God and man in one, Eager now his race to run.
>
> God the Father is his source, Back to God he runs his course;
> Down to death and hell descends, God's high throne he re-ascends.
>
> He leaves heaven to return, Trav'ling where dull hellfires burn;
> Riding out, returning home As the Savior who has come.
>
> God the Father's precious Son Girds himself in flesh to run
> For the trophies of our souls, Longer than this round earth rolls.
>
> Shining stable in the night, Breathing vict'ry with your light;
> Darkness cannot hide your flame, Shining bright as Jesus' name.

Pope Gregory the Great, who reigned from 590 to 604, pioneered churchly establishment in Rome and missionary work far beyond that city by promulgating an orderly liturgy fixed into a Christian year and stimulating the development of music in the church's worship. By the time of the Carolingian renaissance of the eighth and ninth centuries, various musical traditions were fusing into what would become Gregorian chant, a historic art form in itself and one of marvelous fecundity. The eight "modes" or scales of Gregorian Chant became the musical form used in monastic communities, as they chanted their way through all 150 Psalms each week, in the seven daily services of the "Divine Office." The Gregorian impulse did not rest still. The final "a" in a chanted alleluia became a vocalization of human striving for heaven and an artistic impulse to ever greater musical complexity, elongating into ingenious melodies, which then acquired fresh texts as well. Musical improvisation became the germ of drama and the stimulation for Christian poetry. From the musical interlude between Epistle and Gospel readings came new stimulations to hymnody. Chant and then hymns composed in metrical stanzas developed side by side. The mystic Mechtild of Magdeburg would regularly have heard such music and more than the music when she herself sang:

> As the Godhead strikes the note
> Humanity sings.
> The Holy Spirit is the harpist
> And all the strings must sound
> Which are touched in love.

Western Christian music evolved from two foundations. One was the "heightened speech" in which Gregorian chant perfectly molded itself to sacred Latin texts, turning them into "sermons in sound." The other was the free outpouring of song and then instrumental music as the church found its creative way in carrying music far beyond biblical confines and the relatively restrained early Christian practice. *The endless musical ornamentation of earlier forms paralleled the endless ornamentation of the Incarnation in every dimension of lived Christianity and material culture.* By the later Middle Ages, simple chant melodies would elaborate into polyphonic motets. These new musical forms would then acquire elaborate instrumentation during the baroque period (1600–1750). Applauding music as second only to theology in the praise of God and the edification of the Christian community, Luther was fascinated with how music "brings the text to life." He and many others served the wedding of classical rhetoric and musical composition.

The evolution of *music as Christian culture* was not linear, but proceeded on many levels at once, inside the church and outside it. The mass arrival of Germanic peoples proved more than the church could readily swallow, though Christmas culture would accommodate all. These new peoples had no Latin and Greek and no direct experience of the Hellenistic culture that had infused the early church's intellectual life. Gradually, Christian liturgy and theology and the mystical side of Christian spirituality had become the exclusive preserve of the clergy and ecclesiastical hierarchy and later religious orders. Formal worship eventually distanced itself from the people, spatially and linguistically, while musicians developed more as performers than leaders of song. Roles for women diminished, and communal singing in worship nearly died out. But the influx of new peoples into the church's tent mixed Christian doctrine with pagan ideas and practices and also opened up vistas for new musical developments.

Into these ripe fields came a *contagion of vernacular carols*. At first, they were associated with ring dances and secular occasions. They evoked the spontaneity and simplicity of rural life. The carol began as much as a social phenomenon as a musical form, and so it quickly developed beyond narrow definition. From courtly or popular dance-song, it soon became popular religious song in the village and then was embraced as processional song in worship or as a popular substitute to parts of the liturgy. It was not long before it came to sing of Christmas. As such, it is a good example of the hybridization of the liturgy—and of Christmas. During the twelfth to fourteenth centuries, the French carol was a dance-song, and sometimes, as in the court of Henry VIII, an accompaniment of amorous games, as in the song of the holly (male) and the ivy (female). As a festival song, it was perfect for processions, whether down the aisle of a church or carrying the boar's head (the earliest written English carol) to a feast.

Eventually the carol was attached to the imagery of mystery and miracle plays. The Coventry Carol, for example, found its traditional setting in the lament of the mothers of the slain children at Bethlehem in medieval nativity pageants. As they acquired religious themes, carols became ever more popular, in their unpolished reflections and informality becoming a folk music alternative to the formal music of the church. Their content was narrative, contemplative, or celebratory, their spirit simple, and their form a series of verses to a tune. Caroling was stimulated by Franciscan mendicants and the laity under their influence, who brought forth a tradition of *laudi*, simple religious tunes sung to the baby Jesus. These carols were transplanted to England as bittersweet, haunting refrain-songs, written as popular preaching illustrations, intermezzi in religious drama, and for festive group singing. Besides Christian teachings, they sang in affecting and homely ways of the joys and sorrows of everyday life, and evidenced a lighthearted persistence of pagan and folk beliefs. At court or castle and on the village green, they were increasingly associated with the nativity crèche. The intention of the carol is to emphasize the significance of the birth of Jesus for the individual believer, and this it shared with medieval mysticism. They sang the individual's personal relationship to God and celebrated incarnational presence, as manger scenes did, too, in every dimension of daily life.

Nearly 90 percent of surviving carols are religious, with moral or didactic texts, most often Christmas themes. The music of a carol is often described as angular, vigorously rhythmic, with brisk gaiety, freshness, and lilt, often in 6/8 or 3/4 time. Their texts are simple, direct, and unpretentious, often with stock phrases, a perfect accompaniment to popular religious drama. Musicologists think they were written anonymously by men of some education and word-craft but no great intellectual pretensions, for the enjoyment and edification of ordinary people with whom they shared unquestioning assurance in the Catholic faith. Carols were long associated with ritual movement. (More liberal than the present church, clergy of the day were permitted to dance to carols if they didn't lift their feet off the ground.) Carols were about communal joy. But they were also a deliberate effort to see to it that clergy voices were not entirely defiled by theatrical and worldly songs.

They were intended to edify the populace by entertainment and to steal back from the devil many of the good tunes and offer them to God. There grew a large repertory of popular melodies to which carols could be sung. In the twentieth century, Benjamin Britten poured new life into this tradition in his *Ceremony of Carols.* The English church, especially, offers annual harvests of this history in its world-famous and much-recorded Festival of Nine Lessons and Carols late on the afternoon of Christmas Eve day.

The carol is the most emblematic art of Christmas. It is fully religious in its text and fully secular in its origins in medieval dance, as well as in much of its present universal popularity. It is perfectly suited to adorn holy day and holiday, and perhaps indispensable to each. It is thereby an apt icon for the meandering course of Incarnation in European and then American society and culture. The "macaronic" carol, fully vernacular but not giving up some lines in Latin, also suggests the character of Christmas—fully acculturated but always trailing its holier origins. Today, as when they first came to flourish, exquisite but simple carols demonstrate that Christian "taste" does not necessarily equal elitism, and musical resonance does not require an upper-class sensibility or an expensive education. The carol manages to be admired by all, from highbrow musicians to everyone on the street. In the long debate from the late medieval period through Bach's critics to the present, which pits simple and transparent religious music against a florid art music that may obscure the text and render worship for the unsophisticated impossible, the carol is a triumphant entry on one side.

Although the great age of religious folk song was coming to an end in the sixteenth century, the carol tradition poured vigor into the Protestant congregational hymn. (Today churchgoers mostly do not distinguish between a Christmas carol and a Christmas hymn.) Lutheranism immediately developed a rich tradition of hymnody sung by the congregation, but Calvinism restricted itself to metrical Psalms, and the English tradition also was slow to make provision for seasonal hymns. Until the highly successful *Hymns Ancient and Modern* of 1861, hymn-singing was not a staple of Anglican worship. But Tudor England still practiced the after-dinner custom of singing carols of Christmas, and the courts also produced lighthearted frivolous pieces by poet-musicians celebrating sacred and profane muses and interweaving nativity formulae with colorful Yule customs.

Across Europe carols continued to be sung, as developments of liturgical song and as independent folk traditions. But in the England of Puritan ascendancy, growing Protestant opposition forced Christmas song into decline, as English reformers worried about the carols' origins in French ring dances or pre-Christian fertility rites and seasonal songs. But the Methodist revivalism of eighteenth-century England and then the United States produced a great outpouring of fresh congregational song. A new fervent hymn singing provided relief from the dour metrical psalms of the Puritans, and it breathed the warmth and passion of faith and lay preaching. In the nineteenth century caroling was revived as evidence of an old-style celebration of Christmas. As ancient carols were recovered, new ones were being written. Even the middle of the twentieth century saw an explosion of hymnody, confirming that music remained the art form most available for Christian artistic creativity. While evangelical Protestantism remains cautious about the visual arts, it pours considerable energy into new music.

While the carol stands independent of the traditions of Gregorian chant, the latter was developing ever more complex traditions that issued in the elaborate polyphonic sacred music that still today defines a high point of unaccompanied choral music as art song. The greatest composers of the late medieval and Renaissance periods produced a rich harvest of "Masses for Christmas" that convey a religiously focused and liturgically-centered celebration of Christmas as a central holy day of lived Christianity. From within these Latin Masses came also the Christmas motets and sacred songs of William Byrd and Thomas Tallis in the English church and Guillaume Dufay, Jacobus Handl, Orlando de Lassus, Tomas Luis de Victoria, and Palestrina on the Continent. After that, the baroque period, above all in Handel and Bach, but also in Schütz and Praetorius and Monteverdi and their contemporaries, saw the development of elaborately orchestrated oratorios and cantatas that sang the glory of Christmas in almost operatic form. This music specialized in putting across the full emotional power of religious texts, typically through a combination of biblical narrative (recitative) and contemporary poetic amplification (aria).

From colonial America, much attention is currently paid to the robust and infectious music of William Billings. From the nineteenth century come Christmas oratorios by Hector Berlioz and Camille Saint-Saens and Pyotr Tchaikovsky's *Nutcracker Suite*. The twentieith century offers a remarkably wide range of "classical" Christmas music, including Benjamin Britten's *Ceremony of Carols* and *A Boy Was Born*, Hugo Distler's *Weihnachtsgeschichte*, Gian-Carlo Menotti's *Amahl and the Night Visitors*, John Adams's *El Niño*, Ottorino Respighi's *Laud to the Nativity*, and many works by Ralph Vaughn Williams, William Walton, and John Tavener. The Christmas music of the Orthodox tradition, especially Russia, has also gained in popularity. This treasure of Christmas music as Christian culture is widely available on sound recordings and lately on video as well. High school and college choirs and formal concerts in large cities offer opportunities to hear this music as Christian culture live, but, of course, churches are supposed to be the main source and venue for live Christmas music.

Handel's *Messiah*, a religious and even patriotic totem in the English-speaking world, is undoubtedly the most popular piece of classical choral music ever written. While only the first third of *Messiah* treats Christmas and the music's chief intentions are Lent and Easter, it is the Christmas season that today commands the great performances—immense community choral festivals, sing-along marathons, homely church choirs, professional choruses with symphony orchestras, and "early music" ensembles with original instruments all do *Messiah*. Every Christmas new "Messiahs" are born, many surely undreamt by Handel.

The setting in which *Messiah* (and Handel!) first flourished is reminiscent of how the culture of Christmas emerges in any age. When operas stopped making money and were outdone by more popular musical forms, oratorios seemed the promising way to go for musical entrepreneurs like Handel. As religion and government began placing restrictions on theatrical performances by prohibiting operas during Lent and requiring female roles to be played by men, oratorios could be distanced from their operatic origins by adopting a concert style of presentation. To give audiences music during Lent and perhaps to halo the oratorio, *Messiah* was originally intended for performance towards the end of the Lenten season and soon was often being performed on Maundy Thursday.

Like Christmas itself, *Messiah* responded to several cultural problems and opportunities. Oratorio would have two masters, church and theater, the one inspiring choruses and the other arias, the one the subject matter and the other the place and function and style of the performance, altogether holy day and holiday combined. Oratorio might have moved closer to opera, except for the continuing religious insistence that there be no acting or staging. There was also a Puritan resistance to theatrical treatment of Christian themes, so Handel at first wrote oratorios limited to Old Testament themes—Esther, Deborah, Saul, and Israel in Egypt. By intention, Handel's oratorios are not church music but music for an entertainment venue. But though performed far from a churchly setting, Handel's oratorios always featured God as the implied hero and humans as the objects of divine action. That an art form moving away from Italian roots should so capture the English heart was due in no small part to the fact that its texts were in English.

Again like Christmas, *Messiah* is a triumph of the vernacular. At its first London performance at Covent Garden on March 23, 1743, *Messiah* was billed as a new sacred oratorio, but, to minimize religious criticism, not publicized by name. The criticism came soon enough in a letter to the newspaper: "An oratorio is either an act of religion or it is not; if it is, I ask if the Playhouse is a fit temple to perform it in, or a company of players for ministers of God's Word. I fear it gives great opportunity to profane persons to ridicule religion at least, if not to blaspheme it; Is God's word to be prostituted to the perverse humor of a set of obstinate people?" But *Messiah*, like Christmas, would have its way.

In his story "Bach and the Heavenly Choir," Johannes Rueber tells of a French abbot who also happens to be a violinist. When he becomes pope, he wants to canonize Bach. All the obstacles but one are cleared away. It must be demonstrated that Bach had performed miracles. When the pope plays Bach's violin partita, the music itself is perceived to be the miracle. But the paradox of Bach is that he seems to stand for the other Christmas from Handel, the distant, difficult, unrealizable Christmas, the one no longer achievable by modern "audience practice," but at the same time Bach is available to the entire world, as one of the three or four greatest composers in the Western musical tradition.

Merry carolers may be predisposed to avoid thinking about the words they sing. Those who come to Bach (or even Handel) for sheer aesthetic joy may not wish to linger on the texts. When Mendelssohn was reviving Bach's *Saint Matthew Passion*, after a hundred years neglect, one critic complained that the biggest obstacle to enjoying Bach was the "atrocious German chorale texts full of the polemical earnestness of the Reformation and disturbing the mind of the non-believer by smoking him out with the dense fumes of belief which no one really wants nowadays." But for others, Bach, like Christmas, can be swallowed whole, though many concert-goers prefer Bach without the theology. About 75 percent of Bach's music was composed for worship services, but the remaining 25 percent is heard 75 percent of the time today. Bach himself did not care for the distinctions between sacred and secular; he gave it all to God. The second Brandenburg Concerto, with no whiff of sacred text, is a miracle, too.

But contemporary Christianity is not fully comfortable with its legacy of musical culture. The high art of liturgical music makes many Christians uneasy. An English critic has remarked that the glories of English church music evident at King's College Chapel in Cambridge is wonderful for musicians, but its performance is more of a concert than a worship service. Meanwhile, pious churches down the road are singing music that seems weak to musicians but is apparently good for worshipers. In this view, good music is bad if connoisseurs get it but the congregation does not. And bad music is good if it inspires worship of God and fosters spiritual uplift in the community. Musicians, evangelists, ministers, and the laity cannot avoid musical arguments. (Bach was constantly quarrelling with the clergy and school administration in Leipzig.) Every lay person who has felt the brunt of insufferable musicians understands the joke: "What's the difference between a terrorist and a church musician? You can negotiate with a terrorist."

Roman Catholic authorities once attempted to make normative one historical period, the music of the High Renaissance exemplified by Palestrina's masses. Popes praised Gregorian chant as if it had dropped from heaven and declined to ask whether it was suitable for contemporary vernaculars. But to some, Gregorian's wedding to medieval Latin is indispensable. A Latin chant at a midnight mass on Christmas Eve carries unmistakable mystery, whether or not anyone quite gets the words. The implied question is *whether there is a definitive music that is always right for the Incarnation.* If Christ is universal, must not every kind of music praise him? If Christ plays in a thousand faces, must music also?

Many Protestants, and some Catholics too, reject the church's musical past precisely because it now seems elitist and no longer usable. They are unwilling or unable to open these gifts of Christmas past. Their notion is that contemporary worship music must be relevant to the streets, instantly intelligible to anyone just through the door. Music's assignment is to carry texts whose everyday obvious meanings remove all barriers between the church and its visitors. This music avoids liturgical settings and associations because they are perceived as distancing and possibly rote or hypocritical. The hallowed *Dominus vobiscum* ("The Lord be with you") is improved with, "Good morning, how are you feeling today?" Music is a feel-good tool fit to carry instant messaging.

"Real musicians" and liturgical guardians, meanwhile, sniff that such music aspires to the genre of commercial advertising jingles set to billboard messages. They insist that some worship music should be difficult, so that people do not escape the idea that salvation is a long process learned with fear and trembling. They note that colleges insist on instilling in recalcitrant first-year students the glory of arts and humanities past—because it is good for them. Can the church do less?

But this leaves aside the glaring fact that very few Catholic church choirs are capable of performing a Palestrina mass, and almost no Protestant church choir could ever mount Bach's *Christmas Oratorio,* with its huge demand on choir, soloists, and a panoply of instrumentalists. Some performances by church choirs of Handel's "Hallelujah Chorus" are so far off the mark as to be comical. The church seems unable to carry its own legacy in the modern world. (Music is not the only instance of this.) Once, in the fourteenth century, a pope condemned the musical innovations of *Ars Nova* and unintentionally contributed to the development of secular music by driving the best musicians away from the service of the church and into the employment of wealthy and cultured princes. Today's Christianity may be turning its back on the power of its musical inheritance, or concentrating on new (and easier) music. Meanwhile, concert halls in great urban areas (and nearly everywhere in Europe) provide the great classics of Christmas music for December audiences. But the least problematic Christmas music, available to all, and the indispensable accompaniment to every December festival, in church or mall or home, is the Christmas carol.

Caroling Christmas

Now is born the divine Christ Child
Sound forth the oboes with pipes replying

—French carol

Then came the merry masquers in,
And carols roared with blithesome din.
If unmelodious was the song,
It was a hearty note, and strong.

—Sir Walter Scott, "Christmas in the olden time"

The New Oxford Book of Carols displays and annotates 201 carols, though there are many more than that. It gathers "composed carols" and "traditional carols" from all over Europe and then America, too. It is a Christmas cornucopia for readers and singers who want to study familiar carols and discover unknown ones.

To be sure, there are "caroling parties" where participants must negotiate lyrics they no longer believe in. But generally Christmas carols are the ideal entry to Christmas as holy day and holiday. Readily available, new ones easy to learn, often carrying old and almost universal memories, carols somehow, even as accompaniment to shopping pilgrimages, carry the mystery or at least the magic of Christmas into families, parties, streets, and church. To those with an ear for such things, they answer the longings of the heart at this festival.

The texts of some carols are rooted in the church's liturgies. The historic "O Antiphons," sung since the ninth century at vespers on the seven days leading up to Christmas Eve, migrated into the thirteenth-century hymn *Veni, veni, Emanuel.* Today it is a favored hymn of Advent, but is sung by many throughout the Christmas season.

O come, O come, Emmanuel And ransom captive Israel,
That mourns in lonely exile here Until the Son of God appear.
Rejoice! Rejoice! Emmanuel Shall come to you, O Israel.

O come, strong Branch of Jesse, free Your own from Satan's tyranny;
From depths of hell your people save And give them vict'ry o'er the grave.
Refrain

O come, blest Dayspring, come and cheer Our spirits by your advent here;
Disperse the gloomy clouds of night And death's dark shadows put to flight.
Refrain

O come, O Key of David, come And open wide our heav'nly home,
Make safe the way that leads on high And close the path to misery.
Refrain

From the late-medieval Latin liturgy came *Puer nobis nascitur.* In English we sing it jauntily, taking special delight in the repeated last line of each verse:

Unto us is born a Son, King of choirs supernal;
To this world he deigns to come Of lords the Lord eternal,
Of lords the Lord eternal.

Lo! He lies within a stall Where cattle fed before him;
King of heaven and Lord of all They know him and adore him,
They know him and adore him.

Born of Mary on this day By thy grace translate us
To the realm above, we pray, Where endless joys await us,
Where endless joys await us.

Some carols emerged to accompany mystery plays performed in town. A vernacular song from English mystery plays that has survived with text and music intact is the Coventry Carol. Coming at the dramatic moment at the end of the play, the carol is sung to put the babies to sleep so their crying will not alert Herod's marauders. The plaintive song mingles humor and brutality, as the women try to fight off the discovering soldiers. Ironically, the singers were probably a boy and two men; the audience was then accustomed to male performers representing women.

Lully, lulla, thou little tiny child, By by, lully lullay (refrain).
O sisters too, how may we do For to preserve this day
This poor youngling for whom we do sing, By by, lully lullay.

Herod the king in his raging, Charg-ed he hath this day
His men of might in his own sight All young children to slay.
Refrain

That woe is me, poor child for thee! And ever morn and day,
For thy parting neither say nor sing By by lully lullay.
Refrain

One of the most popular Christmas songs in Germany has been sung since the fourteenth century or earlier to two quite distinct texts, "Resonet in laudibus" (Let the voice of praise resound) and "Joseph, Dearest Joseph, Mine." The Joseph song was incorporated into various church dramas, and may originally have been written for them. Following a pre-Reformation Bohemian tradition, German Lutherans on Christmas Eve would sing both texts, alternating between various groups of singers and instrumentalists. Resonet, originally associated with vigorous dancing, came to accompany the medieval custom of cradle-rocking, which spread from Rhineland nunneries to congregational practice, where cradles were enthusiastically being rocked by adults and children at Christmas services. The Joseph text was also sung at weddings, and the text has Mary and Joseph and attendants singing back and forth:

> Joseph, dearest Joseph mine, Help me rock the Child divine;
> God reward thee and all that's thine In paradise, so prays
> the mother Mary.
>
> *Refrain:* He came among us at Christmastide, at Christmastide in Bethlehem.
> Men shall bring him from far and wide love's diadem:
> Jesus, Jesus, Lo, he comes, and loves, and saves, and frees us.
>
> Gladly, dear one, lady mine, I will rock this child of thine;
> Heavenly light on us both shall shine In paradise, as prays
> the mother Mary.

It is said that "In dulci jubilo" (With sweet jubilation) was taught to the German mystic Heinrich Suso, a student of Meister Eckhart, by angels. The combination of leader, refrain, and what sounds like a round dance definitively constitutes this angelic performance as a carol. This is the oldest of all German macaronic (mixed-language) carols, where German and Latin texts alternate in every verse. Text and music come from the thirteenth century. As is often the case, the irresistible last line has a refrain-like quality to it.

> Good Christian men (friends) rejoice, With heart and soul
> and voice;
> Give ye heed to what we say: Jesus Christ is born today;
> Ox and ass before him bow And he is in the manger now.
> Christ is born today! Christ is born today!

Good Christian friends, rejoice With heart and soul and voice;
Now ye hear of endless bliss; Jesus Christ was born for this!
He has opened heaven's door, And we are blest forevermore.
Christ was born for this! Christ was born for this!

Good Christian friends, rejoice With heart and soul and voice;
Now ye need not fear the grave; Jesus Christ was born to save!
Calls you one and calls you all To gain his everlasting hall.
Christ was born to save! Christ was born to save!

Before leaving the German hymn and carol tradition, Martin Luther's hymn written for his family celebration of Christmas Eve is indispensable. The text, with the first five verses sung by parents, standing in for the angels, and the next eight by the children, standing in for the entire Christian community, provides a complete theological account of the Incarnation, in what may be called its objective and subjective dimensions: gospel proclamation and human response. Bach famously set it, with trumpets and kettledrums, in his *Christmas Oratorio*.

Angel (parent)

From heaven above to earth I come To bring good news to everyone.
Glad tidings of great joy I bring To all the world, and gladly sing:

To you this night is born a child Of Mary, chosen virgin mild;
This newborn child of lowly birth Shall be the joy of all the earth.

This is the Christ, God's Son most high Who hears your sad and bitter cry;
He will himself your Savior be And from all sin will set you free.

The blessing which the Father planned The Son holds in his infant hand,
That in his kingdom, bright and fair, You may with us his glory share.

These are the signs which you will see To let you know that it is he:
In manger-bed, in swaddling clothes The child who all the earth upholds.

Children (Christian community)

How glad we'll be to find it so! Then with the shepherds let us go
To see what God for us has done In sending us his own dear Son.

Look, look, dear friends, look over there! What lies within that manger bare?
Who is that lovely little one? The baby Jesus, God's dear Son.

Welcome to earth, O noble Guest, Through whom this sinful world is blest!
You turned not from our needs away, How can our thanks such love repay?

O Lord, you have created all! How did you come to be so small,
To sweetly sleep in manger-bed Where lowing cattle lately fed?

Were earth a thousand times as fair And set with gold and jewels rare,
Still such a cradle would not do To rock a prince so great as you.

For velvets soft and silken stuff You have but hay and straw so rough
On which as king so rich and great To be enthroned in humble state.

O dearest Jesus, holy child, Prepare a bed, soft, undefiled,
A holy shrine, within my heart, That you and I need never part.

My heart for very joy now leaps; My voice no longer silence keeps;
I too must join the angel-throng To sing with joy his cradle-song.

All

Glory to God in highest heav'n Who unto us his Son has giv'n.
With angels sing in pious mirth: A glad new year to all the earth!

From the eighteenth-century English-Catholic tradition comes the now common call to worship at Christmas Eve services. First as "Adeste, fidelis," and possibly intended for Christmas matins, it acquired its English in the nineteenth century.

O come, all ye faithful, joyful and triumphant
O come ye, O come ye to Bethlehem!
Come and behold him, born the King of angels.
Refrain: O come, let us adore him!
O come, let us adore him! O come, let us adore him, Christ the Lord.

The highest, most holy, light of light eternal,
Born of a virgin, a mortal he comes;
Son of the Father now in flesh appearing!
Refrain

Sing, choirs of angels, sing in exultation,
Sing, all ye citizens of heaven above!
Glory to God in the highest:
Refrain

Yea, Lord, we greet thee, born this happy morning;
Jesus, to thee be glory given.

Word of the Father, now in flesh appearing:
Refrain

Isaac Watts was a formative influence on the music and religious poetry of eighteenth-century English and American revivalism, moving English-speaking dissenters and Calvinists beyond the constraints of severe metrical psalm-singing toward the fresh air of newly composed hymns with poetic texts inspired by the Bible, but not literally patterned on it. Almost a century later, there were still many Protestants who refused to sing Watts's hymns because they were of human composition. Watts set out to Christianize the Psalms by reading back into them the glow of the New Testament stories. His text for "Joy to the World" is drawn from his paraphrase of Psalm 98 and, given the continuing inattention to Christmas as a liturgical festival among English and American Protestants, it was not especially written as a Christmas hymn, nor is there any explicit reference to Christmas. Today we cannot hear it apart from Christmas, but the text is a good example of how a poet-theologian sets the Christmas gospel into a larger message of salvation history. Watts's text first united with its present nineteenth-century English tune in America, and then made its way back to England as well. The tune is probably not from Handel, though it has similarities with a chorus from *Messiah*.

Joy to the world! The Lord is come: Let earth receive her King!
Let ev'ry heart prepare him room, And heav'n and nature sing! *Repeat*

Joy to the earth! The Savior reigns: Let men (all) their songs employ,
While fields and floods, rocks, hills and plains Repeat the sounding joy. *Repeat*

No more let sin and sorrow grow Nor thorns infest the ground;
He comes to make his blessings flow Far as the curse is found. *Repeat*

He rules the world with truth and grace And makes the nations prove
The glories of his righteousness And wonder of his love.
Repeat

The brothers John and Charles Wesley wrote the hundreds of hymns that sparked the Methodist, or evangelical, revival in eighteenth-century England. Charles alone wrote about sixty-five hundred hymns, making him the most prolific hymn writer in the history of Christianity. This hymn for Christmas Day is the most popular of Charles Wesley's hymns. The carol only acquired its well-known tune several decades later, and the text went through many editors. Wesley's first verse originally began: "Hark! How all the welkin rings, Glory to the King of Kings"; welkin, an Old-English word for the vault of heaven, was eliminated in favor of the present line by the Methodist preacher George Whitefield. Felix Mendelssohn wrote the tune first for a festival to celebrate the four-hundredth anniversary of the invention of printing and did not think it could suitably be adapted to religious words. In the middle of the nineteenth century, it was suddenly discovered that text and tune were perfect for each other.

Hark! The herald angels sing, Glory to the newborn king;
Peace on earth, and mercy mild, God and sinners reconciled.
Joyful, all you nations, rise; Join the triumph of the skies;
With angelic hosts proclaim, Christ is born in Bethlehem.
Refrain: Hark! The herald angels sing, Glory to the newborn king!

Christ, by highest heaven adored, Christ, the everlasting Lord,
Late in time behold him come, Off-spring of a virgin's womb.
Veiled in flesh the God-head see! Hail, incarnate deity!
Pleased as man with us to dwell, Jesus, our Emmanuel.
Refrain

Hail the heaven-born Prince of Peace! Hail the sun of righteousness!

Light and life to all he brings, Risen with healing in his wings.
Mild he lays his glory by, Born that we no more may die,
Born to raise each child of earth, Born to give us second birth.
Refrain

Never mind that Wenceslas, a Germanized form of Vaclav, was a tenth-century Bohemian king not particularly noted for Christian virtue and that this carol is not based on any known incident in the king's life and that he was canonized for political reasons. Never mind that the nineteenth-century author of the text, John Mason Neale, a distinguished English liturgist and hymn translator, fit the words to a splendid tune about spring that he found in a late sixteenth-century collection of tunes. Together, text and tune are now irresistible, and they make us feel good that Christmas might have a profound moral influence on us. In some homes, the carol is grace before Christmas dinner.

Good King Wenceslas looked out On the feast of Stephen,
When the snow lay round about, Deep and crisp and even;
Brightly shone the moon that night, Though the frost was cruel,
When a poor man came in sight, Gath'ring winter fuel.

Hither, page, and stand by me; If thou know'st it, telling—
Yonder peasant, who is he? Where and what his dwelling?
Sire, he lives a good league hence, Underneath the mountain,
Right against the forest fence, By Saint Agnes' fountain.

Bring me flesh, and bring me wine! Bring me pine logs hither!
Thou and I will see him dine When we bear them thither.
Page and monarch forth they went, Forth they went together,
Through the rude wind's wild lament And the bitter weather.

Sire, the night is darker now, And the wind blows stronger;
Fails my heart, I know not how, I can go no longer.

Mark my footsteps, good my page, Tread thou in them boldly:
Thou shalt find the winter's rage Freeze thy blood less coldly.

In his master's steps he trod, Where the snow lay dinted;
Heat was in the very sod Which the saint had printed.
Therefore, Christian men, be sure, Wealth or rank possessing,
Ye who now will bless the poor Shall yourselves find blessing.

Many, perhaps most, carols are driven by wonderful tunes. "Greensleeves" was for a long time a beloved English folktune, so about 1865, William Chatterton Dix chose it for his new poem. The theologically astute text nicely combines the announcement of the nativity, the cross that is the future of the manger, and the response evoked from Christian believers.

What child is this who laid to rest On Mary's lap is sleeping,
Whom angels greet with anthems sweet While shepherds watch are keeping?
This, this is Christ the King, Whom shepherds guard and angels sing:
Haste, haste to bring him laud, The Babe, the Son of Mary.

Why lies he in such mean estate Where ox and ass are feeding?
Good Christians fear: for sinners here The silent Word is pleading.
Nail, spear shall pierce him through, The Cross be borne for me, for you;
Hail! Hail the Word Made Flesh, The Babe, the Son of Mary.

So bring him incense, gold and myrrh; Come, peasant, king, to own him!
The King of Kings salvation brings: Let loving hearts enthrone him!
Raise, raise the song on high, The Virgin sings her lullaby.
Joy, joy, for Christ is born, The Babe, the Son of Mary.

Although very little Christmas visual art was created in the United States, nineteenth-century America saw the birth of six significant carols: "We Three Kings," "Away in a Manger," "O Little town of Bethlehem," "It Came upon the Midnight Clear," and the African-American "Go Tell It on the Mountain" and "Rise Up Shepherd and Follow." John Henry Hopkins wrote the words and music to "We Three Kings," in which verses 1 and 5 are assigned to all three kings, and 2, 3, and 4 are assigned to each individually, with his gift. Not written by Martin Luther, "Away in a Manger" was probably written for children's programs mounted by American Lutherans. Originally a poem to be recited, it eventually acquired an American tune and a different tune in England, though it too was by an American.

Phillipps Brooks, rector of an Episcopal church in Philadelphia and later in Boston, was inspired to write "O Little Town of Bethlehem" after a visit to the Holy Land in 1865. On Christmas Eve he rode on horseback from Jerusalem to stand in the fields outside Bethlehem in order to imagine the original annunciation to the shepherds, and later listened to the singing at the Church of the Nativity there. He wrote the hymn for children in his Sunday school and asked his church organist, Lewis Redner, to provide a tune, which came to him suddenly, and belatedly, on Christmas morning. An alternative tune, commoner in England, was Vaughan Williams's arrangement of a popular ballad. Edmund Sears, a Unitarian pastor in Massachusetts, wrote "It Came upon the Midnight Clear" in 1849. He was inviting a meditation on humanity's willful deafness to the message of the angels. The proclamation of peace in the first two verses is contrasted with human intransigence in the third and a message of hope in the last two. "Go Tell It on the Mountain" is a Negro spiritual, with several changing verses and a common refrain. "Rise Up, Shepherd, and Follow" is another carol to rise out of black plantation culture, and its tune may be related to a British folksong.

Of course, there are many carols in other languages. The lullaby "Infant holy, infant lowly" comes from Poland, where both its text and melody are anonymous.

> Infant holy, infant lowly, for his bed a cattle-stall;
> Oxen lowing, little knowing Christ the Babe is Lord of all.

Swiftly winging angels singing, Nowells ringing, tidings bringing:
Christ the Babe is Lord of all.

Flocks were sleeping, shepherds keeping vigil till the morning new;
Saw the glory, heard the story, Tidings of a gospel true.
Thus rejoicing, free from sorrow, praises voicing, greet the morrow:
Christ the Babe was born for you.

Much-prized by every group of carolers is the French "Angels, We Have Heard on High," with its wonderful refrain. Both text and melody are an eighteenth-century Noel.

Angels we have heard on high, Sweetly singing o'er the plains,
And the mountains in reply Echoing their joyous strains:
Refrain: Gloria in excelsis Deo.

Shepherds, why this jubilee? Why these joyous strains prolong?
What the gladsome tidings be Which inspire your heavenly song?
Refrain

Come to Bethlehem and see Him whose birth the angels sing;
Come, adore on bended knee Christ the Lord, the newborn King!
Refrain

See him in a manger laid, Whom the choir of angels praise;
Mary, Joseph, lend your aid, While our hearts in love we raise.
Refrain

These and many other enchanting songs are the reason carol singing still survives. Although much of the culture of Christmas has been uprooted from churchly settings and sometimes suffocated by commerce, carolers still gather, in churches, at Christmas parties, and even in the streets. (Singing carols is a far more stirring activity than just listening to them.) The mixed history of carols—doctrinal, personal, mystical, aesthetic, commercial, universal—is the history of Christmas itself. Carols have survived their severance from the dance, ecclesiastical attempts to control them, and Puritan repression (during most of the eighteenth century, "While Shepherds Watched Their Flocks by Night" was the only authorized Christmas hymn, perhaps because the text was a direct paraphrase of Luke, until it was finally joined by Wesley's "Hark! The Herald Angels Sing"). Today carols survive the banalities they often serve in the settings of contemporary consumer religion. Sometimes powerful witnesses to Christian doctrine and sometimes insouciantly blending holy day and holiday, carols keep on singing. Could you read the texts above without singing along?

Musical Reverberations and "Hearing Religiously"

How far into modern culture do carols reverberate? How deep into the aural landscape does the deft touch of the Incarnation reach? Carols will certainly survive as the single most attractive art of Christmas. *Messiah* will be performed throughout the English-speaking world, and in Europe and Asia as well, certainly in concert halls but also in churches. That a single piece of music, *Messiah*, gave rise to "choral societies" devoted just to performing it is a miracle of sorts. Bach's *Christmas Oratorio* will be heard throughout Germany and in concert halls in major Western cities.

The "performance practice" of singers and instrumentalists will keep evolving, but the original "audience practice" remains elusive. As we saw in the case of the infancy narratives in Matthew and Luke, there may be no road back to first sightings and sitings. Bach's religious self-consciousness and the churchly environment in which he worked can scarcely be imagined today. A paradigm shift has occurred since the baroque period, and the modern listener, certainly in a concert hall, is far removed from most of those who heard Bach's music in Leipzig. As far removed as those who stare admiringly at Christmas art in a museum are from those who reverently kiss icons. Still, the aural landscape of Christmas, whatever it means, is compelling and even irresistible. That Bach still lives is not in doubt. In December 2005, BBC Radio 3 broadcasted the entire Bach corpus, with only newsbreaks, during the ten days leading up to Christmas.

But can we hope for more? For something new? Is there still some long-term incarnational deposit in human music in the modern age? Does the *Logos spermatikos* imagined and postulated by the ancient church still fertilize the human imagination? Could one speak, long after Bach or Handel or even after carols are overwhelmed with Santa and Rudolf, of "hearing religiously," a category elusive but suggestive? Is it possible to imagine a next incarnational step?

Could music hesitantly rejoin Christian culture to the modern world? How much traffic between Christmas as holy day and Christmas as holiday can music haul? Modern musicians may believe that music is almost holy, that it grants immediate communion with what lies beyond us, perhaps with God, and musicians sometimes seem to be the priests of this transaction. The arts set the spirit free to explore meanings that lie outside empirical proofs and beyond all other ways of knowing. Is music the way to reestablish an organic connection between the arts and the religious impulse, to reaggregate all the dispersals of incarnational extravagance? Some critics of consumerism are more likely to think that Christmas music is now reduced to ear training for shopping, and some theologians worry that music lures the pilgrim down sidestreets where more enticing wares are on offer.

Religion wants to believe that *music forms the human capacity to listen for God*. This would be a miracle amidst the noise of Christmas. It makes one think about how and where people hear Christmas today. The airwaves of the mall, a car radio, a telephone on hold, a *Christkindlmarkt* in Germany, a happy or contentious home, a television special, an office party, a church, a college choir concert, a ski lift or ice rink.

Sophisticated moderns educated in the "art for art's sake" school will have nothing to do with "hearing religiously." Aesthetes since the Enlightenment assert (though postmoderns do not) that art should be kept formally free and pure and unattached. This is a remarkable idea, actually. Music-and-play and music-and-dance and music-and-festival have stood together for very much longer than music has stood alone. For thousands of years it would have occurred to no one that music is a human artifact that should be contemplated disinterestedly, standing alone without reference to anything but itself. The point is not that music should be absolute and not primarily representational, for that is obvious. Who can keep straight which of Vivaldi's four movements goes with which season? But that is very different from disconnecting music from its social, cultural, and religious settings. Only for the last two centuries has it occurred to people just to go somewhere and listen to music decontextualized, though now the modern concert hall or the living room with a good stereo or ears plugged to an iPod recontextualize the locations where music is most often heard. Does this free or confine the ear?

Of course, the modern period did not really succeed in setting the arts free to live in secure splendor. The visual arts are always produced in an environment of art (economic) appreciation, of buying and selling and impressing, and recently of shocking entertainment. The same is true of music, which, set free from religion, has become more available to advertising or to other cultural constructions. Christmas music that once ritualized a religious festival now becomes, in the melody of shopping, a ritual of secularization. Unencumbered creativity scarcely exists in any of the arts, nor does unencumbered appreciation. No Christmas and no hearer of music escape their social and economic and cultural context.

It is not impossible, however, that the arts open a window on, among other things, meaning. A replete aural landscape could, in fact, invite people to *hear religiously,* to detect more than what is on sale. Artistic beauty has always been an avenue for the mind's ascent, for its quest for more. Music is not reducible to religion and not to commerce, but it can serve either. In a post-religious age, music is as close as many get to God, their clearest experience of being grasped by something precious and good and other than themselves.

The Risk of Incarnation: Fare Well, Christmas

A Valediction to Christmas

Christmas comes wrapped in the culture of the modern world, even if its origins lie in stories written two thousand years ago. When early Christianity first celebrated Christmas, it did so listening to Matthew and Luke read in public worship. The church still understands itself as the appropriate stage for religious festival, though the "audience practices" of former times are scarcely recoverable. But the idea of Incarnation seems to authorize a risky trajectory far beyond Bethlehem, beyond ancient texts, beyond ecclesiastical control. Christmas turned into an entire Christian culture, sedimented into Western civilization, and then took up residence (or captivity) in public square and market and home, as well.

Christianity understands God to have taken a chance on matter. It is a theological conundrum whether the grand tour Christmas has taken is to be celebrated as the ultimate reach of the Incarnation to every material thing or lamented as the eventual ruination of a religious festival by materialism's suffocating embrace. The argument of this book is that the generous material culture of Christianity is not a fall from a spiritual golden age, but a fuller realization of the religious core of Christmas. Imaginative Christians suppose that the God revealed in the New Testament has authorized ever widening vernaculars. To celebrate Christmas today means to embrace an entire and unwieldy Christian (and post-Christian) culture, if also to wonder whether it has lately slipped its moorings.

Now we are at the end of this account of Christmas as a major religious festival. A final *fare well* may express good will and even religious hope for an authentic celebration. But some would say a reluctant *farewell* is more in order, as a great religious performance now sinks beneath the waves of a commodified culture.

Christmas and the Clash of Civilizations

Society's great "cultural performances" reveal the social dramas that run beneath social order and the meanings achieved through the stories we tell ourselves and the rituals we practice. Christmas is such a cultural performance, and its holiday panoply is a form of "deep play" that suggests larger plots hovering over the stage. Christmas is a window on national aspirations, economic meaning, and individual character. One need not be religious to have taken an interest in this drama.

The modern Christmas opens on two rival worldviews, pictures of reality through which we construct, maintain, and experience the world around us. Once worldviews seemed to be neutral statements about the way things are, that we swim in like fish in the sea. Now we are more likely to see them as cultural constructions, even contests over economic power or social meaning. *The contesting worldviews at Christmastime are Christianity (or religion) and consumer capitalism.* The lead story of the last century is how a fabulously successful economic system, outmaneuvering and outproducing its rivals, has morphed into a philosophy of materialism that purports both to define what is real and not and to advertise itself as the fullest meaning of life.

A leading alternative, in this clash of civilizations, is religion, or in this case Christianity, which purports to offer an account of divine initiative and human response that is more adequate and compelling for an understanding of the human condition. The festival of Christmas finds itself positioned between these rivals, or, more precisely, with a foot in both worldviews. Each contests for it, each claims this festival as a sacrosanct inner meaning and legitimization of its own view of life. Especially as Christmas began to come loose from the drama of Christian redemption, it was free to acquire plot and problems from the great rival of the times, the civil religion of materialism and its great edifice, global capitalism.

Modern capitalism sees the earth as a kind of corporation, a collection of individuals drawn together to benefit its members by optimal use of resources. The structures of modern capitalist societies derive from a model that focuses on individual humans bettering themselves. The current neoclassical economics that provides philosophical support is committed to dividing up whatever is scarce among competing users. Claiming to be value-free or neutral on questions of ethics, this worldview uses as its mechanism of achievement the decentralized free market as the allocator of scarce resources. Its faith is that freely acting, acquisitive individuals will ultimately work out the best solutions for production and consumption. Themes like "just distribution" or "sustainability" or "carrying capacity" are externalities not considered intrinsic to this worldview and are left to extrinsic mechanisms, including religion. All intrinsic corrections are in the hands of self-interested individualism operating in a free market.

To be human, in this view, is to partake of a utilitarian individualism that expresses itself mostly apart from community. Its chief goal or value is growth. Sometimes this worldview is characterized as a religion or a philosophy, and then it is called consumerism. In that religion, personal happiness as the ultimate meaning of life is most likely to be achieved through a North-Atlantic style of high-consumption. The players who form the hierarchy of this religion, this "plausibility structure" that makes consumer capitalism workable and believable, are producers, advertisers, the media, national governments, and transnational corporations. To this great stage of cultural and economic performance, advertising draws the audience.

While most human endeavors take place in a market of competing ideas and values, international capitalism wants to monopolize the celebration of Christmas. Lively alternatives that compel the imagination are in short supply. A religious Christmas has mostly lost the ability to defend itself against a hostile takeover that has uprooted it from its original traditions, carried it to new sites, and put it to work on behalf of a rival system of meaning. There is no doubt that a secular culture, at least since the eighteenth century, has seriously weakened religion as a worldview and source of meaning. Atheism achieved an "empire of the mind" in the two centuries from 1789 to 1989, perhaps less through forceful intellectual argument than through a sympathetic cultural mood. But the culture of atheism has mostly failed to produce adequate substitutes for discarded religious symbols. This has produced a civilizational crisis, as the plausibility structures within which religious systems of meaning should thrive become eroded, and images of God and humanity destabilized. But a world disenchanted soon becomes disenchanting. Materialist ideologies ultimately fail as comprehensive systems of meaning, while becoming cancerous in attempts to succeed. Because every system of meaning requires ritualization, capitalist materialism borrows from its host. Christmas becomes the civil religion of consumer capitalism. Of the approximately two hundred countries in the world today, one hundred and fifty observe December 25 as a legal holiday, a materialist sacrament everyone wants a piece of.

Consumer capitalism's success is not an accidental, serendipitous, unplanned circumstance. Its status as the leading worldview comes from the apparent success of its claims. The argument that the truest significance of human culture, including Christmas, is the accumulation of material goods has caught on. Consumerism is the modern way of life. If "way of life" sums the organizing principles that constitute the definition of the good life, define human obligations, and elaborate right and wrong, then consumerism has outdistanced its religious and moral competitors—and left the rival economic system of socialism far behind. In the modern liberal democracy, everything is and ought to be for sale. Whatever people want the most must be the best for them, and advertising puts together for them the sum of things required for a good life. Brand commodities are brought together to become the wardrobe of a coherent selfhood. Once consumption was what one did in secular life, or part of what constituted holiday; now it has swallowed holy day whole.

The consumer capitalist worldview is not untroubled. By encouraging people to put a monetary value on everything, market values undermine ties of human solidarity and interdependent definitions of the good and foster social isolation and selfishness. The new creed professes that happiness arises from prosperity in economics and individualism in politics, potentially disconfirmable assumptions. Its necessary doctrines are high profits, weak labor rights, deregulation, ever extending markets, and a world system shaped for making money. Since such a creed could be seen as destroying the environment and condemning the poor and the lower middle class and creating for many others a false life, its affirmations claim to be made on behalf of freedom and choice and populism. No doubt most celebrators of Christmas as the civil religion of capitalism believe it is good for them—and for all.

Just as any advertised product competes for shelf space, one competitor religion attempts to displace another. If the truest meaning of human life is the accumulation of material goods, Christmas becomes an obliging sacrament put to new uses. Economic forces dislocate the historic incarnational account of the meaning of life and erode its religious substance. *A capitalist Christmas focuses on all the materials that claim to be good instead of on the Good that claims to be material.* The original Christmas placed God; the modern Christmas displaces God and buries the lead of a religious festival.

There is no shortage of political, economic, and theological analyses of the present state of Christmas and its situation between clashing worldviews, as we saw in chapter 7. In one analysis, it is not the materialism of Christmas that troubles but the fate of religion itself in consumer culture. Consumer capitalism re-trains believers to act like consumers *precisely when they are behaving religiously.* All cultural goods, even religion, are commodified, distributed, and consumed in highly individualistic acts and portions. Beliefs and practices removed from their ground in a living Christian tradition and dispersed as additional consumer products lose their aggregative power to reshape lives—to offer a compelling alternative to religion's chief rival. The material culture of religion and the religious symbol system that supports it are rendered as things one can choose and buy as accoutrements to a lifestyle. Believers learn to interact with them as they do with all purchasable things selected for decorative use and display. Consumerism's bandwidth far exceeds that of the church, as everyone becomes a terminal of network outreach. Holy day is another opportunity for holiday outfitters.

In this ethos, holy day has no organic and cumulative impact and loses its ability to assert itself in the face of overpowering economic forces. Consumerism as the great rival system of meaning does not need to face religion in a head-on contest. It simply renders Christian symbols freestanding commodities selected for self-aggrandizement. Christmas sermons still get preached, but they are unframed by a tradition and inattentive to their modern context, so their power to construct and maintain a rival universe is sluiced away. Religion disarmed loses its potential to subvert the status quo and to create an alternative world.

In another analysis, modern Christianity functions not to transcend or resist the leading dominant system, but to constitute and establish it. Christmas authorizes consumerism as the meaning of life, and capitalism is its delivery system. In a seasonal miracle, Christmas is aligned with economic existence even as a capitalist empire appears to be holding religion sacrosanct. Capitalism's close embrace of Christmas goes unnoticed because of the subterfuge of the separation of church and state, the labeling of all challenges to capitalist world domination as dangerously "fundamentalist" (or earlier, "communist"), and the fencing of economic life from religious inspection. Those who insist religion is purely a matter of personal belief also do their part. Because a consumer-capitalist Xmas is in fact the dominant *religious* festival, capitalism appears not as a rival to genuine Christianity but the chief and well-meaning manifestation of it. To pose as ultimate meaning, a penultimate, secular enterprise requires significant religious support.

With an irony few notice, the celebration of Christmas provides precisely that. But because Xmas looks simply like a secular shopping festival, its *religious function* as the legitimization of capitalism goes unnoticed. In a subtle process that nicely evades the American fixation on church versus state, a once religious festival now appears to be mostly secular, but in that evolution from one to the other achieves *the religious establishment of capitalism. Christmas, a quasi-religious and splendidly secular festival, has become socially compulsory*. Participation in the Church of Christmas Capitalism is nearly mandatory for most Americans. Neither the ostensibly religious nor the clearly secular can any longer opt out. Because the way of capitalism is to cannibalize every dimension of the public sector, turning all of culture into commodities, it should not surprise that religion, too, has been invaded and taken over. Much more powerfully and effectively than the church, the mass media control the means of (symbol) production. They define what Xmas is, filling or emptying it of content, and they depict salvation as the acquisition of products, though they prefer that the citizenry see the mirage of Christmas as a unifying winter festival for a pluralistic society. They preach a convincing story about shopping as the achievement of higher meanings and purposes. Religion lends its magic, its aura, and its mystery to consumption.

In this clash of civilizations, Christianity's voice is now a minor theme. Historically, the church has claimed that God initiated a new relation with humankind at the Incarnation, that in the life, death, and resurrection of Christ human redemption and redirection was effected. The two pillars of Christ's significance are celebrated in the great Christian festivals of Christmas and Easter. As regards the Incarnation, Christianity claims that a God who created the world good has reestablished the divine presence on earth by "bodying forth" in the life of the world. This means that matter—and hence the material culture of Christianity—is good and a finite vessel fit for the infinite. The cultural substance laid down in human civilization through the impetus of the Incarnation and which Catholic theology especially treasures should be embraced, retrieved, and renewed. But operative as well is the Protestant principle that guards against any and every penultimate that makes pretensions of ultimacy, including particular biblical interpretations, varieties of Christian culture, and the manifestations of the institutional church itself. Attentive to both approaches, *Catholic substance and Protestant principle*, Christmas may be seen, among other things, as the reaffirmation of every earthly good, including matter and bodily existence on a real earth, while also insisting that every good becomes authentically religious only as its godward dimension is recovered and honored. Thus, the Good that hallows every good also relativizes every good.

But Christianity, like capitalism, suffers from its own internal contradictions. Given the all-embracing materiality of the Incarnation, Christian theology and practice seems in retreat when it narrows the scope of Incarnation to the believer's heart, or to communities disconnected from the real world, or to a moral ethos that allows politics and economics to stand outside its purview. The incarnational wager appears to be declined whenever Christianity abandons the field of human interactions to economic or political forces, rendering them, in effect, autonomous and off-limits to the prophetic claims that are essential to the biblical witness in both the Old and New Testaments. The way one interprets the world, or leaves it uninterpreted, is the way it becomes. A Christmas without theological or worldview claims attached is holy day already ceded to holiday. The New Age spirituality often thought to be a promising dialogue partner to Christianity and other world religions narrows religion to inner experience, while Christian fundamentalism often narrows it to personal morality. A distant supernatural God leaves believers and their embrace of consumer capitalism unexamined. By contrast, the Jesus of the New Testament proclaimed a kingdom of God where everyone gets a place at the table.

In this clash of civilizations, the normative claims of Christianity and its festival seem to have little effect. Cultural critics observe that *happiness as limitless material acquisition is denied by every known religion and preached incessantly by every American television set.* It may be that the theological claims of capitalist advertising simply occupy a much wider bandwidth than religion. It may be that they acclimate much more readily to felt human aspirations. Students of religion—any world religion—might expect a great potential for countering consumerism as the de facto meaning of life, but contemporary Christianity seems strangely ineffectual, for reasons discussed above.

Christianity seems to be searching for strategies that would renew Christmas as a religious festival. Censoring capitalism as falsehood, though there is some truth to that, seems less promising in a liberal society than attempting to tell larger truths—persuasively. An ironic move is for Christianity to offer itself as the savior of capitalism by freeing it from its impossible pretensions.

The "contradictions of capitalism" have become commonplace discussions in the social sciences, and not on religious grounds. Many note that capitalist claims to ultimacy are doomed to fail for reflective human beings, and certainly for the poor, and that they are destructive to the earth as well. While a highly productive economic system easily outdoing its competitors, capitalism sows cultural (and religious) destruction when it implies that its survival requires the additional claim that happiness and well-being can be reduced to material acquisition, that the commodification of all cultural goods is the end strategy, and that all earthly good is determined and measured by market values. A Christianity with nerve might presume to save capitalism from itself. Its Christmas good news would be that capitalism mitigated and stripped of its mission to provide an entire account of life could thrive again, without doing untold damages to the poor and the earth and the quest of all humans for ultimate and transformative meaning.

Believable Christian Performance

Jesus famously admonished those intent on picking out a speck in their neighbor's eye to attend first to the log in their own. Criticism is most believable when it comes from a believable critic: "Physician, heal thyself." A revitalized festival of Christmas would provide a vividly imagined alternative world and an authentic way to live in it. It would require a newly vigorous Christianity fully in touch with its roots and historic vision. The sociology of religion uses the term "plausibility structure" to refer to the communities and institutions required by any ritual or worldview that wishes to remain believable. Inside the plausibility structure of a happy marriage, for example, a given outlook and behaviors make sense. If the structure falters, the worldview becomes unsustainable and its rituals hollow. The theatrical troupe that stages Christmas would have to ring true to the characters it plays. The church is heavily charged by its sacred texts *to look like the body of Christ in the world.*

A return to Western Christendom is not a promising strategy. There is no way back to that time in Europe and in Puritan America when Christianity suffused culture and even government. The religious manipulation of politics and culture in the modern age and religion's corruption by power in every age are not promising examples. All contemporary celebrations of Christmas occur in a secular world that has discovered how to live outside the sacred canopy of Christian symbols. Of course, the establishment of secularism (and the disestablishment of Christianity) is never the whole story. The postmodern world is now filled with competing stories, many of them religious.

Still, there may be a temptation to once-each-year triumphalism in which the church gets to dress the December commons in the exclusive fashions of Christianity. But holy day will be holiday, and holidays resist boundary-tending. The membrane between holiday and holy day is highly permeable, as an un-ghettoed Incarnation appears to suggest. In the imaginations of some religious thinkers and actors, the New Testament call to "bring every thought captive to the obedience of Christ" is not a secret call for Christian cultural hegemony but a beguiling invitation to every art and intellect to lavish incarnational wagers. These would have to exceed a one-night-stand on Christmas Eve. Abraham Heschel saw that the Sabbath could not survive in exile from everything else, a lonely stranger among days of profaneness. In this view, Christmas would have to claim the entire year. Heschel believed that it was not Jews who kept the Sabbath, but the Sabbath that kept the Jews. This would be the charter of Christmas for the people of God in the world who call themselves Christians.

In the clash of civilizations at the turn of the third millennium, the Christian worldview would have to unmask, name, and engage the economic forces and the ideology of materialism that claim to be the entire meaning of life. Mounting rival accounts is not a matter of ecclesiastical scoldings, but of religious imagination and authentic living.

The Orthodox churches believe they are staging heaven in every Sunday's liturgy, and above all at Christmas and Easter. This seems an audacious effort to the modern mind. It is a task for which most individual Christians appear to have lost heart and art. When ancient Israel was in exile, they sat down by the rivers of Babylon, hung their harps upon the willows, and lamented, "How can we sing the Lord's song in a strange land?" It is a wild hope to believe that *liturgy can save the world*. But liturgists say that to participate in a Christmas Eucharist is to venture inside God's imagination. There, the Protestant deal that cedes the accoutrements of Christmas to secular culture and domesticates its religious power as good family times—is off. Novice playwrights learn not to *talk* the drama ("Jesus is the reason for the season"), but to make it play on stage.

Bent on protecting the grace of divine initiative, Christian theology tends to be frightened by the idea that a platform for divinity must be erected by human hands. In the Old Testament, God was "enthroned on the praises of Israel." If that were so, the Christmas zeppelin would have to be kept high by human breath and effort. Christmas seems to need the church like a black preacher needs the amens of the congregation. In another age, a pipe organ stopped sounding if the boys pumping the bellows reneged. The organist was helpless to make music on his own. The drama in the clash of rival worldviews means watching whether Christianity will buy the idea that an authentic festival of Christmas depends on the believability of an authentic church. God's incarnational wager still requires human response. There is no Plan B, but humans are a necessary part of Plan A.

Retrieving Christmas Past

The "hermeneutics of retrieval" refers to a leap of interpretive imagination through which the past is recovered and then reclaimed. The modern visitor to St. Paul's Cathedral in London finds at the grave of the cathedral's architect, Christopher Wren, the admonition: "If you seek his monument, look around." But museum directors who mount contemporary exhibitions of religious art comment on how much this requires modern viewers to relearn of the past and unlearn of the present. Like the acres of space where modern museums conserve all the art they have no room to display, Christian liturgies and traditions are open archives waiting to be plumbed. The gold is there, and withdrawals are permitted.

In a Jewish tale, a Polish rabbi dreams there is gold under the bridge in the great city. He sets out the very next day, arrives at the bridge, and begins digging. A soldier questions him. As they talk, the soldier confides that last night he himself dreamed there was gold hidden behind the stove of a Jew in a small village. Astonished, the Jew hurries home and finds the gold. It has been noticed lately by media critics that formerly religious symbols become most usable for modern advertising precisely when the church no longer tends to them. They can easily be cherry-picked when no one is watching. *The modern Christmas may seem a plundered archaeological site,* everything removed from its original setting and disaggregated. Retrieving this legacy requires an imagination beyond the determinism of the present. Current fashions and market capitalism are not the only permanent exhibit of Christmas.

Some ages *were* better, at certain things. Great times are worth retrieving. We do not fault the Renaissance for returning *ad fontes,* to the sources. It was an act of hermeneutical imagination, not a reactionary move, when they recovered the fruits of classical civilization missing from the current diet. Americans reinvigorate national life by returning to the unparalleled times of their eighteenth-century founders. Christianity prizes great ages of faith, which were, not coincidentally, great ages of the arts as well. Theater returns for revitalization to the inspiration of the Globe Theatre in Shakespeare's day. It is not a burden to listen, still, to Mozart and Beethoven and Brahms. Viewing Michelangelo and Fra Lippo Lippi and Dürer and Riemenschneider and Rembrandt does not require a forced march.

It appears that some ages (and individuals) get some things better than others. Does one resent that Shakespeare all by himself achieved an advance in the evolution of humanity? Or pout that Bach single-handedly still defines the literature of the organ and of much other musical invention as well? Should one pass over the fact that Dante brought together in one great epic personal spirituality and public culture as no one else had ever done? If Thomas Aquinas wrestled together nature and grace in a magnum opus, might not rereading it be just the thing for an age in which a one-sided naturalism has made us homeless in the cosmos? Did anyone nail God to earth more persuasively than Luther? A canon in literature or religion comes about when later generations feel chosen and influenced by earlier figures. The disdain of a commercial

Christmas for the riches of the past is not a mark of maturity. No age provides the complete range of options for being fully human.

Every ransacking of the past may be an implicit critique of the present. But it is not sufficient just to hold on to early music, or old theology, or nostalgic festivals. That way resembles orchestras and opera houses that never challenge their audiences for fear of the wrath of season ticket-holders. Christ will play in ten thousand faces, as the poet Hopkins saw. Retrieval requires an opening up to the past. While the Enlightenment thought the Middle Ages horrible and dark, the Romantics found them luminous. A valid question for any culture is, What is missing from the current menu.

A great German collector of liturgical artifacts characterized his trove as a survival station. Just in case it turned out that he was assembling a dying art form, he was motivated to create a new context for his beloved objects, supplying a new environment for articles that had lost their functions in earlier religious life. Then he scattered his collected objects around in country churches, hoping that objects sanctified by long use in religious practice might imbue new settings with a sense of recovered tradition. He wanted to let his fellow Catholics experience the life of these objects. It was as if these were his Christmas presents to a culture that no longer knew. Museums, too, are survival stations, and we may need to make our pilgrimages to beautiful monuments to experience the faith that once made art. The memories of all that Christmas has been are kept alive in the presence of its cultural display, its ornamentation of the Incarnation, over time. If the church is a storehouse with most of its goods not on display, is this the result of ignorance, poor promotion, an inadequate advertising budget?

A hermeneutic of retrieval is like a pilgrimage, always including the roundtrip. In India pilgrims understand that the journey is not over and its meaning registered until they return with water from the Ganges to pour into the ritual life of the village. Pilgrims to Christmas past would presumably return bearing gifts. How to pass on retrievals is the question. The German language nicely creates a connection between gift (*Gabe*) and task (*Aufgabe*). To be gifted is to be tasked.

Imagining Christmas Future

Every year on Epiphany, at the Drury Lane Theatre in London, a special twelfth-night cake is carried to the actors in the green room by wigged and liveried theatre servants, fulfilling a bequest made in 1794. The bequest was of a hundred pounds in 3 percent funds, the interest to be used each year for the cake tradition. In Jewish life there is an "ethical will," in which a moral rather than a financial legacy is left to the next generation. The church's bequest of religious holy day was the beginning of the ancient Christian culture of Christmas.

Over the last fifteen hundred years the Incarnation has taken root and acquired ever new variety. To many contemporary watchers, it seems that God stubbornly refuses delivery from the womb of divine seclusion, so it must be human contractions that deliver a new birth of Christmas. Or not. The patron saint of saying yes is Mary, whose existential choice concretized divine initiative. Not accepting the role is the other choice.

It would be a theological claim, postponed to the end of this study so as not to annoy the reader prematurely, that *getting Christmas right improves the chances of getting ourselves right.* Plotting the human course in the world requires triangulation, positioning humans, their great festivals, and divine presence, each a story to be told. Let it be said that a weak divine biography tends to produce tiresome humans. Luther was so fixated on a God who would not speak that he (Luther, not God) suffered chronic constipation. It seemed God was waiting for a good story to appear. The implication was that if humans perform it, God will come. Christmas should not, like Churchill's pudding, be sent back to the kitchen for lack of a theme. Around the time of Jesus, the community at Qumran had gone to the desert to find God. Seers always go there, to see more clearly the mystery in the night sky. The last prophet went there, too, John the Baptist, whose season is Advent. The earnest seekers at Qumran hoped to create the ideal conditions that would lure God back. The desert would be the landing strip. The American John Muir, in a different context, thought that journeying into the wilderness was necessary to preserve the world.

It cannot be denied that Christmas comes in an uncertain season of Western civilization, where worldviews clash by night. Amidst capitalist splendor, there is much loss of light. A new solstice ceremony is required no less than when European ancestors valiantly attempted to haul back the sun. Many live "in the bleak mid-winter" of metaphysical and metaphorical loss. In such a situation the poet Dante once worked. "In the mid-path of my life, I woke to find myself in a dark wood," he began. Commentators say that *Paradise* is what Dante did with loss. He turned the tragedies of lost love and exile into the comedy of pilgrimage. He brought back to familiar embrace faith and reason, grace and nature. He overcame the tension between material and spiritual, between poetry and what poetry handles. He set out to "pick up the scattered leaves of God's book" and reunite what is dispersed throughout the universe in a single volume. Intending to imitate God, he bound them together with love.

Dante's way is not to renounce life in this world but through his art to give back a humanity viewed from earth's heavenward side. His own work epitomizes incarnational synergy, material culture as a divine-human venture. His vision and his hopes are large and inclusive, anticipating the coming autonomous forces of the Renaissance and also historic Christianity as a community on its way to the city of God. He sets an example of intellectual and artistic courage, capturing an entire civilization—the classical heritage, Italian painting, Gothic architecture, the age of the troubadours, scholastic philosophy and theology, the conflict of church and empire, monastic piety. He re-gifts the Incarnation with his own unifying vision. He means to render intelligible not only the union of humanity and divinity in Christ, but our own union between matter and spirit, between religion and culture. In his poetic pilgrimage, he overcomes the distance between heaven and earth. Dante the poet is the return gift of Dante the pilgrim.

Like the spotted owl, Christmas is an indicator species. The fate of Christmas becomes a symbol through which the reader can ponder how religion, or humans themselves, or the God who is thought to have taken the chance to leave home, are faring in the life of the modern world. My own conclusion is that Christmas will survive if we survive, if religion survives, in a world where there is so much material and cultural good to be celebrated, an abundance of the natural, and wherein all that good threatens to overwhelm the Good. So I close saying, “Fare well, Christmas.”

Notes for Further Reading

Preface

Of the thousands of books on Christmas themes, a hundred new ones every year, almost none of which offer a full religious and cultural appraisal of the festival itself, a good encyclopedia-style work is Gerry Bowler, *The World Encyclopedia of Christmas* (Toronto: McClelland and Stewart, 2004). Paying equal heed to historical traditions and to contemporary popular culture, this book offers a thousand entries in 288 pages. Another is Mary-Ann and Tanya Gulevich, *Encyclopedia of Christmas*, 2nd ed. (Detroit: Omnigraphics, 2003). Named an Outstanding Reference Source, this book offers 240 short entries on a thousand pages, emphasizing ancient customs and traditions.

In her catalog essay for an exhibition of religious art, *Divine Mirrors: The Virgin Mary in the Visual Arts* (New York: Oxford University Press, 2001), Melissa R. Katz claims that a contemporary understanding of religious art requires more attention to knowledge lost than to the kind of knowledge likely to be gained in the modern world. Amidst the brouhaha that accompanied the 1999 Sattchi display at the Brooklyn Museum that featured a Madonna collage daubed with elephant dung, it was noticed that dung on a religious icon could not shock a New Yorker, only the sincere expression of religious belief.

1. The Original Texts of Christmas

Jack Miles's psychological portrait of the God of the Old Testament, *God: A Biography* (New York: Vintage, 1996), won the Pulitzer Prize. His succeeding book, *Christ: A Crisis in the Life of God* (New York: Vintage, 2002), portrays the New Testament story as God's change of heart.

Modern New Testament commentaries vary widely in form and purpose, such as devotional meditation, moral application, guide to preaching. Scholarly commentaries focus on the original Greek text, the oral and written forms that may have preceded the present text, the literary style of a given book like Matthew or Luke, the historical and social settings of both the original stories and their later roles as written texts in the life of early Christianity, and the meaning of the texts as theological proclamation. Among commentaries of this latter kind, I am heavily indebted to the following: Francois Bovon's *Luke 1: Commentary on the Gospel of Luke* (Minneapolis: Fortress, 2002); Raymond Brown's *The Birth of the Messiah: Commentary on the Infancy Narratives in the Gospels of Matthew and Luke*, updated (New Haven: Yale, 1993); Frederick Danker's *Jesus and the New Age: A Commentary on St. Luke's Gospel*, revised (Minneapolis: Fortress, 1998); W. D. Davies's *Matthew 1–7 Critical and Exegetical Commentary on the Gospel according to St. Matthew* (London: T&T Clark, 2004); Edwin D. Freed's *The Stories of Jesus' Birth: A Critical Introduction* (London: T&T Clark, 2004); Robert Horton Gundry's *Matthew: A Commentary on His Literary and Theological Art* (Grand Rapids: Eerdmans, 1982); Gundry's *Matthew: A Commentary on His Handbook for a Mixed Church under Persecution*, 2nd ed. (Grand Rapids: Eerdmans, 1995); Richard Horsley's *The Liberation of Christmas: The Infancy Narratives in Social Context* (New York: Crossroad, 1989); Ulrich Luz's *Matthew 1–7: A Commentary* (Minneapolis: Fortress, 2007).

A commentary of a different type is Thomas C. Oden's editing of *Ancient Christian Commentary on Scripture* (Downer's Grove, Ill.: InterVarsity Christian Press). The proposed twenty-eight volumes in this series collect Christian exegesis of biblical texts from the first eight centuries of Christianity. This escapes the dominant "presentism" of contemporary scholarship while retrieving the wisdom of the ancient church.

Besides commentaries, biblical studies also call attention to the Bible as a stimulus to spiritual growth, a treasured object of material culture, an inspiration to religious art, or as an instance of the current emphasis on doing theology as story. To those ends, I have drawn from the following: Raymond Brown's *A Coming of Christ in Advent* (Collegeville, Minn.: Liturgical Press, 1988); Raymond Brown's *An Adult Christ at Christmas* (Collegeville: Liturgical Press, 1988); Andreas Fingernagel's and Christian Gastgeber's *In the Beginning Was the Word* (Cologne: Taschen, 2003), a display of the most famous illuminated Bibles in the Austrian National Library and a splendid example of "the culture of the book"; Eugene H. Peterson's *Eat This Book: A Conversation in the Art of Spiritual Reading* (Grand Rapids: Eerdmans, 2009), a good example of contemporary admonitions to recover the discipline of spiritual reading of the Bible that has characterized monastics, mystics, and the pious over the centuries; Anne Rice's *Christ the Lord: Out of Egypt* (New York: Ballantine, 2005), a novelistic attempt to imagine the Jesus story, told from the point of view of Jesus as a seven-year-old child—by a best-selling novelist re-embracing her Catholic faith; Philip and Sally Scharper's *The Gospel in Art by the Peasants of Solentiname* (New York: Orbis, 1984), a collection of the famous examples of Christian peasant folk art in Nicaragua, a visual liberation theology and evidence of how Third World peoples can seize religious narratives from their dominant interpretive settings in the First World middle class and make them their own; H. Stephen Shoemaker's *Godstories: New Narratives from Sacred Texts* (Valley Forge, Pa.: Judson Press, 1998), one of many efforts to recover "theology as story"; Samuel Terrien's *The Magnificat: Musicians as Biblical Interpreters* (New York: Paulist, 1994), a scholarly examination of Mary's song and an interpretation through musical settings of the last six hundred years.

Two recent studies establish the role early Christianity played in shifting information technology towards the culture of the book, as we know it today. Anthony Grafton and Megan Williams, *Christianity and the Transformation of the Book: Origin, Eusebius, and the Library of Caesarea* (Cambridge: Harvard Belknap Press, 2008); Megan Hale Williams, *The Monk and the Book: Jerome and the Making of Christian Scholarship* (Chicago: University of Chicago Press, 2006). Eamon Duffy, in his review article "Early Christian Impresarios" in the *New York Review of Books* (March 29, 2007), highlights the Christian generation and use of the book as an indispensable and prized object of material culture.

2. The Human Play of Christmas

Joan Wester Anderson, *Angels We Have Heard on High: A Book of Seasonal Blessings* (New York: Ballantine, 1997). A good, somewhat credulous example of the current fascination with angels. Short, heartwarming accounts of seasonal miracles.

Dawson W. Carr, *Andrea Mantegna: The Adoration of the Magi* (Los Angeles: Getty Museum Studies in Art, 1997). This is an excellent example of a brief book devoted to a single painting, the Getty Museum's recent acquisition of Mantegna's "The Adoration of the Magi."

Caroline H. Ebertshauser et al., *Mary: Art, Culture and Religion through the Ages* (New York: Crossroad Herder, 1997).

Cynthia Hall, *Portrayed on the Heart: Narrative Effect in Pictorial Lives of Saints from the Tenth through the Thirteenth Century* (Berkeley: University of California Press, 2001). The saints are, in effect, extensions of the Incarnation, ongoing exemplars of God's assumption of humanity.

Lesley Hazlton, *Mary: A Flesh-and-Blood Biography of the Virgin Mother* (New York: Bloomsbury, 2004). Hazleton's method is to show the modern reader what Mary might have seen, heard, and experienced in everyday Galilean peasant life, but based on a very uncertain grasp of the scholarship of first century Judaism and Christianity.

Ann Dorian Brice Hunt, *The Mythic Meaning of Christmas: Oh come, let us become Him* (Mansfield, Mass.: Center for Inner Gardening, 2001). A New Age approach to recovering the spiritual potential of celebrating Christmas. The reader enters the sacred story and becomes each character, in order to examine the reader's own life. Sample response to the Virgin Mary: "What am I going to birth at this time in my life?"

Melissa R. Katz, *Divine Mirrors: The Virgin Mary in the Visual Arts* (New York: Oxford, 2001). This is a catalog, with interpretive essays, of a museum display of images of Mary over time and how they disclose cultural preoccupations. Robert Orsi's essay is especially good at depicting the evolution of Mary in the "lived religion" of Christianity.

Norbert King, *Mittelalterliche Dreikonigsspiele* (Freiburg, Switzerland: Universitatsverlag, 1979). This study of the development of magi themes in Latin, German, and French plays from the middle ages to the end of the sixteenth century demonstrates the fascination with and endless embellishment of the three kings, indeed more than of any other biblical narrative. Essentially, these plays took the form of stations on a journey, of the magi and of life.

Martyn Lloyd-Jones, *My Soul Magnifies the Lord: Meditations on the Meaning of Christmas* (Wheaton, Ill.: Crossway Books, 1998). Argues that Christmas, and Mary's Magnificat, are stories of reversal, not of the apex of human striving.

Jaroslav Pelikan, *Mary through the Centuries* (New Haven: Yale, 1996). Following the path taken by "historical Jesus" research, this study portrays the different faces of Mary in each age.

Jaroslav Pelikan, *The Illustrated Jesus through the Centuries* (New Haven: Yale, 1997). A sophisticated historical and theological account of how each age achieves or invents a different Jesus. A superb and lavish collection of images complement a brilliant text.

Richard C. Trexler, *The Journey of the Magi: Meanings in History of a Christian Story* (Princeton: Princeton University Press, 1997). Thorough study of the political, social, and economic uses of the magi symbol over the history of Christianity. A good example of how biblical characters evolve and come to serve abundant new purposes.

Marina Warner, *Alone of All Her Sex: The Myth and Cult of the Virgin Mary* (New York: Vintage, 1983). An early and very influential work in modern feminist studies of Mary.

3. Christian Worship as Theater

In so-called liturgical churches like Roman Catholic, Orthodox, Anglican, and Lutheran, and in churches trending towards more liturgical worship, there are never-ending efforts to produce not only works on the history and theory of liturgy, but also liturgical "helps" to enrich worship according to the Christian Year. Among those that influenced this chapter are the following:

New Zealand Prayer Book (San Francisco: Harper, 1997). This is a much-cited example from the Anglican Church in New Zealand and Polynesia of attempts to pray the liturgy in ways relevant to the modern world and to indigenous peoples.

Catherine Aslanoff, ed., *The Incarnate God: The Feasts of Jesus Christ and the Virgin Mary,* vol. 1 and 2, translated from the French edition by Paul Meyendorff and illustrated by Andrew Tregubov (New York: St. Vladimir Seminary Press, 2004). This set presents a catechism of Orthodox Christianity derived from the liturgical year, drawing on scripture readings, hymns, and icons and leading the reader into the mysteries of the faith. Volume 1 is organized around Advent, Christmas, and Theophany (Epiphany).

Susan A. Blain, ed., *Imaging the Word: An Arts and Lectionary Resource,* Vols. 1–3 (Cleveland: United Church Press, 1995). A superb (Protestant) example of contemporary attempts to enrich liturgical worship through the arts, arranged according to the three cycles of lectionary readings for the church year.

Raymond Chapman, *Stations of the Nativity* (Harrisburg, Pa.: Morehouse, 1999). Attempts to take the well-known practice of Lenten piety surrounding the stations of the cross and use it in Advent.

Days of the Lord: The Liturgical Year (Collegeville, Minn.: Liturgical Press, 1991). This is a good example of the outpouring of Roman Catholic scholarship on the meaning of the church year. This first volume is devoted to Advent, Christmas, and Epiphany.

Aidan Kavanagh, *Elements of Rite: A Handbook of Liturgical Style* (Collegeville: Liturgical Press, 1990). Occasionally acerbic but wonderfully wise, this is a guide to the liturgy and the mind of the church by a Benedictine professor of liturgics.

Patrick Kelley and Lawrence Boadt, *Stations of the Nativity* (New York: Paulist Press, 2002). Attempts to take the well-known practice of Lenten piety surrounding the stations of the cross and use it in Advent.

Robin A. Leaver and Joyce Ann Zimmerman, eds., *Liturgy and Music: Lifetime Learning* (Collegeville: Liturgical Press, 1998). This excellent collection of articles by leading Roman Catholic liturgical scholars pays equal attention to liturgy and to music and advocates a normative pattern of Christian worship that can be called a "musical liturgy."

Thomas J. O'Gorman, ed., *An Advent Sourcebook* (Chicago: Liturgy Training Publications, 1988). A superb collection of devotional and theological readings to recover and enrich the liturgical season of Advent.

Frank C. Senn, *Christian Liturgy: Catholic and Evangelical* (Minneapolis: Fortress, 1997). Roman Catholic, Lutheran, and Anglican theologians are the chief contributors to liturgical study and reflection. This is a recent work by a Lutheran.

Frank C. Senn, *New Creation: A Liturgical Worldview* (Minneapolis: Fortress, 2000). Not limiting his study to liturgical churches, Senn argues that liturgy is what happens whenever Christians gather for any kind of worship. It always means, in some way, the performance of a religious worldview.

Mary Ann Simcoe, ed., *A Christmas Sourcebook* (Chicago: Liturgy Training Publications, 1984). A rich compendium of prose and poetry readings that are not only pious and devotional but theologically astute.

Watch for the Light (Farmington, Pa.: Plough Publishing House, 2001). An excellent collection of meditations for Advent and Christmas by Christians from many traditions.

Among works reconnecting Christmas and solstice and other "pagan" festivals are the following:

Samuel L. Macey, *Patriarchs of Time: Dualism in Saturn-Cronus, Father Time, the Watchmaker God, and Father Christmas* (Athens: University of Georgia Press, 1987). An attempt, through a mélange of customs and quotations, to suggest the direct continuity of Saturnalia and Christmas, but without critical scholarship.

John Matthews, *The winter solstice* (Wheaton, Ill.: Quest Books, 1998). A New Age meditation on the solstice.

Daniel Miller, ed., *Unwrapping Christmas* (Oxford: Oxford University Press, 1993). The editor's opening essay, "A Theory of Christmas," offers an extensive account of the seasonal celebrations that preceded the Christian Christmas.

The emergence of medieval drama from the life and liturgy of Christianity is an example not only of how biblical texts of Christmas turn into mystery tales played on carts moving through the streets, but also of how Christmas itself, as a great religious festival staged in the church, relentlessly migrates down every avenue of arts and material culture. I have drawn from the following important works on this development.

John Allen, ed., *Three Medieval Plays: The Coventry Nativity Play, Everyman, and Master Pierre Pathelin* (London: William Heinemann, 1953). A valuable study of the famous Coventry Nativity Play of 1534.

Emilia Batschmann, ed., *Das St. Gallen Weinachtsspiel* (Bern: Francke Verlag, 1977). A valuable study of the oldest German language Christmas play and the circumstances in which it arose.

Dorothe Krieger, *Die mittelaltlichen deutschprachigen Spiele und Spielszenen des Weihnachtstoff Kreise* (Frankfurt: Peter Lang, 1990). A valuable study of how Christmas plays grew out of earlier Easter plays. Locates the *officium pastorum* (shepherds) and *officium stellae* (wise men) in the liturgies of Christmas. For instance, the three kings play comes at the eucharistic procession that brings the gifts of bread and wine to the altar.

A. M. Nagler, *The Medieval Religious Stage: Shapes and Phantoms* (New Haven: Yale, 1976). A very technical study of theater history, with elaborate attention to performance practices, stage directions, and places of performance.

Karl Schubert, *Das Alt-Egerer Krippentheater: Ein Beitrag zur Geschichte des Krippenspiels* (Munich: R. Oldenbourg Verlag, 1986). Studies the development of shepherd and magi plays, from liturgy to outdoor theater, from clerical to lay, from church to public, from Latin to the vernacular.

Lowell Swartzell, ed., *The Twelve Plays of Christmas* (New York: Applause, 2000). This anthologizes three traditional plays, three contemporary religious plays, including Menotti's "Amahl and the Night Visitors" and Langston Hughes's "Black Nativity," and nine nonreligious plays, with introductions. Demonstrates that Christmas continues to stimulate theater.

William Tydeman, *The Theatre in the Middle Ages: Western European Stage Conditions, 800–1576* (Cambridge: Cambridge University Press, 1978). A thorough scholarly study fully conversant with all the relevant literature of the dynamic interaction between liturgy and drama, church, and the development of theatre.

Glynne Wickham, *The Medieval Theatre* (New York: St. Martin's Press, 1974). One of the finest studies of the evolution of liturgy as music-drama to plays in the street, carefully attending also to the role of actors, staging, costumes, and translations to the vernacular. The three most significance forces in the development of dramatic art from the 10th to the 16th centuries are religion, recreation, and commerce.

Karl Young, *The Drama of the Medieval Church,* 2 vols. (Oxford: Clarendon Press, 1933). A seminal discussion of the course from the dramatic qualities of liturgy to street theater. It builds on the metaphor of troping, in which final notes of liturgical sequences acquire infinite expansion, first musically and then textually, as artistic input plays an ever greater role in the life of the church.

In anthropology and religious studies especially, but also across the humanities and social sciences, there is developing a rich literature on ritual, its history, theory, promise, and impediments in the modern world. Among those that have influenced this chapter are the following:

Roland Delattre, "Ritual Retrospective and Cultural Pluralism," *Soundings* (Fall 1978). Delattre develops the idea that ritual is a vehicle through which humans pass through the world and, simultaneously, the world passes through their humanity.

Tom Driver, *The Magic of Ritual* (San Francisco: Harper, 1991). Ritual offers three gifts not available in other ways, the ordered cosmos of an established and shared worldview, the social world of human connectedness in community, and the transformation beyond ourselves that comes with the performance of the magic of religion.

Ronald Grimes, *Beginnings in Ritual Studies* (Lanham, Md.: University Press of America, 1982). Grimes is one of the most prolific writers on ritual in modern life, its impediments, and its possibilities.

Ronald Grimes, *Research in Ritual Studies: A Programmatic Essay and Bibliography*. ATLA Bibliography Series, no. 14 (Metuchen, N.J.: Scarecrow, 1985).

Ronald Grimes, *Ritual Criticism: Case Studies in its Practice, Essays on its Theory* (Columbia: University of South Carolina Press, 1990).

Donald Heinz, *The Last Passage: Recovering a Death of Our Own* (New York: Oxford University Press, 1999). In the last three chapters Heinz applies much of the work in contemporary ritual studies and their possibilities to the context of death and dying.

Susanne K. Langer, *Philosophy in a New Key* (Cambridge: Harvard University Press, 1957). Langer sees in rituals "a disciplined rehearsal of 'right attitudes,'" without which we lack "mental anchorage" (pp. 153, 290).

Jonathon Z. Smith, *To Take Place* (Chicago: University of Chicago Press, 1987). Develops the notion of ritual as a mode of paying attention.

Henry David Thoreau, *Walden: 150th Anniversary Illustrated Edition of an American Classic* (New York: Houghton Mifflin, 2004). Thoreau saw in carefully rehearsed motions a spiritually formative power, a way to resist the distracting commotion of life. He proposed to dwell in the world according to the rhythms of an alternative reality, to renew the resources for such a life by frequent journeys upon the "inward sea."

Victor Turner, ed., *The Anthropology of Performance* (New York: PAJ, 1987). The anthropologist Victor Turner collaborated with theater practitioner Richard Schechner in a very influential work that has connected ritual and theater.

Victor Turner, *The Ritual Process: Structure and Anti-Structure* (Chicago: Aldine, 1969).

4. Motley Crew: Pilgrims on Holiday

I have depended on the following works for the history, theory, and practice of Christian pilgrimage:

Craig Bartholomew and Fred Hughes, eds., *Explorations in a Christian Theology of Pilgrimage* (Burlington, Vt.: Ashgate, 2004). A superb collection of articles, though decidedly Protestant in its clear exaltation of the person of Christ over sacred place. Focusing primarily on Jerusalem, the anthology offers twelve articles under the three themes of biblical, historical, and theological perspectives on pilgrimage.

Horton and Marie-Helene Davies, *Holy Days and Holidays: The Medieval Pilgrimage to Compostela* (Lewisburg, Ohio: Bucknell University Press, 1982). An exemplary study that significantly influenced the discussion of holy day and holiday throughout my book. Scholarly, widely-sourced, gracefully written, every dimension of pilgrimage is examined in detail. Discussion ranges over pilgrims and their motives and practices, inevitable profiteers, the role of the church, routes and relics, the influence of the Reformation and the Enlightenment.

J. G. Davies, *Pilgrimage Yesterday and Today* (London: SCM, 1988). Early pilgrimage practices and suggestions for contemporary Christian pilgrimage, lacking social science theory and aspiring to be theologically normative. Pilgrimage as a spiritual exercise and imitation of Christ; veneration of the saints as a celebration of grace in real time; shifts in pilgrimage between Catholic and Protestant spiritualities.

John Eade and Michael J. Sallnow, eds., *Contesting the Sacred: The Anthropology of Christian Pilgrimage* (London: Routledge 1991). Sees pilgrimage as an allegory of the journey of the soul to God and sacred sites as the spatialization of charisma. Excellent accounts of theory and practice.

Rivka Gonen, *Biblical Holy Places: An Illustrated Guide* (New York: Collier Books, 1987). This is a guide to sacred sites named in the Old and New Testaments, with 250 color photographs and detailed maps. A good example of a manual for Christian tourism.

James Harpur, *Sacred Tracks: Two Thousand Years of Christian Pilgrimage* (Berkeley: University of California Press, 2002). Lavishly illustrated and organized around early paths, medieval roads, and modern ways, the book describes the saints and pilgrims, shrines and cathedrals, relics and practices of the pilgrimage traditions.

Susaan Signe Morrison, *Women Pilgrims in late Medieval England* (London: Routledge, 2000). Argues that pilgrimage breaks down distinctions between sacred and secular, performer and audience, body and society; that women's pilgrimage represented transgressive mobility and social disorder against those who want to keep constant surveillance of women's bodies; that pilgrimage is about journeying to new space to encounter the other and escape the quotidian; that pilgrimage is entry into the liminal and escape from ecclesiastical control.

Mary Lee and Sidney Nolan, *Christian Pilgrimage in Modern Western Europe* (Chapel Hill: University of North Carolina Press, 1989). Though not rich in anthropological theory or theology, offers exhaustive survey research or actual visits that take into account 6,150 pilgrimage sites in sixteen European countries. Data on numbers and purposes of pilgrims all coded by site.

Victor and Edith Turner, *Image and Pilgrimage in Christian culture* (New York: Columbia University Press, 1995). Together with his wife, the great anthropologist of religion set pilgrimage into theoretical work on ritual and public ceremony.

Diana Webb, *Medieval European Pilgrimage* (New York: Palgrave Macmillan, 2002). Excellent history of pilgrimage practices.

For pilgrimage as a psychological or devotional or New Age concept, I have profited from the following:

Jean Shinoda Bolen, *Crossing to Avalon: A Woman's Midlife Pilgrimage* (San Francisco: Harper, 1994). This is a Jungian and feminist account of pilgrimage as a quest for meaning missing from one's life and culture. Mythic journeys begin when exceptional circumstances initiate a heroic response. A provocative and inspiring account.

Ann Dorian Brice Hunt, *The Mythic Meaning of Christmas* (Mansfield, Mass.: Center for Inner Gardening, 2000). Utterly New Age, but quite enchanting and with good ideas about personalizing the Christmas story.

It is always useful to compare a root metaphor like pilgrimage with its use across other world religions. I have learned much from the following:

Sabita Acharya, *Pilgrimage in Indian Civilisation* (New Delhi: Manak, 1997). This is an excellent window on lived religion, including sacred geography, sacred performance, and sacred specialists. With astonishing detail, the book offers an ethnography of how, as also in the evolution of Christmas, holy day and holiday, spiritual and material culture constantly jostle each other.

Duncan Forbes, *The Buddhist Pilgrimage* (Delhi: Motilal Banarsidass Publications, 1999). Though short on critical reflection, this book is good on narrative details.

Ann Grodzins Gold, *Faithful Journeys: The Ways of Rajasthani Pilgrims* (Prospect Heights, Ill.: Waveland, 2000). Very useful discussion of pilgrimage as a roundtrip: the pilgrim returns with material and spiritual gifts for the home community.

Stephen P. Huyler, *Meeting God: Elements of Hindu Devotion* (New Haven: Yale, 1999). Beautifully illustrated, features both pilgrimage and household shrines. Good discussions of *darshan,* seeing and being seen by God; *puja,* reverence through invocation, prayer, song, ritual contact with images and material culture; and the process in which sacred shrines accumulate a rich material culture from the vows of pilgrims.

Jha Makhan, ed., *The Social Anthropology of Pilgrimage* (New Delhi: Inter-India Publications, 1991). Strong on theory in first chapter, the rest of the book less compelling but with exhausting details.

Brij Tankha, *Buddhist Pilgrimage* (New Delhi: Lustre Press, 1997). A good discussion of the theory and practice of Buddhist pilgrimage as an adventure in time and place, recapitulation and rediscovery, outward and inward journey.

5. Staging Incarnation: Material Culture and the Traveling Manger Scene

E. N. C. Zarur and Charles Muir Lovell, *Art and Faith in Mexico: The Nineteenth Century Retablo Tradition* (Albuquerque: University of New Mexico Press, 2001). Lavishly illustrated, this study includes introductory essays and extensive notes on the paintings. Very good on how religious symbols acquire and stimulate new meanings in domestic settings.

Laura Chester, *Holy Personal: Looking for Small Private Places of Worship* (Bloomington: Indiana University Press, 2000). This is a manual for locating spirituality in the home.

University of Dayton (udayton.edu), Nativity collection. This Catholic university has a large and impressive collection of nativity scenes, frequently stages exhibits, and has a very useful educational Web site.

6. Re-Presenting Incarnation: The Role of Theology

Athanasius, *On the Incarnation*, translated and edited in English (Crestwood, N.Y.: St. Vladimir's Seminary Press, 2003). A seminal treatise by an important father of the Greek church.

Augustine, *Sermons for Christmas and Epiphany*, translated and annotated by Thomas Comerford Lawler, vol. 15 of Ancient Christian Writers (Westminster, Md.: Newman Press, 1952).

Roland Bainton, *Martin Luther's Christmas Book* (Minneapolis: Augsburg, 1948). Bainton was the dean of earlier Luther scholarship in America and here offers a winsome picture of Luther, his theology, and his favorite liturgical season.

Robert Boenix, translation and introduction, *Anglo-Saxon Spirituality* (New York: Paulist Press, 2000). With an excellent and long introduction to Anglo-Saxon culture, literature, and religion, shows it to be muscular more than mystical and certainly eclectic in its accommodation of Christianity to the cultures of northern Europe.

Stephen Davis, et al., eds. *The Incarnation* (New York: Oxford, 2002). Twenty-four essays by international scholars at an Incarnation Summit that follows themes from an earlier British debate: logical coherence of belief in the Incarnation, evidences from foundational Christian literature, impact of cultural conditioning. New themes: Could the Incarnation have occurred more than once, expressing it in art and preaching, influence on ethics. Other books joined the debate: Brian Hebblethwaite, *The Incarnation* (Cambridge: Cambridge University Press, 1987); John Hick, ed. *The Myth of God Incarnate* (Louisville: Westminster John Knox, 1977); Hick, *The Metaphor of God Incarnate: Christology in a Pluralistic Age* (Louisville: Westminster John Knox, 1993); Michael Goulder, ed., *Incarnation and Myth: The Debate Continued* (London: SCM Press, 1979); Michael Green, ed., *The Truth of God Incarnate* (London: Hodder and Stoughton, 1977); John A. T. Robinson, *The Human Face of God* (London: SCM Press, 1973).

Mircea Eliade, ed., *The Encyclopedia of Religion* (New York: Macmillan, 1987). The most important encyclopedia of world religions in English, with, of course, extensive treatment of Christian themes.

Alejandro Garcia-Rivera, *The Community of the Beautiful: A Theological Aesthetics* (Collegeville, Minn.: Liturgical Press, 1999). One of many works, especially from Catholic theologians, to connect theology to the arts through a theological aesthetic of divine beauty in the world.

Stanley Hauerwas, *A Community of Character* (South Bend, Ind.: University of Notre Dame Press, 1981). In this and other works, the notable Protestant ethicist argues that the church is called to a unique non-assimilationist stance in the world and that its character must be uniquely formed and shaped by the theological stories it tells.

Larry W. Hurtado, *How on Earth Did Jesus Become a God?* (Grand Rapids: Eerdmans, 2005).

Larry W. Hurtado, *Lord Jesus Christ: Devotion to Jesus in Earliest Christianity* (Grand Rapids: Eerdmans, 2003). Hurtado argues that from earliest Christianity to the end of the second century Christians were already engaging in a pattern of devotional practices that treated Jesus as God. This comes in the face of some modern assumptions that the growth of Jesus the man into the Son of God was a product of much later Greek ontology.

Rene Latourelle and Rino Fisichella, eds., *Dictionary of Fundamental Theology* (New York: Crossroad, 2000). This complements *Sacramentum Mundi* as an excellent dictionary of Roman Catholic theology. I have especially depended on the article "Inculturation: The Problem," by Marcello de C. Azevedo, and "Inculturation of the Gospel," by Herve Carrier. Both are unusually good accounts of the issues involved when the gospel is proclaimed in new cultural settings.

Martin Luther, *What Luther Says: An Anthology*, compiled by Ewald M. Plass (St. Louis: Concordia, 1959). A very useful compendium of pithy Luther statements on hundreds of important issues in Christian theology and practice.

Sallie McFague, *The Body of God: An Ecological Theology* (Minneapolis: Fortress, 1993). This and several other works by McFague stake out an incarnational theology that ultimately transcends Christianity and also makes a sacrament of nature. She is one of the most influential and groundbreaking feminist theologians who take Christian theology well beyond its previous categories and ambitions.

Alister E. McGrath, ed., *The Blackwell Encyclopedia of Modern Christian Thought* (Oxford: Basil Blackwell, 1993). Very useful treatment of the main themes and issues in contemporary Christian thought. I have especially profited from articles on Karl Barth, Christology, Schleiermacher, and above all Incarnation.

Jack Miles, *Christ: A Crisis in the Life of God* (New York: Knopf, 2001). This sequel to the author's Pulitzer Prize-winner, *God: A Biography*, offers a literary interpretation of the coming of Christ that is thought-provoking and disturbing and amazing.

Donald W. Musser and Joseph L. Price, eds., *A New Handbook of Christian Theology* (Nashville: Abingdon, 1992). I have drawn from this well-regarded book on the following topics: Christ, liberation theologies, theology and the arts, and worship.

Donald W. Musser and Joseph L. Price, eds., *A New Handbook of Christian Theologians* (Nashville: Abingdon, 1996). I have used articles in this well-regarded book on the following theologians: Karl Barth, Karl Rahner, and several liberation theologians.

Jaroslav Pelikan, *The Christian Tradition: A History of the Development of Doctrine,* vols. 1–5 (Chicago: University of Chicago Press, 1971–89). The magisterial history of the Christian Tradition for the twentieth century. I have especially depended on volume one.

Stephen Prothero, *American Jesus: How the Son of God Became a National Icon* (New York: Farrar, Straus & Giroux, 2003). Jesus has slipped the bonds of Christianity to become an American icon and brand.

Karl Rahner, ed., *Encyclopedia of Theology: The Concise Sacramentum Mundi* (New York: Seabury, 1975). An indispensable encyclopedia of systematic theology, especially excellent for the Roman Catholic tradition. Extraordinarily good articles on "Incarnation" by Karl Rahner and on the many dimensions of doing theology.

Philip Scharper, ed., *The Gospel in Art by the Peasants of Solentiname* (Maryknoll, N.Y.: Orbis Books, 1984). A visual example of liberation theology.

Friedrich Schleiermacher, *Christmas Eve* (Richmond, Va.: John Knox Press, 1967). Chatty philosophical and theological reflections on Christmas set in an upper-class German home, by Protestantism's greatest nineteenth century liberal theologian.

Friedrich Schleiermacher, *The Christian Faith,* vols. 1–2 (New York: Harper Torchbooks, 1963). An attempt to reinterpret the Christian tradition in the context of the nineteenth century.

7. Second Thoughts on Incarnation: Taking Christmas Back

For good discussions of the Puritan suppression of Christmas, I have depended on the following:

John Ashton, *A Righte Merrie Christmasse: The Story of Christ-Tide* (New York: Benjamin Blom, 1968). Though not a scholarly work, this pleasing account is packed with anecdotes from the fifteenth century to the present. It is particularly telling on the English Puritan suppression of Christmas.

J. H. Barnett, *The American Christmas: A Study of National Culture* (New York: Macmillan, 1954). Good on the opposition to Christmas among American Puritans.

Stephen Nissenbaum, *The Battle for Christmas: A Cultural History of America's Most Cherished Holiday* (New York: Vintage, 1997). A Pulitzer Prize finalist, this very influential book offers a more searching analysis than Restad of how the American Christmas came about. The opening chapter, "New England's War on Christmas," is a good account of the American Puritan suppression of Christmas.

Penne L. Restad, *Christmas in America: A History* (New York: Oxford, 1995). A comprehensive work that traces the evolution of the American Christmas, especially through the nineteenth and early twentieth centuries. In addition to a standard historical account, Restad offers chapters on the domestication of Christmas in the American home, trees and giving, Christmas in the slave South, national holiday, gifts, charity and commerce, and Santa Claus.

For examples of social scientific or journalistic, but not necessarily religious critique of holiday ritualizations, see the following:

Amitai Etzioni and Jared Bloom, *We Are What We Celebrate: Understanding Holidays and Rituals* (New York: New York University Press, 2004). Building on the work of Durkheim and Weber, this anthology takes up the issue that public holidays and rituals provide important indicators of who we are as a people. The view is that if holidays deteriorate, so do moral and social order. The book is a good example of how a modern critique of holiday may arise not from religion but from a moral vision of community rooted in the social sciences.

Maud Lavin, ed., *The Business of Holidays* (New York: Monacelli Press, 2004). Short pieces on thirty American holidays ask what their celebrations say about Americans as a society. The answer seems to be that the business (purpose) of holidays is business.

For the problems of Christmas symbols in a secular public square, see:

Noah Feldman, *Divided by God: America's Church-State Problem—And What We Should Do About It* (New York: Farrar, Straus and Giroux, 2005). This legal history of the American church-state conflict defines "legal secularism" and "values evangelicals" and assumes everyone seeks a national unity that includes religious diversity. His solution to the "religious establishment" dilemma is "no coercion and no money," allowing unlimited religious symbolism in the public square, but eliminating all federal funding of "faith-based initiatives."

Stephen M. Feldman, *Please Don't Wish Me a Merry Christmas: A Critical History of the Separation of Church and State* (New York: New York University Press, 1997). A Jewish protest that seems naïve about religion, power, and dominant cultures, and succumbs to a victim ideology. Argues that the separation of church and state manifests and reinforces Christian domination, "normalizes" American Jews, and requires them to define themselves in relation to it.

John Gibson, *The War on Christmas: How the Liberal Plot to Ban the Sacred Christian Holiday Is Worse Than You Thought* (New York: Sentinel HC, 2005). A sensationalist account by a Fox News anchor digs up evidence of the war on Christmas, for example: Illinois state government workers are forbidden to say "Merry Christmas" while at work; a New Jersey school board bans even instrumental versions of Christmas carols; Arizona school officials think it unconstitutional for a student to make any reference to the religious history of Christmas in a class project. Suggestions for fighting back.

A. J. Menendez, *The December Wars: Religious Symbols and Ceremonies in the Public Square* (Buffalo, N.Y.: Prometheus Books, 1993). Covering court cases on manger scenes on public property and carols in public schools, this study argues for the predominance of the Establishment Clause over the Free Exercise Clause of the First Amendment.

For critical examinations in the humanities and social sciences, including theology, of the modern evolution of Christmas as the civil religion of consumer capitalism, I am indebted to the following:

Catherine Bell, *Ritual Theory, Ritual Practice* (New York: Oxford, 1992). This excellent and influential book on the history and theory of ritual offers a compelling analysis of how ritualization can both produce powerful internal social norms and also render them obvious and unquestionable.

Hassan M. Fattah, "Ramadan Ritual: Fast Daily, Pray, Head to the Mall," *New York Times* (October 12, 2005). Suggests Islam is as vulnerable to consumer capitalism as Christianity. The holy month of Ramadan has taken on the commercial trappings of Christmas, from hanging lights to greeting cards to special sales and advertising campaigns.

Richard A. Horsley, ed., *Christmas Unwrapped: Consumerism, Christ, and Culture* (Harrisburg: Trinity Press, 2001). This anthology argues against a golden age of an American Christmas that was spiritual and in favor of the view that Christmas relentlessly grew into the religious expression of consumer capitalism. Max A. Myers's chapter, "Christmas on Celluloid," shows how Hollywood helped to construct the American Christmas. In "Still Dreaming," Kathleen M. Sands analyzes how America invented new traditions for Christmas which ostensibly paid homage to a past ideal but in fact smoothed the way for new ritualizations that were essentially "rituals of secularization." In "Christmas," Horsley establishes this festival as the religion of consumer capitalism, in part by comparing it to the public festivals of ancient Mesopotamia.

Richard A. Horsley, *Religion and Empire: People, Power, and the Life of the Spirit* (Minneapolis: Fortress, 2003). American religion constitutes the imperial reality of international capitalism. A consumer-capitalist Christmas has become the dominant religious festival, allowing capitalism to take over the national civil religion.

Vincent J. Miller, *Consuming Religion: Christian Faith and Practice in a Consumer Culture* (New York: Continuum, 2004). Abjuring the typical argument that Christmas is excessively commercialized, this study focuses on modern consumerism as a normative behavior that dominates all cultural consumption and thoroughly corrupts the practice of religion. Analyzes the "commodification of culture" and the ways in which religious belief and practice have morphed into a consumerist model.

For examples of the "alternative celebrations" movement, I have depended on the following:

Edward and Faith Andrews, *The Shaker Order of Christmas* (New York: Oxford, 1954). An endearing description of the first Shaker Christmas in the new world, 1776, it is an excellent example of how saying no to Christmas can be radiant and positive rather than negative and dour.

Joseph Cusumano, *Scrooge: Dickens' Blueprint for a Spiritual Awakening* (St. Paul: Llewellyn, 1996). The author's thesis is that both Dickens and Scrooge share a wounded inner child, parental neglect, and abandonment.

Jo Robinson and Joan Staeheli, *Unplug the Christmas Machine: A Complete Guide to Putting Love and Joy Back into the Season* (New York: William

Morrow, 1991). This is among the better how-to-save-Christmas books, with many interesting suggestions for alternative celebrations.

Steve Russo, *Keeping Christ in Christmas: Helping Families Find Their Focus* (Eugene, Ore.: Harvest House, 1989). After a very useful popular history of Christmas, the author turns to preacherly admonition with digressions into modern education and family dynamics.

Elaine St. James, *Simplify Your Christmas: 100 Ways to Reduce the Stress and Capture the Joys of the Holidays* (Kansas City: Andrews McMeel, 1998). One of the calls for dismantling present Christmas practices, simplifying life, and creating new approaches in family and home.

www.simpleliving.org. This is one of several Web sites that promote simple living at Christmas and throughout the year as an antidote to a debased culture of conspicuous consumption.

8. Ornamenting the Incarnation: The Popular Culture of Christmas

I have benefited from the following books for their discussions of material culture, both in its particularities and in its larger meanings.

John Ashton, *A Righte Merrie Christmasse: The Story of Christ-Tide* (New York: Benjamin Blom, 1968). Not a scholarly work, but packed with anecdotes and quotations from the fifteenth century to the present, displaying the British material culture of Christmas.

Frank Burch Brown, *Good Taste, Bad Taste, and Christian Taste* (New York: Oxford, 2000). This considers art as an alternative to religion, the pervasiveness of material culture, and the role art could play in its redemption.

Damien Cave, "How Breweth Java with Jesus," *New York Times* (October 23, 2005). Starbucks tried a line on its drink cups from mega-church pastor Rick Warren, "You were made by God and for God, and until you understand that, life will never make sense." If religion is good for Starbucks, is Starbucks also good for religion?

Alain Corbin, *Village Bells: Sound and Meaning in the 19th century French Countryside,* translated by Martin Thom (New York: Columbia University Press, 1998). This is an extraordinarily evocative study of a lost aural culture, with implications for the understanding of the material culture of Christmas, transitioning from sacred to secular.

W. F. Dawson, *Christmas: Its Origin and Associations* (Detroit: Gale Research Company, 1968). First published in London in 1902, lacks footnotes or bibliography, but provides an interesting history of how English kings celebrated Christmas, filled with poetry and court chronicles.

Cynthia Hart, John Grossman, and Priscilla Dunhill, *A Victorian Christmas* (New York: Workman, 1990). Nobody did material culture like the Victorians. This lavish book is pure delightful eye-candy, every page crammed full of images.

Judith Martin, *Miss Manners' Guide to Excrutiatingly Correct Behavior* (New York: Athenium, 1982). The quotation is from page 521.

Karal Ann Marling, *Merry Christmas!* (Cambridge: Harvard, 2000). This book is very good on the material culture of Christmas, such as wrapping paper, greenery, lights, ornaments, Christmas windows, Dickens and Irving, charity, cards and gifts, films, and ethnic celebrations.

Material Religion: The Journal of Objects, Art and Belief. Published three times a year by Berg, in the United Kingdom. Founded in 2005, this journal, bridging the world of scholarship and museum practice, "explores how religion happens in material culture—images, devotional and liturgical objects, architecture and sacred space, works of art and mass-produced artifacts.

Colleen McDannell, *Material Christianity: Religion and Popular Culture in America* (New Haven: Yale, 1995). One of the seminal books that began to turn scholarly attention to visual and material culture as disclosive locations for understanding lived religion.

Daniel Miller, ed., *Unwrapping Christmas* (Oxford: Oxford University Press, 1993). This book offers sophisticated analyses with extraordinarily useful bibliographies. Pertaining to this chapter are the following articles: James Carrier, "The Rituals of Christmas Giving"; Russell Belk, "Materialism and the Making of the Modern American Christmas," which also has a useful analysis of Dickens; Adam Kuper, "The English Christmas and the Family." Miller's opening essay, "A Theory of Christmas," also takes up the role of the family.

Stephen Nissenbaum, *The Battle for Christmas: A Cultural History of America's Most Cherished Holiday* (New York: Vintage, 1997). A Pulitzer Prize finalist, it offers a searching analysis of how the American Christmas came about. Excellent chapters on the domestication of Christmas as a family-centered celebration, gift-giving, the Christmas tree, Christmas charity, and Christmas in the antebellum South.

P. R. Rulon, *Keeping Christmas* (Hamden, Conn.: Archon Books, 1990). This good collection of short stories about Christmas includes Earl Hammer's well-known "Home coming" and, most surprisingly, a Marxian reading of an egalitarian-bent Santa Claus.

William Sansom, *A Book of Christmas* (New York: McGraw-Hill, 1968). A collection of Christmas poetry and stories, lavishly illustrated with material culture.

Rudiger Vossen, *Weihnachtsbrauche in aller Welt* (Hamburg: Christians Verlag, 1985). A superb catalog of a museum exhibition in Hamburg, including the thick November–December calendar of saints, including St. Martin and St. Nicholas, on manger scenes, and especially on the Christmas Tree.

Many of the books above look at gift-giving, but the following book focuses exclusively on it.

William B. Waits, *The Modern Christmas in America: A Cultural History of Gift Giving* (New York: New York University Press, 1993). This is a study of gift giving 1880–1940, based on a random sample of mass circulation periodicals of that period, analyzing 1,720 articles and also gift ads from the *Ladies' Home Journal* and *The Saturday Evening Post,* 1900–1938.

I have drawn from books mentioned above and the following for the treatment of the Christmas tree.

D. J. Foley, *The Christmas Tree* (Philadelphia: Chilton, 1960). Poorly reproduced but abundant images. Good on the role of Prince Albert in the Victorian Christmas, Hans Christian Andersen, and other short stories.

9. Saint Nicholas and the Enchantment of the World

Russell W. Belk, "Materialism and the Making of the Modern American Christmas," in *Unwrapping Christmas,* ed. Daniel Miller (Oxford: Oxford University Press, 1993). This article sees Santa as "a sacred figure for a secular world."

Gerry Bowler, *Santa Claus: A Biography* (New York: McClelland & Stewart, 2005). Amidst all the fluffy accounts of Santa Claus, this captivating and well-researched biography of "the world's most influential fictional character" is the one to read.

Robin Crichton, *Who is Santa Claus: The True Story Behind a Living Legend* (Edinburgh: Canongate, 1987). Filled with woodcuts by Margaret Nisbet, offers bittersweet nostalgia for the eclipse of St. Nicholas by Santa.

Donald E. Glover, *C. S. Lewis: The Art of Enchantment* (Athens: Ohio University Press, 1981). A good study of the Christian writer who brought enchantment as well as religious sensibility to his adult and children's literature.

Adam Gopnik, "Prisoner of Narnia: How C. S. Lewis escaped," *The New Yorker* (November 21, 2005). Argues that Lewis was drawn to Christianity by the likeness of the Christian story to pagan myth, not in spite of it, hoping that conveyance would carry us on to religion. In dialogue with two important recent biographies of Lewis: the American Alan

Jacobs, *The Narnian* (New York: HarperOne, 2008) and the British A. N. Wilson, *C. S. Lewis: A Biography* (New York: W. W. Norton, 2002).

Eric Hobsbawm and Terence Ranger, eds., *The Invention of Tradition* (Cambridge: Cambridge University Press, 1992). This highly influential anthology develops the concept of the invention of traditions in the last two centuries and offers many recent examples.

Ann Dorian Bryce Hunt, *The Mythic Meaning of Christmas* (Mansfield, Mass.: Center for Inner Gardening, 2001). A New Age approach that attempts to recast Christmas as above all a means to enchantment.

E. W. Jones, *The Santa Claus Book* (New York: Walker, 1976). Lavishly illustrated in poor quality images. A good history of Santa Claus.

Claude Levi-Strauss, "Father Christmas Executed," in *Unwrapping Christmas,* ed. by Daniel Miller (Oxford: Oxford University Press, 1952).

Alister McGrath, *The Re-enchantment of Nature: The Denial of Religion and the Ecological Crisis* (London: Galilee Trade, 2003). McGrath argues for a renewed sense of wonder that will come from Christianity, not reductionistic atheism.

George McKnight, *St. Nicholas: His Legend and His Role in the Christmas Celebration and Other Popular Customs* (Williamstown, Mass.: Corner House, 1974). Though not at all a work of critical scholarship, this is an interesting compendium of stories and allusions to European artistic portrayals of Nicholas.

Max A. Myers, "Santa Claus as an Icon of Grace," in *Christmas Unwrapped: Consumerism, Christ, and Culture*, ed. by Richard Horsley and James Tracy (Harrisburg, Pa.: Trinity Press International, 2001). Myers argues that the American Christmas is less a Christian festival than the religion of global consumer capitalism, and that Santa Claus is a rival icon to the crucified Christ, the former mystifying commerce as religion.

Stephen Nissenbaum, *The Battle for Christmas: A Cultural History of America's Most Cherished Holiday* (New York: Vintage, 1997). The chapter "Revisiting 'A Visit from St. Nicholas'" is a revisionist look at Clement Moore's poem and its setting in early nineteenth century New York, on which I am deeply dependent.

Penne L. Restad, *Christmas in America: A History* (New York: Oxford, 1995). A very good study with individual chapters on the early American development of Christmas, Christmas in the slave South, the domestication of Christmas as a family festival, gifts and charity, and Santa Claus.

Leigh Eric Schmidt, *Consumer Rites: The Buying and Selling of American Holidays* (Princeton: Princeton University Press, 1995). Argues that protesting commercialism is a tired old theme and that, in fact, there has always been the church's time (holy day) and the merchant's time (holiday), and that gift-giving, exchange, and the culture of festival are longstanding human themes much studied by anthropologists.

Mark A. Schneider, *Culture and Enchantment* (Chicago: University of Chicago Press, 1993). This study of Geertz and Levi-Straus argues that symbolic anthropology is a kind of enchantment in the social sciences that does not yield ultimate ground to rigid empirical studies.

Jeremy Seal, *Nicholas: The Epic Journey from Saint to Santa Claus* (New York: Bloomsbury, 2005). Part travelogue and part detective story, this book traces the history of St. Nicholas, fancifully conceiving that Nicholas himself is managing his career and trying to save Santa as well.

J. R. R. Tolkien, *Letters from Father Christmas* (New York: Houghton Mifflin, 1999). Between 1920 and 1943 Tolkien (*Lord of the Rings*) wrote wonderfully imaginative letters to his fortunate children, as if from Father Christmas, and beautifully illustrated them with his own drawings.

James B. Twitchell, *Twenty Ads That Shook the World: The Century's Most Groundbreaking Advertising and How It Changed Us All* (New York: Three Rivers Press, 2000). This study has an important chapter on "Coke and Christmas: The Claus that refreshes," showing how Santa was drafted to sell a cold drink during winter and how Haddon Sundblom, drawing a new Coca-Cola Santa each year from the 1930s on through the '50s and '60s, became one of the most important iconographers of Santa Claus.

G. Weightman and S. Humphries, *Christmas Past* (London: Sidgwick & Jackson, 1987). Strongly argues that the Christmas we know today is the invention of the Victorian middle class and reflects their preoccupations.

Lois Parkinson Zamora and Wendy B. Faris, eds., *Magical Realism: Theory, History, Community* (Durham, N.C.: Duke University Press, 1995). My treatment of magical realism is fully indebted to this seminal work that is replete with the history of this movement, definitions, and many studies of individual works.

10. Seeing Christmas: Visual Incarnations

Annunciation (London: Phaidon, 2000). Small in size, but an extraordinary collection of paintings on the theme of Gabriel's appearance to Mary.

James Luther Adams, *Paul Tillich's Philosophy of Culture, Science and Religion* (New York: Schocken, 1970). Of twentieth-century Protestant theologians, Tillich took the most interest in the arts and offered the most influential treatment of them, as seen in chapter 3, "The Theology of Art and Culture."

Diane Apostolos-Cappadona, ed., *Art, Creativity, and the Sacred* (New York: Continuum, 1995). An anthology of short essays by artists, art historians, and theologians.

Robert Bartlett, *Medieval Panorama* (Los Angeles: J. Paul Getty Museum, 2001). A superbly illustrated example of the rich Christian material culture of the Middle Ages, with extraordinary detail and commentary.

Giulia Bartrum, *Albrecht Durer and his Legacy: The Graphic Work of a Renaissance Artist* (Princeton: Princeton University Press, 2002). An important study with elaborate illustrations and abundant commentary.

Susan A. Blain, ed., *Imaging the Word: An Arts and Lectionary Resource,* vol. 2 (Cleveland: United Church Press, 1996). Well-chosen examples of recent religious art, prose, and poetry as aids to liturgical worship.

Susan A. Blain, ed., *Imaging the Word: An Arts and Lectionary Resource,* vol. 3. (Cleveland: United Church Press, 1995).

Thomas Bodkin, *The Virgin and Child* (New York: Pitman, 1949). A good history of how images evolve, from Mary's holiness, purity, simplicity, tenderness, and majesty in the Middle Ages to human portraits of peasant girls in the Renaissance.

Friedrich Buechner, *The Faces of Jesus* (New York: Riverwood, 1974). Richly illustrated, this features Buechner's devotional meditations on art, photographed by Lee Boltin.

Heather Child, *Christian Symbols Ancient and Modern: A Handbook for Students* (New York: Charles Scribner, 1971). A standard work that interprets the symbols one sees in Christian art.

Holland Cotter, Review of a gallery sale of Ethiopian art, *New York Times* (October 19, 2005). The reviewer finds the images fierce and gorgeous, a category-scrambling encounter with centuries of Africa's oldest Christian culture, distinctive in its beliefs, worship, and art and provoking spiritual interaction with the viewer.

John of Damascus, *Three Treatises on the Divine Images,* translation and introduction by Andrew Louth (Yonkers, N.Y.: St. Vladimir Seminary Press, 2003). One of the most important pro-art arguments during the eighth-century iconoclastic controversy, this treatise helped establish the place and future of Christian visual art, in the face of those who counted it blasphemous idolatry.

Helen De Borchgrave, *A Journey into Christian Art* (Minneapolis: Fortress, 2000). One of many recent attempts to demonstrate that Christianity owes much to visual images and not just to written texts. This is a chronological, well-illustrated account of how Christianity grew into a lavish visual culture.

Jane Dillenberger, *Secular Art with Sacred Themes* (Nashville: Abingdon, 1969). Looking for works of art with religious subject matter by major artists 1900–1970, Dillenberger finds very little. The exemplary works of Thomas Eakins, Diego Velasquez, Andre Derain, Marc Chagall, Manzu, Picasso, and Barnett Newman do not treat Christmas themes.

Jane Dillenberger and Joshua C. Taylor, *The Hand and the Spirit: Religious Art in America 1700–1900* (Berkeley: University Art Museum, 1972). Examines seven hundred pieces of American religious art, including "naïve" or folk art. Why has a nation so fervent with religion produced so little religious art? Protestantism is too simple an explanation. Almost none of this art treats Christmas themes.

John Dillenberger, *The Visual Arts and Christianity in America: From the Colonial Period to the Present* (New York: Crossroad, 1989). Very important analysis of the British origins of the disinterest in and undervaluation of art in the first two centuries of American Protestant Christianity.

John Drury, *Painting the Word* (New Haven: Yale, 1999). This work by an Anglican theologian selects examples of great Christian art and offers extensive commentary on its meanings.

Eamon Duffy, *The Stripping of the Altars,* 2nd. ed. (New Haven: Yale, 2004). Argues that pre-Reformation English Christianity was religiously and culturally rich at all levels of society and deplores the plundering of that legacy by Henry VIII and Elizabeth I.

Gabriele Finaldi, *The Image of Christ* (London: National Gallery, 2000). Since one-third of the images in London's National Gallery are on Christian themes, this work attempts to set them into their original contexts, of which most visitors know little or nothing. This book demonstrates the changing meanings images acquire when transplanted from a religious setting to a museum setting.

Daniel Johnson Fleming, *Each with His Own Brush: Contemporary Christian Art in Asia and Africa* (New York: Friendship Press, 1938). A good selection of images, with commentary, that demonstrate that Christian art did not come to an end in early modern Europe and that Christmas, for example, continues to indigenize in non-European vernaculars.

David Freedberg, *The Power of Images* (Chicago: University of Chicago Press, 1989). An influential work that positions visual culture at the center of contemporary social science analysis.

Frank and Dorothy Getlein, *Christianity in Modern Art* (Milwaukee: Bruce, 1961). Many illustrations of modern religious art, with commentary.

Jeffrey F. Hamburger, *Nuns as Artists: The Visual Culture of a Medieval Convent* (Berkeley: University of California Press, 1997). Nicely demonstrates personal "vision" as determined women's response to male "supervision."

Jeffrey F. Hamburger, *The Visual and the Visionary: Art and Female Spirituality in Late Medieval Germany* (New York: Zone, 1998). A fine study, with noteworthy attention to the role of images in nuns' theology and mysticism and the implications for a feminist Christian art history.

Colum Hourihane, ed., *Insights and Interpretations: Studies in Celebration of the 85th Anniversary of the Index of Christian Art* (Princeton: Princeton University Press, 2002). These essays honor the Princeton project that assembled 100,000 images under 27,000 subject headings, attending both to image and text.

Colum Hourihane, ed., *Objects, Images and the Word: Art in the Service of the Liturgy* (Princeton: Princeton University Press, 2003). An important scholarly study that shows that liturgical art has a life of its own and that such art is not simply word-controlled.

H. W. and Anthony F. Janson, *History of Art*, 5th ed. rev. (New York: Harry N. Abrams, 1997). Part two, "The Middle Ages," and part three, "The Renaissance through the Rococo," document the seminal presence of Christianity and the church in the evolution of Western art.

Robin Margaret Jensen, *Understanding Early Christian Art* (London: Routledge, 2000). This book usefully shows the reader how to "look" at a tradition and read it visually, rather than concentrating on texts, as other kinds of scholarship do.

Melissa R. Katz, *Divine Mirrors: the Virgin Mary in the Visual Arts* (New York: Oxford, 2001). This is a catalog, with interpretive essays, of a museum display of images of Mary over time and how they disclose cultural preoccupations. A contemporary understanding of religious art is more about knowledge lost than gained in the modern world.

Neil MacGregor and Erika Langmuir, *Seeing Salvation: Images of Christ in Art* (New Haven: Yale, 2000). A study of how artists over the centuries continuously image and re-image Christ and thus affect the unfolding of Christian culture, for the religious and for the general public.

Thomas R. Martland, *Religion as Art: An Interpretation* (Albany: SUNY Press, 1981). Not yet taking a postmodern approach, this is a very useful book full of delicious quotes and allusions on art, aesthetics, and religion.

Comelis Monsma (Monsmaart.com). This artist and his Web site are examples of the turn to Christian visual art by some modern artists. The artist seeks to "unearth the deeper truths of the Christian faith and relate to a much broader audience than Christianity only."

David Morgan, *Visual Piety: A History and Theory of Popular Religious Images* (Berkeley: University of California Press, 1998). A very important and influential work on the role that visual culture plays in religious life. It is an excellent example of the turn to the visual in the study of popular religion.

David Morgan and Sally M. Promey, eds. *The Visual Culture of American Religions* (Berkeley: University of California Press, 2001). A very important anthology on the contemporary analysis of visual culture that looks at how religious visual culture shapes public identity, constructs new meaning, and addresses modernity.

Richard Muhlberger, *The Christmas Story* (New York: Metropolitan Museum of Art, 1990). Lavish illustrations and excellent commentary.

Peter and Linda Murray, *The Oxford Companion to Christian Art and Architecture* (New York: Oxford, 1996). This valuable dictionary offers articles on all the significant issues and themes in the Christian tradition in Western art.

Seth Mydans, "Russia peels the veils from antiquity and gazes, awed," *New York Times* (October 16, 2005), from *International Herald Tribune*. The reporter describes Russian icons arriving in restoration studios as small blackened boards, slightly warped, their holy images hidden behind a veil of spoiled dark patina. Thousands of icons are entering the warehouses of historical museums throughout Russia, as the painting and restoring of icons has flourished since the fall of Communism, when many died trying to save them.

Nancy Netzer and Virginia Reinburg, *Fragmented Devotion: Medieval Objects from the Schnutgen Museum Cologne*. (Chicago: University of Chicago Press, 2000). Superb brief essays that discuss how medieval objects as signifiers of religious meaning can be uprooted from their original settings and end up in bourgeois collections, where they acquire new meanings that contribute to the romantic valorization of the Middle Ages or to artistic sensibilities on display in modern museums. Indispensable background for the changing meanings that Christmas symbols acquire in new times and places.

Aidan Nichols, *The Art of God Incarnate: Theology and Image in Christian Traditions* (London: Darton, Longman, Todd, 1980). A Christian aesthetic requires the coming together of theology and image.

Ron O'Grady, ed., *Christ for All People* (Maryknoll, N.Y.: Orbis Books, 2001). This book provides lavish evidence that the Incarnation is well rooted among non-Western indigenous peoples and that religious art carries religious meanings into new settings.

Jaroslav Pelikan, *The Illustrated Jesus through the Centuries* (New Haven: Yale, 1997). I have depended, in the opening paragraphs of this chapter, on Pelikan's account of how the complexification of the church's understanding of Jesus Christ went hand in hand with an ever widening Christian visual culture, especially the outpouring of art after the conversion of Constantine in the fourth century and then the justification and resolution of the role of Christian art during the iconoclastic controversies of the eighth and ninth centuries.

David Price, *Albrecht Durer's Renaissance: Humanism, Reformation, and the Art of Faith* (Ann Arbor: University of Michigan Press, 2003). Many key woodcuts, including those on Christmas themes, and accompanying commentary.

Olga Raggio, curator, *The Nativity* (New York: Doubleday, 1969). These are photographs, by Lee Boltin, of the famous Christmas creche at the Metropolitan Museum of Art in New York, demonstrating how people place themselves into the nativity scenes.

Patrick Reyntiens, *A Stained-Glass Christmas* (New York: Stewart, Tabori & Chang, 1998). A charming little book with six removable stained-glass windows.

Masao Takenaka, *Christian Art in Asia* (Kyoto: Nissha Printing, 1975). One hundred-twenty works by one hundred-seven artists from eighteen Asian countries. Twenty-two are on Christmas themes.

Elizabeth Cover Teviotdale, *The Stammheim Missal* (Los Angeles: J. Paul Getty Museum, 2001). A fine study of a famous illuminated manuscript. Excellent commentary and illustrations demonstrate the book as an example of Christian material culture.

M. Thomas, *The Golden Age* (New York: George Braziller, 1979). Wonderful reproductions and excellent commentary on illuminated manuscripts in the age of Jean, Duke of Berry.

Vatican Museums, *The Mother of God: Art Celebrates Mary* (Washington D.C.: Pope John Paul II Cultural Center, 2001). Beautifully reproduced images with excellent layout, also offers excellent commentaries on the evolution of Marian visual imagery and her religious roles.

Richard Viladesau, *Theology and the Arts: Encountering God through Music, Art and Rhetoric* (New York: Paulist, 2000). A very good study of aesthetics and theologies of beauty, of paradigms in theology and art, of art as theological "text," and of preaching as a rhetorical art.

Ingo F. and Norbert Wolf Walther, *Codices illustres* (Cologne: Taschen, 2001). Possibly the best available, superbly reproduced collection of illuminated manuscripts 400–1600, a major period in the material culture of the book.

Helen Woodruff, *Index of Christian Art at Princeton University* (Princeton: Princeton University Press, 1942). This is a history of the collection of images begun in 1917 that aspires to cover the whole of medieval art to 1400. A major contribution to the science of iconography, the pictorial illustration or description of a subject by means of figures and drawings.

Robert Wuthnow, *Creative Spirituality: The Way of the Artist* (Berkeley: University of California Press, 2001). This study by the leading authority in the empirical sociology of religion reports on interviews with one hundred artists who are seeking transcendence or spirituality, often via nature and not typically through institutional religion.

Robert Wuthnow, *All in Sync: How Music and Art Are Revitalizing American Religion* (Berkeley: University of California Press, 2006). This study suggests that one of the reasons American religion did not suffer predicted decline in the last thirty years is a renewed relation between religion and the arts. Based on national survey research and four hundred in-depth interviews, the book suggests that "those with greater exposure to artistic activities are more likely than those with less exposure to be seriously committed to spiritual growth."

Museum of Biblical Art. This new museum in New York intends to display art related to the Bible and to encourage a religious and not just aesthetic viewpoint.

Vatican Museums. In particular, the "Collection of Modern Religious Art" and the "Missionary-Ethnological Museum" offer ample evidence that Christianity continues to stimulate religious art in the modern age and also that this is occurring, as well, outside Western precincts.

11. Hearing Christmas: Musical Incarnations

The following works inform my discussion of music as Christian culture:

Jeremy Begbie, *Music in God's Purposes* (Edinburgh: Handsel Press, 1989). A brief devotional pamphlet.

Jeremy Begbie, *Voicing Creation's Praise: Toward a Theology of the Arts* (Edinburgh: T & T Clark, 1991). This superb theology of art begins with an analysis of Paul Tillich, then moves to neo-Calvinist aesthetics, and finally offers the author's own unique analysis.

Jeremy S. Begbie, *Theology, Music and Time* (Cambridge: Cambridge University Press, 2000). A deft philosophical argument about the timeboundedness of music and how it thereby relates to Christian theology's negotiation of life in the world.

Albert Blackwell, *The Sacred in Music* (Louisville: Westminster John Knox, 1999). Like all the other joys of Christmas, music and religion are always ambivalent—voice of God or devilish cacophony, pure spirituality or sensual depravity?

David N. Power, et al., eds., *Music and the Experience of God* (Edinburgh: T & T Clark, 1989). An uneven, mostly Roman Catholic anthology on music and religion, offering much analysis on pastoral versus aesthetic considerations and on Gregorian chant.

Robin A. Leaver and Joyce Ann Zimmerman, eds., *Liturgy and Music: Lifetime Learning* (Collegeville, Minn.: Liturgical Press, 1998). This excellent collection of articles by leading Protestant and Roman Catholic liturgical scholars locates Christian music within the liturgical life of the church. I have especially depended on the treatment of Don E. Saliers in his chapter, "Liturgical Musical Formation,"

Andrew Wilson-Dickson, *The Story of Christian Music* (Minneapolis: Fortress, 1996). This is a well-illustrated and extremely useful history of Christian music for worship from Gregorian chant to black gospel, covering all the major Christian traditions.

For my discussion of carols and hymns, I have depended on the following:

Hugh Keyte, Andrew Parrott, and Clifford Bartlett, *The New Oxford Book of Carols* (Oxford: Oxford, 1998). The indispensable work on carols.

Stanley Sadie, ed. *The New Grove Dictionary of Music and Musicians* (New York: Grove, 1980). The article on the carol is by John Stevens and Dennis Libby.

Christopher A. and Melodie Lane, *Christ in the Carols: Meditations on the Incarnation* (New York: Tyndale House, 1999). Carols can be prized for their singability and their Christmas spirit, but also because they attest to Christian theology.

J. R. Watson, *An Annotated Anthology of Hymns* (Oxford: Oxford University Press, 2002). This is a selection of 251 hymns, under twelve mostly chronological headings, that includes about one page of valuable remarks on each.

For Handel and *Messiah* I have depended on the following:

Roger A. Bullard, *Messiah: Gospel According to Handel's Oratorio* (Grand Rapids: Eerdmans, 1993). A bit of musicology together with observations from New Testament theology make a not altogether satisfying book.

D. Burrows, *Handel: Messiah* (Cambridge: Cambridge University Press, 1991). A very good book in the Cambridge handbook to music series.

J. P. Larsen, *Handel's Messiah* (New York: W. W. Norton, 1972). This is the original work of scholarship that influenced all subsequent twentieth-century studies of Handel's Messiah.

Richard Luckett, *Handel's Messiah: A Celebration* (New York: Harcourt Brace, 1992). A good study.

Michael Steinberg, *Choral Masterworks: A Listener's Guide* (New York: Oxford, 2005). Steinberg wrote program notes for several major American symphony orchestras. In this very useful book he takes the reader and music lover through famous accompanied choral works and asks what it means to have secular audiences listening to religious music. What does it mean to have a chardonnay or a cappuccino between parts I and II of Bach's *St. Matthew Passion,* when the Leipzig Lutherans would have had a sermon. He calls Bach and Handel entertainments with "high spiritual potential."

David Willcocks, ed. *Messiah Highlights and Other Christmas Music* (New York: Metropolitan Museum of Art, 1987). A good example of two artforms, music and visual art, brought together in the service of Christmas delight. Each carol and chorus from Handel's *Messiah* has corresponding Christmas visual art.

For Bach and the *Christmas Oratorio,* I have depended on the following:

Friedrich Blume, *Two Centuries of Bach: An Account of Changing Taste,* translated by Stanley Godman (London: Oxford University Press, 1950). Bach is bringing to fruition monuments of the Western musical tradition, while his own age is passing him by.

Malcom Boyd, ed., *J. S. Bach: Oxford Composer Companions* (Oxford: Oxford University Press, 1999). A standard work in this series, organized by dictionary entries.

Eric Thomas Chafe, *Analyzing Bach Cantatas* (New York: Oxford University Press, 2000). Highly technical, this study argues that Bach's music follows allegorical types refined by Luther's law-gospel dialectic as the appropriate mode for biblical and religious interpretation.

James R. Gaines, *Evening in the Palace of Reason* (New York: Harper Collins, 2005). Alternates chapters on the life of the Prussian King Frederick the Great with that of J. S. Bach, culminating in Bach's visit to the Prussian court in 1747 and his instant improvisation of an amazing fugue on a fiendishly difficult melody offered by Frederick. Riffs on Bach's religious world, for God's ears, and Frederick's Enlightenment world, for audience delight.

Jaroslav Pelikan, *Bach Among the Theologians* (Minneapolis: Fortress, 1987). Sets Bach in the Lutheran theological context of his time.

G. Stiller, *Johann Sebastian Bach and Liturgical Life in Leipzig* (St. Louis: Concordia, 1984). This study of Bach in Leipzig positions him as fundamentally a church musician, situates his music in the eighteenth-century development of the Lutheran liturgy, and perhaps overplays Bach as deeply orthodox Lutheran, making for a good contrast with Handel's religious music, written for the concert hall.

Conrad Wilson, *Notes on Bach* (Grand Rapids: Eerdmans, 2005). The "Notes on" series views a great composer through twenty important works, in this case including both Bach's *Magnificat* and the *Christmas Oratorio.*

Christoph Wolff, *Johann Sebastian Bach: The Learned Musician* (New York: W. W. Norton, 2000). The most important modern and now indispensable biographical study of Bach.

I suggest the following as one example of modern artists still grappling with the meaning of Christmas:

John Adams, *El Nino* (2003). This oratorio, with a libretto in English, Spanish, and Latin drawn from sacred texts and modern poets, depicts the annunciation from the perspective of a sixteen-year-old girl. It was staged at the Brooklyn Academy of Music as a multimedia production, conducted by Esa-Pekka Salonen and directed by Peter Sellars.

The Risk of Incarnation: Fare Well, Christmas

Harold Bloom, *The Western Canon: The Books and School of the Ages* (New York: Harcourt Brace, 1994). In this magisterial and much-debated work, Bloom identifies twenty-six authors central to the Western canon, as antidotes to much that Bloom finds objectionable in the present. One of Bloom's telling notions is "the anxiety of influence," through which he accounts for how the canon comes to be and what effects it has.

Eamon Duffy, *The Stripping of the Altars,* 2nd ed. (New Haven: Yale, 2004). Recovers the lost world of pre-Reformation English Catholicism by examining the abundant art-historical evidence of ordinary people's rich and vital religious life, full of festivals, rituals, and images that bound them together in a Christian society. Even deeply rooted religious life is fragile.

John Freccero, *Dante: The Poetics of Conversion,* ed. and with an introduction by Rachel Jacoff (Cambridge: Harvard University Press, 1986). My allusions to Dante are indebted to this collection of essays by a distinguished Dante scholar.

Frank and Dorothy Getlein, *Christianity in Modern Art* (Milwaukee: Bruce, 1961). Images of modern Christian art, with commentary.

Richard A. Horsley, *Religion and Empire: People, Power, and the Life of the Spirit* (Minneapolis: Fortress, 2003). Sees religion as transcending political and economic reality, resisting it, or constituting it. The chapter "Christmas, the Festival of Consumer Capitalism" argues that American religion *constitutes* the imperial reality of international capitalism.

Philip Jenkins, *The Next Christendom: The Coming of Global Christianity* (New York: Oxford, 2002). While my book focuses on the Christian culture of the West, this book concentrates on the explosive southward expansion of Christianity in Africa, Latin America, and even Asia, The author claims that by 2050 only one Christian in five will be a non-Latino white person. What will this mean for the course of Incarnation?

Sallie McFague, *Life Abundant: Rethinking Theology and Economics for a Planet in Peril* (Minneapolis: Fortress, 2001). I am indebted to this book for its portrayal of the regnant contemporary economic model and worldview, that of international capitalism, locked in conflict with the ecological economic model and worldview, which she attributes to an awakened and enlightened Christian planetary theology.

Alister McGrath, *The Twilight of Atheism: The Rise and Fall of Disbelief in the Modern World* (New York: Doubleday, 2004). This book focuses on two centuries of atheism weakening Christianity and perhaps softening it up for the blows capitalism would rain on it. But the author argues that the two-century-long cultural mood for atheism as an empire of the mind, 1789–1989, has now passed and that religious belief is reasserting itself around the world.

Vincent J. Miller, *Consuming Religion: Christian Faith and Practice in a Consumer Culture* (New York: Continuum, 2004). After analyzing consumerism as a normative behavior that dominates cultural consumption and corrupts the practice of religion, the author proposes a renewed and theologically and culturally dense Catholic Christianity as the antidote. Liturgical worship embedded in living traditions and communities is the answer, countering the disaggregating effects of commodification and reinforcing the interconnections between religious symbols and practice.

Walter Wink, *Naming the Powers: The Language of Power in the New Testament* (Minneapolis: Fortress, 1984).

Walter Wink, *Unmasking the Powers* (Minneapolis: Fortress, 1986).

Walter Wink, *Engaging the Powers: Discernment and Resistance in a World of Domination* (Minneapolis: Fortress, 1992). These three books call for an aggressive theological and churchly engagement with "the powers" of the world arrayed against Christianity. I have adopted Wink's approach to suggest how Christianity must take on the rival forces and worldviews arrayed against an authentic celebration of Christmas in the modern world.

Index

A

B

T

V

W

X

Y

Z

3 1170 00849 4381